The Territory of the Historian

for Jim from Lucia
Christmas 1982

The Territory
of the Historian

EMMANUEL LE ROY LADURIE

TRANSLATED FROM THE FRENCH BY
BEN AND SIÂN REYNOLDS

THE UNIVERSITY OF CHICAGO PRESS

The University of Chicago Press, Chicago 60637
The Harvester Press Ltd, Hassocks, Sussex

Originally published in France as *Le territoire de l'historien*
by Editions Gallimard, 1973

The present translation published by the Harvester Press Ltd
and the University of Chicago Press, 1979

Printed in Great Britain by Redwood Burn Limited

Library of Congress Cataloging in Publication Data
   Le Roy Ladurie, Emmanuel.
      The territory of the historian.
      Translation of Le territoire de l'historien.
      Includes bibliographical references.
      1. France—Historiography.   I. Title.
   DC36.9.L3713 1979   944'.007'2   78-31362
   ISBN 0-226-47327-9

CONTENTS

History without People: The Climate as a New Province of Research

PUBLISHER'S NOTE

It should be noted that certain chapters of the French edition have been omitted from this translation. They include "Système de la Coutume", which appeared in translation in *Family and Inheritance*, edited by J. Goody *et al* (Cambridge, 1976), entitled "Family Structures and Inheritance Customs in Sixteenth Century France". Some articles on the climate were left out because the author has published a book in English on the subject: *Times of Feast, Times of Famine* (Doubleday, New York, 1971 and Allen & Unwin, London, 1973).

TRANSLATORS' NOTE

In some of the articles in this book, particularly those concerned with French history, a number of French terms appear for which there is no accurate (or brief) English equivalent. We have therefore left them in French; sometimes the meaning is clear from the context or is explained, but in any case a full glossary appears at the end of the book.

Siân Reynolds would like to thank the Director and staff of the Humanities Research Centre, Australian National University, Canberra, for the generous hospitality and facilities offered to her as a Visiting Fellow while she was working on this translation.

T.B.R.

S.R.

PREFACE

The articles and papers contained in this volume, written at different times and in the course of various study projects, are concerned with a number of provinces, as it were, of historical research, different from each other, yet often adjacent and in some cases overlapping. Prominent among such provinces are for instance the material, sociological and cultural history of rural societies during the "modern" period (i.e. from the end of the Middle Ages to the early nineteenth century); and serial or quantitative history, using statistical data and methods and applied, for example, to demography. Then there are the interdisciplinary zones, territory where the historian rubs shoulders and establishes contact with—indeed sometimes rather rudely jostles—the other social sciences (anthropology, economics) as well as the natural or environmental sciences, whether biological (phytogeography, dendrochronology) or purely physical (climatology, glaciology). Such interdisciplinary and serial excursions have led me on many occasions to take part in collective projects, in collaboration either with my colleagues in the Sixth Section of the *École Pratique des Hautes Études*, or with individual specialists in "the other camp" (botanists and nuclear physicists for example.) My thanks therefore to Y. Pasquet, N. Bernageau, P. Dumont, J.-P. Desaive, J. Goy, P. Couperie, A. and J. Gordus and D. Richet, who have given permission for articles prepared with their assistance in the course of joint research to be included in this collection.

I might just add, incidentally, that some of the studies referred to in this collection required the use, as long ago as 1966, of the computer as an instrument of historical discovery, something that is today taken for granted.

E.L.R.L.

PART ONE

LEARNING TO LIVE WITH COMPUTERS: THE QUANTITATIVE REVOLUTION IN HISTORY

I

The Historian and the Computer[1]

ONCE upon a time, not so very long ago, a specialist in German history decided to use a computer to analyse *the social composition of the entourage of Wilhelm II*. So he compiled biographies of all the individuals at the Kaiser's court, encoded their particulars, with details of their family ancestries and birthplaces, then took a deep breath and fed all his material, duly transferred to punched cards, into a computer. The machine's verdict was categorical: Wilhelm's entourage was composed essentially of . . . *aristocrats born east of the Elbe*. The computer had told him what everyone knew in the first place.

This anecdote illustrates an obvious point: in history as in everything else, what matters is not so much the machine as the question one asks it. A computer is only interesting in that it allows one to tackle problems that are new and original in their subject matter, method and above all their scope.

This said, many promising research possibilities are of course opened up to those historians who have access to computer science. One that immediately springs to mind is the analysis of those vast deposits of documents, containing vital data, but whose sheer bulk has until now daunted all researchers.

One such is the 1427 *Catasto* (land register) of Florence: it has been waiting five hundred years for historians to take any notice of the prodigious wealth of demographical data contained in its bulging registers. For in these documents the Florentine inspectors of the fifteenth century had listed in detail information about the family circumstances of 50,000 households.

Two medievalists, D. Herlihy and C. Klapisch, have now taken the opportunity offered by modern techniques for analysing the contents of these ancient files. Thanks to these historians, the university computer at Madison, Wisconsin, will shortly have made a mere mouthful of the *Catasto*. For the first time, massive records of a medieval population in the century following the Black Death will be fully revealed. What is more, a machine-readable tape, easily stored and reproduced, and containing all the information collected, will make available for further research, calculations and correlations, data previously buried in the massive and unreadable Florentine documents, which by good fortune survived the flooding of the Arno.

Not only has it a voracious appetite for data, but the historical computer can also accommodate any number of approaches or ideologies. One of the earliest "machine-history" studies, which appeared some time ago in the review *Annales*, was the work of a Soviet historian seeking to establish the degree to which the Russian peasants were exploited by wealthy landowners in the past: this was pure Marx or Lenin, but tailored to the computer age. In a somewhat different perspective, the new generation of radical historians like Lockridge in the United States, who are engaged in re-interpreting the 1776 Revolution, putting greater emphasis on its revolutionary or even Castroist content, are using the most sophisticated technology in their work. With the aid of computers which can digest the hundreds of thousands of figures contained in the tax records of the thirteen colonies, they are seeking to show that the upheavals of the War of Independence had their origins in a situation of social crisis as the small farmers, victims of the depression and impoverished by the division of their land, directed their concentrated resentment against their British masters.

In Europe, particularly in England and above all in France, where quantitative history has made so much headway in the last thirty years, the computer is gradually becoming central to one of the most promising disciplines of the new school: historical demography. The most difficult and above all exhausting task in this area always used to be the laborious reconstitution of families who were alive in, say, the seventeenth and eighteenth centuries.

Researchers who embarked upon this task were until now obliged to card-index all the records for any village they were studying: the marriages, baptisms and burials entered in the registers kept up over a period of two hundred years by successive parish priests. These tens of thousands of entries then had to be reclassified on files for each family, so that for every couple the births, marriages and deaths of parents or children were recorded. This labour of classification was both Herculean and depressing: it could last months or more, without the slightest glimmer of an intellectual discovery on the horizon. Only afterwards, when all the families had been reconstituted, did it become possible to make any meaningful calculations of fertility, family size, mortality etc. A number of researchers in Cambridge and Paris are now working out programmes so that the computer can take care of this thankless preliminary phase, from the initial data-collection to the reconstitution and statistical analysis of the family files. The historian will then have virtually nothing to do but apply thought: which should after all be his or her proper task.

To take another kind of research, a team of historians from the *École des Hautes Études* recently completed a study of Parisian rents from the fifteenth to the seventeenth century. Here again, the computer was the key to success. The basic data on these rents had been lying unread in notarial files or in hospital and convent accounts. Thanks to this study, which was considerably accelerated by the use of computers, the data could at last be extracted from these dusty ledgers and some of the basic questions which preoccupy quantitative historians could be asked of them—for instance: when did the real economic renaissance occur in Paris? Is it true that the city experienced a "sixteenth-century boom", a "seventeenth-century crisis", or a depression at the end of the Middle Ages? The computer made it possible for these problems to be tackled with a far greater margin of safety than the traditional procedures of reckoning. And indeed within a fairly short time the team had obtained not merely a single graph of average Parisian rents, but over a hundred graphs, providing corroboration for each other and casting light on all kinds of aspects of the question; charting rent movements according to occupation of tenant, district, type of housing or landlord, etc.

Computer-based history does not merely lead to a single,

well-defined category of research. It can also bring about
the institution of a new kind of archive. Once information has
been placed on computer cards or tape and used by one trail-
blazing historian, it can be stored for the purposes of future
researchers seeking to make previously unattempted comparisons. An "archive bank" of this kind already exists in the
Interuniversity Consortium for Social Sciences at Ann Arbor
University: the Consortium at present holds census returns
and American election records since the beginning of the
nineteenth century. A new kind of archivist is to be found
there too—a sort of historical technologist very different from
the traditional scholarly graduate of the *École des Chartes.*

I need hardly add that, here as elsewhere, there is an
"American challenge". For twenty or thirty years the French
school of history has been living—rather well—on the
heritage of the founding fathers, Lucien Febvre and Marc
Bloch. And, in the field of social, economic and quantitative
history at least, this school has come to be regarded as a
pacemaker and an avant-garde for historians of other countries. The technological revolution we are now experiencing
bids fair to change all that. In the United States, every
university of any importance now has its computer centre
and young graduates are quite accustomed to handling the
new machinery, from their very first work as historians—
whether research, article or Ph.D. thesis. These young
scholars are thoroughly at home in the computer age. And
in France too, one can venture to prophesy, looking forward
to the quantitative history of the 1980s, that in this area at
least, tomorrow's historian will have to be able to programme
a computer in order to survive.

2

The Quantitative Revolution and French Historians:[1] Record of a Generation (1932-1968)

SPECIALISTS in French economic history have always worked with figures since the days of Levasseur, Hauser and Mantoux: they could hardly do otherwise. But it was only after about 1932, with the publication of the major works of Simiand and Labrousse that the systematic use of measurement became virtually obligatory among historians. Of course our procedures have remained simple, primitive even, by the sophisticated standards of the econometricians and "historio-metricians" of the USA. Even so, the quantitative revolution has completely transformed the craft of the historian in France.

In retrospect, it appears to have been articulated around several key concepts. Originally developed in the context of considerations about price-changes, it has led in more recent years to a study of economic growth analysed by means of the factors of supply and demand—population, production and incomes.

The grand old man of prices in the 1930s was François Simiand—the inspiration, directly or indirectly, of a whole generation of historians. The central concept in his work is the long-term perspective of price movements, which he took to be indicators of the first importance. If over the long term (30 years or more) prices rise, usually under the impact of imported gold and silver, they necessarily carry with them, according to Simiand, both profits and eventually production, in the same upward movement towards prosperity. This is the *A phase*. But if, by contrast, they should, following a "monetary famine", move downwards over several decades (the *B phase*) the result is depression, collapse, unemployment and subsequently a decline in gross product. *A phases* (rising prices and economic prosperity) alternate over the

7

centuries with *B phases* (falling prices, hence recession and a series of lean and hungry years). The combination of A and B phases forms the very web and substance of economic history and sometimes of all history: what may be termed the *conjoncture*.

Simiand's ideas, which I have over-simplified in summary, were often schematic and sometimes one-dimensional. Even so, they were nevertheless illuminating. They acted as a stimulus to research at a time when the collapse of the market, and the American and world depression of the 1930s, had understandably impressed a generation of historians. A number of important books and articles set out to resurrect and reconstruct whole areas of the economic past, the years of plenty along with the years of starvation. Postan and Abel, whose direct or indirect influence on French medievalists was immense, contrasted the triumphs of the Gothic age and the thirteenth century with the long periods of depression which lay so heavy on the rural areas of the West, stifling them with price collapses between the crisis of 1310–1320 and the beginning of the Renaissance. The Hundred Years War, the disastrous reign of Charles the Mad, the massacres by the Armagnacs and the burning of Joan of Arc ceased to be thought of by the new generation of French medievalists as symptoms of a tragedy peculiar to France during the terrible years of the fifteenth century. Despite these troubles, France under Charles VII, for all its agony, when viewed through the dispassionate eyes of the quantitative historian now seems to have been merely a particularly hard-pressed area within a Europe itself on the rack, a Europe everywhere suffering from the rural crisis of the *Trecento* and *Quattrocento*.

And then, in the wake of these misfortunes, came the brilliant compensations of the Golden Age: Hamilton in 1936, and Braudel in 1949 pointed out the material foundations of the Renaissance, to be seen in the sudden rise in prices and the more than proportionate increases in rent and capital gains, (realized on the backs of wage-earners) between 1500 and 1600. The "price revolution", according to these historians, was the result of heightened demand, itself caused by a population increase and by the influx of precious metals from the mines of Mexico and Potosi.

With the seventeenth century, as the young (and not so young) researchers of the 1940s and 1950s discovered, we were once more in a B phase: prices had levelled off by about 1630 or 1660; the so-called *Grand Siècle* of Louis XIV was in fact caught in an interminable rut of economic depression. Seen against the unflattering background of the downward price curves, Colbert turns out not to be the history-book figure we all learnt about in school: no longer is he the great administrator from whose hands the manufactures of France sprang fully armed. Rather he is the grim agent of deflation. After his death, matters went from bad to worse. True, inflation returned after 1690, but in the form of such violent price rises that they put bread far beyond the purse of the poor, many of whom were thus sent to their graves.

This miserable seventeenth-century reality, which is described without embellishment in the work of Meuvret and Goubert, was not entirely over until after 1730. After this date, if we apply Simiand's still-useful model, the horizon seemed to brighten again, with the new splendours of an A phase which has been depicted in great detail in many works by Ernest Labrousse and later writers. Mexican silver and Brazilian gold, mined in large quantities during the Age of Enlightenment, helped to get the wheels of the economy moving again. While currency remained stable— as it was to do, apart from the brief interval of the *assignats*, from 1726 to 1914—prices, profits, rents and production began to move up once more. An unprecedented wave of prosperity swept over the bourgeoisie, the Atlantic shores of France and colonial trade. All this only came to an end, and then briefly, in about 1780, when wine and grain prices collapsed, spreading crisis, overproduction, unsold surpluses and poverty, the breeding-ground for the popular discontents which were to explode in 1789 and thereafter.

To summarize in this way is of course to misrepresent. The thought of such men as Labrousse, Braudel, Meuvret and Goubert goes far beyond the narrow confines of a study of price movements. It can take the historian, depending on his interests, towards social history, Marxism, perhaps geography or the study of civilization, demography, etc.

But it would not perhaps be entirely misleading to say that, apart from a general wish to go beyond the history of events, the common denominator in the work of these four historians is a concern to study the *conjoncture*, for which, at the time when they were writing, the price records offered the surest signposts. The conceptual framework proposed by Simiand over thirty-six years ago has had at all events the unquestionable merit of providing, for a while at least, a coherent theory of periodization covering more than five centuries: a considerable achievement in itself. But this approach was gradually and logically bound to transcend its own terms; it would have to look to more complex indicators than prices if it was not to collapse under the pressure of the new data being unearthed every day, the cumulative weight of relentless facts which were gradually making cracks everywhere in the structure. Already the nineteenth century was looking like a glaring counter-illustration of Simiand's ideas. The period from 1820 to 1850—a B phase if ever there was one—was characterized by a long period of price stagnation. But this sluggishness of the market, far from paralysing the economy, was on the contrary accompanied by a fantastic increase in gross production. The B phase of price recession was not, in the particular example of France under Louis-Philippe, the mother of depression, but on the contrary the daughter of prosperity. The source of this B phase was the steadily growing supply of goods produced, which kept prices down and prevented them from rising. Simiand's model was in this case caught in flagrant contradiction to the real world. Something else would have to be found.

The "something else" though turned out to be more than simply the consequence of disproving a theory, as in the case just mentioned. What has happened, since 1960, is that quantitative history has been granted a new lease of life. This revival can be attributed to the new theories of economic growth introduced quite recently to France. The general tenor of these theories has been popularized, thanks to the instructive, though somewhat oversimplified, concept of *economic take-off*. Economic historians and historical economists now generally distinguish between stable, traditional types of society—before take-off (for example rural Europe in the seventeenth century); and growth societies, after take-off: those in which the gross disposable per capita product grows steadily and slowly but surely. In the years 1960–1965, historians such as Baehrel, Chaunu, Delumeau, Vilar, and in particular Marczewski, centred their work on this new kind of data, systematically setting alongside the price indicator the indices of trade and production in the form of total or per capita income.

Nowadays the concept of growth (or in more traditional societies, non-growth) has won its place in historiography. When applied, it considerably modifies the notions we once had of French modernization in the nineteenth century.[2] The concepts of "industrial" and "technological revolution" which were so popular for so long, have now been pushed into the background. The economic expansion which was so marked in this country during the first two-thirds of the nineteenth century was in fact very largely fuelled by the traditional sectors of the economy (agriculture, building, international trade in agricultural products) which were not modified by technological innovations of any importance for a very long time. On this issue (though with some reservations) French historians are at one with their "historiometric" colleagues in the United States, of whom Fogel is one of the leading representatives. Fogel has tried for instance to establish the truth about the famous legend of the railroads, which is still a powerful force in popular imagery, as addicts of westerns will know. By the use of figures and what he calls "counterfactual hypotheses", he claims to demonstrate that, even if there had been no railroads at all, the impressive expansion of the American economy during the first eighty years of the nineteenth century would still have taken place in very much the same way. It was not the steam engine or the locomotive, he says, that created the wealth of America in the last century, but the efforts of the farmer and the ancient institution of slavery (which remained profitable right to its last gasp). If we can rely on Fogel's concepts and equations—which are possibly too ingenious to be totally convincing—the battle for the frontier had nothing to do with the epic of the railroads: it was an expansion of a traditional type—not so very different in certain respects from that of rural Europe in the eleventh century. Whether this is the case or not, the new quantitative studies of growth certainly emphasize the role of traditional elements in the apparently revolutionary take-off of the economy in the nineteenth century. At the same time by way of contrast, they are mapping the features of societies without growth as these once functioned in the west.

One such society was the French countryside from approximately 1330 to 1730. Many writers, from Marc Bloch to Poitrineau, have made us familiar with it. In some respects it deserves the name of a stable society. True, the stability was very relative: rural society in the past was constantly subject to immense, slow-moving fluctuations; and was also from time to time beset by alarming convulsions. It was nevertheless distinguished by its unwillingness to change—or, to put it another way, its incredible capacity for recovery. Even when disturbed or seriously damaged, this type of society has a powerful tendency to rebuild itself, to heal the wounds, along the lines of the original archetype. Fourquin and Tulippe have convincingly demonstrated this apropos of the Hundred Years War. The last trooper and the last Englishman had hardly left before the peasants of the Ile-de-France were beginning to reconstruct their parishes, their landscape and their population, in an exact replica of the time-honoured patterns which had flourished a century and a half before. In the reigns of Louis XII and François I, these country people were quite unapologetically reviving the age of Philip the Fair.

What statistical studies have recently brought to light about these *ancien régime* societies is the presence of a number of insuperable barriers and limitations. The most evident type of barrier (finding concrete expression in the shape of famine) concerned the production of subsistence foodstuffs and more particularly agricultural productivity which stubbornly refused to grow. A recent debate between the historians Slicher von Bath and Morineau has shed much light on this question: Morineau and several others have demonstrated, with the aid of documents and accounts, that the wheat yield per hectare—even on the richest of French soils—did not rise by so much as a quintal between the age of Saint Louis and that of Louis XV—or even that of Louis-Philippe. The study of tithes, those venerable and much-challenged measures of overall production, as recently undertaken by Goy and several other historians, leads towards similar conclusions: for long periods, between the fifteenth century and the early years of the eighteenth, grain production, measured by the tithe, failed to increase, thus imposing certain insurmountable limits on the expansion of the society as a whole. This does not mean of course that dynamic islands of growth did not exist within that society; but such islands were, under these conditions, long to remain exceptional or altogether insignificant.

Similar obstructions can be found at various levels, paralyzing the entire social body. Wage-rates for example, even in Paris, a city of rapid growth, were held down extremely rigidly between the fifteenth and the eighteenth centuries. Micheline Baulant has quantified them: between 1470 and 1750, wages kept falling: then at the very lowest point on the graph there was a long period of wage stagnation, which persisted heartbreakingly throughout the classical period. Marx saw the pauperization of the workers as the baptismal act of capitalism; in fact it seems to have been above all the distinctive mark of a blocked society, one incapable of raising productivity and hence the living standards of the lower classes.

Other blocks and barriers in traditional societies were the result of authoritarian or parasitical levies demanded from above in rent, tithes or taxes. Every time the royal administration, for example, tried to increase its share of the national cake, in the form of taxes, while the cake in question remained the same size or grew only very slowly, it triggered off as if by reflex action a number of violent disturbances. Richelieu was to find this to his cost: having turned the fiscal screw rather sharply, and without warning, in the period 1625–1630, he automatically received in reply the series of popular revolts which have received much recent attention following the work of Porchnev and Mousnier. And under the next cardinal, the response was —the Fronde.

In this context, the notion of fluctuation takes on a rather different meaning from that given it by Simiand. Price movements in particular, while certainly not negligible, are no longer accorded such predominant and exclusive importance: the historian is becoming increasingly aware that these occur (before 1700) within a primitive economy in which many products are bartered or consumed on the spot, without ever entering the market economy with its prices. So price changes during A and B phases cannot be regarded as explaining everything. Besides, to the extent that they nevertheless remain important, they necessarily refer the historian elsewhere, since they are located at the intersection of supply and demand. Demand was generally elastic: expressed in varying conditions by a fluctuating population; while supply was on the whole inelastic: consisting of subsistence production.

It is this basic contradiction—demand-supply, population-subsistence, population growth-gross product—which has, for the time being, provided the economic history of rural regions with a model of periodization in so far as it can be approximately mapped by quantified indicators. In general terms (if I can trust my own experience which is certainly very partial and localized) I see two great multisecular cycles, separated by the falling blade of the Black Death. First the medieval cycle, with its topical contradictions on the one hand: rising demand, which might or might not be backed by the ability to pay, and a rising population, between the eleventh and the early fourteenth centuries; and then the counterpart to this upward movement, the growing inadequacy of subsistence production, leading to famines between 1310 and 1340 and finally culminating in a wave of epidemics and disasters which relieved demographic pressure tragically between 1348 and 1480. Once this apocalyptic time of plague and misery is over, towards the end of the fifteenth century, the second great cycle begins. This moves through various phases from the time of Louis XII to Louis XIV. It is characterized by a demographic recovery, a new rise in the population rate and, once more, saturation point in the Malthusian sense is reached in land, subsistence and employment, because of this human overload. The only way out of this dilemma and the harsh depressions that inevitably followed would be through growth, which eventually got under way, gradually, during the Age of Enlightenment. And for this growth it seems that the non-agricultural sector was initially responsible.

I have restricted myself in this survey to the area of economic history, where quantitative research is both essential and, nowadays, recognized as such. Statistical or "serial" history as it is sometimes called, has nevertheless spread to other fields of enquiry: former patterns of religious observance and the history of attitudes have both been the subject of statistical studies (see the work of P. Pérouas and that of François Furet and his collaborators on *Livre et société au XVIIIe Siècle (Books and society in the eighteenth century)*.) But certain pioneering and promising disciplines (for instance the field of historical psychology) remain resolutely qualitative, and very properly refuse to be quantified. They are still at the stage of conceptualizing their approach, seeking to build coherent and operational models, in short acquiring their credentials which must always, in any area, be a necessary preliminary for statistical analysis. Without such preliminary precautions, the numerical approach might run the risk of becoming platitudinous or ridiculous. But in the long run, even in the more esoteric branches of history, it must surely be the case that there will always come a moment when the historian, having worked out a solid conceptual basis, will need to start counting: to record frequencies, significant repetitions, or percentages. For only calculations of this kind, however tedious and even elementary they may seem, can in the end validate the data that has been collected and show whether this goes beyond the anecdotal to the typical or representative. To put it in its most extreme form (and it is an extreme so remote and in some cases so beyond the scope of present research as to be perhaps only imaginary), history that is not quantifiable cannot claim to be scientific.

3

Quantitative History:[1] The 6th Section of the École Pratique des Hautes Études

ROBERT FORSTER originally suggested as a title for this lecture: "Aims and methods of the 6th Section". That title might seem a little mysterious to the many people, both here and in France who do not as a rule know what the 6th Section (economic and social sciences) of the *École Pratique des Hautes Études* actually is. To those who do know, the same title might seem somewhat provocative. Well, never mind. I have kept the same wording, slightly modified, but I would warn my audience that my paper will be principally concerned with the *publications* and *research* associated with this Institution, which does not claim to hold the monopoly of certain *methods*.

The 6th Section was founded in 1947, within the confederal framework of the *École des Hautes Études*. Its aim was to promote research and teaching of the most advanced kind in the area of economics and the social sciences.

The enterprise was a challenging one, since in the area of "human sciences" at any rate, French scholarship had much to do if it was to approach what had already been achieved in the English-speaking countries. And much was done: with men like Claude Levi-Strauss, Roland Barthes, Pierre Bourdieu and many others, and the wave of enthusiasm for structuralism, the 6th Section has certainly been in the forefront of French research in the areas of anthropology and sociology (sociology as such, with the work of Pierre Bourdieu, or sociology combined with linguistic methods and applied to literary methods, as associated with Roland Barthes).

But today we are here to talk about historians. And the fact remains that the 6th Section, in spite of its title (economic and social sciences) which does not necessarily suggest a

17

historical bias, is one of the key places in France for the development and publication of active historical research. There are many reasons why this should be so. Some may appear to be accidental: successive presidents of the 6th Section have been, or are, themselves distinguished historians. But the more fundamental reasons probably go beyond the question of individuals, however eminent. These reasons have to do with the special place that history has long occupied in France, under the influence of successive currents of thought and sensibility. In the past, many intellectual trends have been profitable to French historians—from Romanticism in the days of Michelet and Thiers to the Hegelian-Marxist wave of the 1930s. When the social sciences first began to be developed in our country, French historians had the advantage of an already established position; and they were able, quite simply, to take the lead in the new movement and to cooperate with these younger disciplines which promised so much for the future. Such strategic intelligence (so clearly displayed in the years 1930–50 in the review *Annales*) was very much to the credit of the initiators of the movement, Marc Bloch, Lucien Febvre, Fernand Braudel and Ernest Labrousse. In other European countries, as we know, history has been by no means so fortunate.

Its ill-wishers may perhaps suggest that the dominant position held by the 6th Section in the world of historiography is basically explained by the fact that it receives grants for research and publication. This charge is easily answered: the CNRS for example has also acted as a stimulus to the financing of historical research and publication. And yet the name of this institution—an extremely useful and beneficial one—has not become attached to any particular school of historical study, as has that of the 6th Section.

The reasons for the success (and by the same token the aims and methods) of the 6th Section are clearly of an intellectual nature. Let me therefore list them, not necessarily in any logical or chronological order.

The first positive aspect on which I would remark is: openness to the world. It is fascinating, when one visits the Department of History at Princeton for example, to discover the virtually worldwide scope of the research that is carried on there.[2] And many professors at that university are quite ready, in a friendly way, to criticize the supposed provincialism of French historical research. One such professor said to me: "Your colleagues are in a class of their own on French history. But outside France you are like Mao Tse-tung's fish—lost out of water." The accusation might be true in some individual cases, but it is undeserved in a wider sense; and it would be easy to refute it by mentioning some of the recent works published in the universities of Paris and the French provinces. In this connection, the entire corpus of work of Fernand Braudel, the president of the 6th Section, has been devoted to breaking down the constricting barriers of national historical studies. With *The Mediterranean and the Mediterranean World in the age of Philip II*, French historiography took its place in world history. Since this book first appeared (there is now a second, revised edition)[3] the Iberian world has become a favourite area for published studies and as it happens for the researchers of the 6th Section. *Séville et l'Atlantique* by Pierre Chaunu, *La Catalogne dans l'Espagne Moderne*, by Pierre Vilar, *Simon Ruiz* and *Géographie de l'Espagne morisque* by Henri Lapeyre, *La Population catalane de 1553 à 1717* by Nadal and Giralt,[4] all represent different aspects of a continuous effort to provide new bases for the historiography of Spain and the Iberian world—that is America and the Philippines—between the sixteenth and the eighteenth centuries. In this sense, it would be true to say that the initiative launched by Earl J. Hamilton[5] in the 1930s found a sequel in France as much as, or perhaps even more than, in his native country. More recently, we have published two new books, Bennassar's *Valladolid au Siècle d' Or* and Carrère's *Barcelone*,[6] which illustrate both the vitality of this vein of research and the fruitfulness of cooperation between the *École des Hautes Études* and the great provincial universities like Toulouse.

Even more important however than extension of the range of research is the development of methods. Essentially of course this concerns the use of quantitative techniques. The works published by the 6th Section make absolutely no claim to have a monopoly of these. But it is only right to recognize that they have put them to particularly systematic and productive uses.

The actual progress made by the quantitative method in French historiography deserves a brief mention here, since the circumstances of its perfection and triumph as applied to France itself are not necessarily widely known. The best historians of the 1930s in our country were, to a very great extent, "qualitative" historians. Among them was Georges Lefebvre, whose excellent books received such attention in the United States that they have sometimes overshadowed other major developments of French historiography. Lucien Febvre and Marc Bloch (the founders of the *Annales* review and "School", where the group of historians attached to the 6th Section in some ways originated) were themselves too, for the major part of their careers, qualitative writers. What was essentially new about the work of Febvre and Bloch was not a move from "quality" to "quantity", but much more the fact that both historians systematically ignored the "event" and concentrated instead on data of more profound significance, on *structures* and on the *long term*. The very logic of such an undertaking inevitably meant working with figures and statistics (as can be seen very clearly in the case of *The Mediterranean*,[7] a "structural" book in the full force of the term, where the sections devoted to statistics, already substantial in 1947, were much enlarged in the second edition of 1966). To return to the "founding fathers", Febvre and Bloch, however the transition to statistics took place outside their immediate circle. It was another group, or sub-group, of historians who began moving in the direction of "numerical" history—which was however already implicit in the conception underlying Febvre's *Rabelais*[8] or Bloch's *Caractères originaux*[9]. The first stimulus towards the pursuit of the quantitative in history came from a third man: Ernest Labrousse.

Labrousse, who subsequently became director of studies at the 6th Section and a professor at the Sorbonne, had already outlined, in his *Esquisse du mouvement des prix au XVIIIe siècle*,[10] a rigorous and substantial model of quantitative history. A second book: *La Crise de l'économie française*

... *au début de la Revolution*,[11] which had a tremendous scientific impact in France, inspired literally countless students to become quantitative historians between 1945 and 1960. For this rapidly-growing group of scholars, the 6th Section was to become a haven; sometimes only a port of call; occasionally a sanctuary; at all times a meeting-place and in most cases a providential publisher. We can also say that it was a training centre, since many students and researchers, young and not so young, went there to attend the seminars conducted by Braudel, Labrousse, Meuvret, Vilar and Goubert.

A record of the final success of the section must simply mention some of the works it has produced. Take for instance Pierre Goubert's *Beauvais et le Beauvaisis au XVIIe siècle*.[12] Goubert started from an idea: that one could apply the quantitative method not merely to prices, as had been mainly the case until then, but to a different set of documents: parish registers. The result was a completely new picture of the life of ordinary families under the *ancien régime*.[13]

Another type of quantitative history is concerned with economic development: for many years, as I have said, historians studying the French economy, having fallen under the spell of François Simiand, almost unanimously devoted themselves to the history of prices. And indeed this interest proved to be very stimulating—we published for example *La Mercuriale de Paris* by Jean Meuvret and Micheline Baulant.[14] But this enthusiasm carried with it the risk of neglecting other variables.

More recent research has therefore tackled *trends in trade*: Pierre Chaunu, one of Fernand Braudel's pupils, has, by using the archives in Seville,[15] reconstructed the entire movement of Spanish shipping in the Atlantic between 1500 and 1650—and in the Pacific as well (see his excellent and too-little-known book on the Philippines).[16] He has thus been able to establish the limits of the sixteenth-century expansion and the seventeenth-century crisis within the areas under Iberian influence. A whole set of studies (of ports, routes and trade) resulted from similar initiatives and were published by the 6th Section. In this collection, or closely attached to it, there is for example P. Jeannin's work on the accounts of the Sund;[17] or the study of Livorno by Braudel and Romano.[18] Particularly interesting from the methodological point of view which is our present concern, is Jean Delumeau's *L'Alun de Rome*:[19] Delumeau charts, decade by decade, the production and world sales of an important commodity (alum) which was indispensable in the cloth industry: he has thus managed to give for the first time a view of the secular and even multisecular (fifteenth to eighteenth century) progress of the textile industry in various European countries and particularly southern France. One final example in this area: Louis Dermigny's book on China,[20] in three volumes, ending with a series of graphs which give a very clear picture of the trend of the "China trade" from 1650 to 1800. As with Chaunu's *Séville*, this is a book which it would be perfectly reasonable to begin at the end, by "reading" the magnificent collection of graphs.

In a related area, I should mention as an example of international collaboration carried out within the 6th Section, Frank Spooner's book on monetary movements and the minting of currencies.[21] Here again, some crucial graphs and a series of brilliant maps (in which the masterly touch of Jacques Bertin, the 6th Section's cartographer, can be detected) give a remarkable précis of trends in the history of currency in France in the sixteenth and seventeenth centuries.

The quantitative breakthrough achieved by Pierre Chaunu had consequences of great significance. Carrying further the work that he had accomplished with the assistance of the 6th Section (which made it possible to publish a monumental work in ten volumes, unthinkable in any other circumstances) Chaunu founded, at the University of Caen where he now teaches,[22] a quantitative history group; the group has set about quantifying all kinds of regional problems: past developments in agricultural production, population, building etc. One remarkable project on which Chaunu's young disciples have embarked is a statistical history of crime from the sixteenth to the eighteenth century.[23]

Chaunu's example clearly shows that "quantitative" history is so to speak contagious: it is a method which conquers one area after another. Let us concentrate for the moment on economic history. It is clear that research should go beyond commercial exchange—to the very basis of economics, that is production itself. In this respect René Baehrel's pioneering but not always properly appreciated book was a landmark.[24] It was published by the 6th Section at a time when its ideas ran counter to "received opinion"; despite its somewhat chilly reception in academic circles, this study, which is unfortunately not always easy to follow, now seems more and more to have been breaking new ground. Taking as the basis for his research the ecclesiastical accounts, Baehrel was led straight away to absolutely basic data such as agricultural production and income (as ascertained through the tithes), wages, land rent, and payments exacted in taxation, seigniorial dues and usury. He was also the first historian to elaborate a completely original chronology of the seventeenth century, producing a series of long-term graphs. Until (and *not*, for obvious reasons, including) Baehrel, historians had put their faith essentially in price curves; and it was thought that because of the long period of falling prices in Europe after 1600 or after 1630 and 1650, a large section of the seventeenth century was dominated by economic depression. Perhaps rather hastily, terms like "the seventeenth century crisis" or "the tragic conditions of the seventeenth century" had been bandied about—terms which were certainly valid in the case of Spain, but which seemed much less applicable to French problems, at least in the south of France. Baehrel plunged purposefully into the ecclesiastical accounts and extracted from them production curves proving beyond dispute that Provençal agriculture had experienced moderate but steady expansion until about 1680, give or take a few years.[25]

One could hardly therefore talk about the "seventeenth century crisis", since the depression actually occurred somewhere between 1680 and 1720. If I may be permitted to quote my own work,[26] since I too have been a member of the 6th Section and have published under its auspices, I must say that my research on quantitative questions, carried out quite independently in the Languedoc, has confirmed Baehrel's conclusions on this question (though not on all the others): the reversal of the secular trend in the case of the Languedoc takes place in about 1680. It seems that the Dutch war—that World War I of Louis XIV's personal reign—played an extremely important role as detonator in this respect. Our graphs thus concur with the purely qualitative but extremely pertinent evidence published by the American historian Rothkrug in his admirable book, *Opposition to Louis XIV.*[27]

*

   Comparable in terms of methodology, but this time relating to the eighteenth century, is Pierre Vilar's major work, *La Catalogne dans l'Espagne moderne,*[28] which should be given an important place in this account. Vilar, director of studies in the 6th Section, uses the quantitative method at several different levels: his demography is based on census returns which, when compared, show a doubling of the Catalan population in the eighteenth century; on production, as in Baehrel's work, the key sources are the incomes of the ecclesiastical communities, hospitals and seigniorial and royal farmed offices. In addition, Vilar has also included wage series for the period. The combined effect of this *total* investigation (that is one which brings together, in a collection of unique graphs, vital factors of supply and demand) is extremely striking. Vilar establishes that, in the heart of a traditional society, eighteenth-century Catalonia, the pheno- menon of economic take-off occurred. Population increased, but production rose even more. As a result, however great the obvious inequality of distribution, the gross product available for per capita consumption increased; in spite of the increase in the number of mouths, the classical pheno- mena of pauperization that one expects in under-developed societies going through a population explosion, did not take place. The proof is that the Catalan wage curve went up, (faster than the price curve) thus demonstrating the progres- sive improvement in the standard of living of wage earners— a standard that remained low, of course, in spite of this slight improvement. Many economic historians will be surprised and even shocked by the appearance of this "take- off" within a typical traditional economy. They can take heart from Pierre Vilar's suggested explanation—a simple though not an exhaustive one: that among other things it was irrigation, extensively developed in eighteenth-century Catalonia, that made possible the rise in agricultural productivity and the upward surge of production.

Very different is the picture that emerges from works on quantitative history published by the 6th Section on earlier centuries (from the fourteenth to the eighteenth century). One book, which I can quote from my own experience as a researcher, is Baratier's *La Démographie provençale*.[29] Working from fiscal returns, the author establishes that the population of Provence, numbered in round figures, hardly increased at all between the thirteenth and the sixteenth century. There were massive fluctuations—the collapse after the Black Death and so on. But numbers by 1540 had merely caught up with and somewhat exceeded those of 1300. This image of a society of country people remaining stable over the very long term (in spite of some violent temporary upheavals) seems to me to be one of the fundamental results to emerge from the works of quantitative history which we have produced or published. In the sixteenth century for instance, in the south of France as I have come to know it, there was no economic take-off. The population rose very quickly, regaining the level it had reached before the Black Death. But wheat yields remained constant, agricultural production and productivity were held in check. In consequence, the processes of pauperization were triggered off: these were reflected in the fall in real wages and in the division into tiny plots of peasant smallholdings—two logical consequences of demographic expansion when it is not accompanied by a corresponding increase in gross product. In the long run, these processes eventually cause poverty to increase, thus putting a stop to demographic expansion itself. This then appears to be a society in possession of its own Malthusian mechanisms for self-limitation: it is a society of stability—as compared to the societies of growth which were beginning to appear here and there in the eighteenth century and which became the dominant model in the nineteenth. The accurate description of such phenomena and the elaboration of models corresponding to these different types of development is, I believe, one of

the most helpful contributions made by French historiography as practised or published in the 6th Section.

Central to almost all works of this nature is the concept
of what in French is called *la conjoncture*, a term hard to
translate into English. To study the *conjoncture* of a period
means more than simply taking a few indicators (such as
prices); it requires the historian to compare the various
trends discernible in the different variables (population,
production, prices and wages) and on this basis to construct
a dynamic model. It is on such foundations that many of the
books published under the auspices of the 6th Section have
been written.

The most powerful objection that could be made in this
respect is that in these books, the *conjoncture* is overwhelm-
ingly agricultural. This is plain to see in Baehrel's work, and
mea culpa, in my own research. But it looks as if this perhaps
over-exclusive preoccupation is being changed. We have just
published an important book which throws much light on the
dark side of the *conjoncture*, on changes in industrial production in the *ancien régime*, Deyon's study of the textile industry
in Amiens in the seventeenth century.[30] In seeking to establish
trends in manufactured production, Deyon had no basic data
concerning the number of pieces of cloth woven. But he
convincingly filled this gap by using and putting into graph
form statistics relating to indirect data, such as the figures for
working looms, local tolls and the numbers of young appren-
tices. He was thus able to demonstrate by looking at the shape
of the curves, that textile production was indeed, at least in
part, influenced by the cycle of agricultural production.[31] Another conclusion that emerges from his Amiens study is that
seventeenth-century industry, locally at any rate, cannot be
described by the blanket terms *crisis* or *growth*: there seems
to have been a good period lasting until about 1628, some
disastrous vicissitudes in mid-century and a degree of
revival in the last decades—preparing the way for the take-
off of the eighteenth century.

Conclusions of this kind are closely related to the history
of material civilization. And indeed this area of historical
study has inspired some important individual or collective
research within the 6th Section: for example Fernand

Braudel's most recent work, *Civilisation matérielle et capitalisme*,[32] and the international project on *deserted villages*[33] which has brought together contributions concerning France, England, Germany and Italy. This study has proved, it seems, that the disappearance of entire villages, notably during the fourteenth and fifteenth centuries, was comparatively rare in France, a demographic island in western Europe, while it occurred with devastating frequency in the surrounding countries.

Quantitative history, as practised in the 6th Section, has however gone well beyond the bounds of the study of material life as such, as its achievements in the area of social history show. In 1961, François Furet and Adeline Daumard produced their first study of social structures in Paris, based on notarial archives.[34] Using the marriage settlement as the cornerstone of their research, these two young scholars defined social groups within the capital according to a double scale of references: hierarchical differences and wealth. Within this framework, they re-located a number of variables: family mobility, choice of marriage partner etc., and thus formulated some new conclusions about the internal articulations of Parisian society. And other works followed the first (Daumard: *La Bourgeoisie parisienne de 1815 à 1848*; Meyer: *La Noblesse bretonne*; Bennassar: *Valladolid au siècle d' or.*)[35]

Even psychological history has been infected, in France as elsewhere, by the quantitative revolution. This branch of history, which was brilliantly launched by Lucien Febvre and is carried on today by historians like Jacques Le Goff, Robert Mandrou and Alain Besançon,[36] has deep roots in the *École des Hautes Études*. And in this area, which has already been explored in the past, the introduction of quantitative methods has represented a classic case of cultural migration: coming from economic and social history where he had produced several important works, François Furet undertook to apply to the eighteenth century the statistical methods which had already proved their worth in historical sociology. By classifying and breaking down, according to genre, the tens of thousands of book-titles published in France during the Age of Enlightenment and up to the Revolution, Furet was able to quantify, step by step, the process of de-clericalization, the "rejection of the super-natural" which characterized French consciousness at the time of the *philosophes*. In the same study, Roche gave us for the first time a quantitative analysis of a "cultural milieu" —that of the provincial academy. He proved statistically among other things that the frontier of the Enlightenment world ran through the middle of the bourgeoisie: excluding manufacturers and tradesmen, but including on the other hand, in a cultural community with the Nobility, the enlightened bourgeoisie of the *grands Notables*.[37]

*

Perhaps at this point I should conclude this record of publications—although it is still incomplete (I should for instance have mentioned studies like Pérouas's *La Diocèse de La Rochelle au XVIIe siècle*,[38] which applies the methods of quantitative religious sociology to the centuries of the Counter-reformation and the Enlightenment). But I ought now to give some indication of the current projects of the Centre for Historical Research in the 6th Section. Quantitative history remains very much the dominant preoccupation.

One of the main studies in progress at the moment is entitled "Agricultural production and income from the sixteenth to the eighteenth century". The basic source for this is the tithe agreements which enable one to build up a picture over the long term (a very approximate one to be sure) of the movement in production and also in revenue from land.[39] The first results are about to be published; they help us to define with more precision the economic *conjoncture* of the seventeenth century.

Another investigation under way concerns "Houses and building in economic history". This started from recognition of a gap in our knowledge. Of the two basic industries in the *ancien régime* economy, we know quite a lot about one— textiles; but much less about the other—the building industry. So in collaboration with researchers from the quantitative history group at Caen University, we have tackled a whole series of problems in connection with this area: for instance, the geography of the building industry in traditional France (seventeenth to nineteenth century) and the construction of the modern rural dwelling (in the eighteenth century). In particular we have studied the history of rents in several towns, notably Paris. The interesting thing about urban rents is that through their rise and fall they enable us to estimate the long-term economic fortunes of the town in question. From the point of view of *demand* for lodgings, a *rise* in rents could reflect demographic pressures and the existence of sufficient disposable income to be able to pay them. Looking at the *supply* side of lodgings, a *fall* in rents may be caused by large-scale new building. The problem is to be able to chart the rents in question!

What we have done therefore is to consult the ecclesiastical and hospital archives and pick out the rents of several hundreds of houses in Paris which we then follow individually wherever possible over several decades or more; the entire project covers roughly three centuries (1450–1789). Since the establishment of average rents raised many problems (we had to work out averages according to district and to the institutional landlord; averages both in nominal money values, that is in *livres tournois*, and in deflated values, by using a grain-equivalent; and also to try to establish correlations between the level of rents and the occupation of the tenants) we used a computer to extract these various temporal series from our impressive pile of index-cards. This study, when published, will be one of the first in France to use a computer for a historical project. It will give us more accurate information of great importance about economic trends in Paris (the *conjoncture*): the brief expansion during the Renaissance, the development of Paris between 1600 and 1671, despite the Fronde, the upsurge of the eighteenth century, and the deep depressions of the years 1565–1595 and 1672–1715.[40]

In a general way, like other teams of historians in other countries, we are increasingly turning to computers. One of the interesting problems here is the development of an *ad hoc* method for the entering of documents on punched cards or tapes for the memory bank of the computer. The historical document, even when it is easily quantifiable (notaries'

inventories for instance, marriage settlements, etc.) does
have a specificity and complexity, not to mention an archaic
character, which distinguishes it from the better classified
and formalized material that social scientists—statisticians,
sociologists, political scientists—feed into computers. A
researcher in the 6th Section, Marcel Couturier, has therefore perfected a technique which contains both some useful
tricks for simplifying the data and a number of real innovations : the formalization of the document, the use of "definers"
and "descriptors" which make it possible to avoid numerical
coding before the data is entered into the machine.[41]

One of the first testing-grounds for this method has been
the French military archives. We wanted to carry out a
series of cross-sections of the French population. And we
wanted the cross-sections to fulfil the following requirements :

1. To give a picture of France while it was still traditional
and before it had been completely altered by the industrial
revolution.

2. To give a national and not merely regional sample (so
as not to fall into the habitual tendency of French social
history which is rather too regional in emphasis).

3. But in spite of this nation-wide scale, to preserve the
individual within the sample (this is in order to avoid the
"ecological fallacy"[42] which has been rightly criticized by
sociologists: correlations established on an individual
"baseline" are always more relevant than those based on the
administrative unit).

4. To contain a sufficient number of variables.

5. To be based on documents assembled centrally in
Paris—since our funds did not allow us to go round the ninety
or so departmental archives.

The documents which most fully met these requirements
were those of the first military census (of conscripts) in
1868, now held in Paris. These contain data on the 300,000
men of that year's call-up, listing their occupation, their
wealth (defined simply by whether or not they could afford
to pay for a substitute to do their military service) their
literacy or educational level, their illnesses, their past or
future criminal offences in civilian life (since their files were
kept up to date during the twenty years they were on the

reserve), their past or future changes of address and those of their parents, and lastly data of physical anthropology, some of which at least partly depend on living standards (stature for instance) while others, which do not directly concern the historian, can nevertheless be noted and stored in case they interest biologists (genetic details like colour of eyes and hair). So here we have what amounts to an anthropological document that enables us to carry out a high number of correlations, to study and put in perspective each of the variables listed above. We have already analysed the years 1868 and, for purposes of comparison, 1887, that is two massive surveys covering the entire surface of France, region by region and referring, in each of the two years mentioned, to 10,000 men out of the 300,000 of the total conscript army.[43]

A project like this though, goes well beyond the publication of another volume of social history. It implicitly leads to the establishment of a set of quantitative archives. The cards or tapes on which the collected data have been punched should be made available in the future to other researchers, who may find in them correlations unpublished, ignored or unsuspected by the historians responsible for the initial collection and publication. This "archives" project is remarkably akin to the herculean labours currently under way at the *Inter-University Consortium for Political Research* at Ann Arbor, which is amassing American electoral and census data for the use of future historians. It is not impossible that the similarity between our enterprises should one day lead to some direct form of cooperation[44] on an equal footing between the Archives at Ann Arbor and the data collection of the 6th Section. Such cooperation, which is in the mutual interests of both parties, should not cause any major diplomatic problems, and would in return offer some very promising perspectives for quantitative history and for the academic community of American and French historians.

4

The Conscripts of 1868: A Study of the Correlation Between Geographical Mobility, Delinquency and Physical Stature, and other Aspects of the Situation of the Young Frenchmen called to do Military Service in that Year.[1]

THE following article continues the study of which the preliminary and methodological section appeared in *Studi Storici*[2] in 1969. The earlier publication analysed only a fraction of our sample (1,637 conscripts) as an exemplary and exploratory exercise. The present article is based on the complete survey—a total of 11,819 conscripts, representing one-tenth, selected at random, of those young Frenchmen who in the year 1868 received a "bad number" in the national draw for military service. Our survey covers all the bad numbers ending in 5.

We have attempted to analyse relationships between various phenomena. Of these, delinquency offers some of the most interesting data. The information on delinquency, it must be borne in mind, is extremely varied, since it appears on the conscripts' record cards in the recruiting registers under a wide range of headings:

—begging
—drunkenness
—insulting or assaulting the police
—failing to pay (for a meal etc.)
—causing a disturbance
—fraud, fraudulent extortion of money
—breach of close (trespass)
—resisting the forces of order
—vagrancy
—theft (from "crop-stealing" to "armed robbery")
—wilful bodily harm

—aiding and abetting theft
—indecency or indecent assault
—rape or attempted rape
—arson
—murder

The offences recorded in the file may refer to convictions before, during, or even after military service (during the twenty years spent on the reserve). As can be seen, they may be grouped under a certain number of general headings as follows:

—rural offences
—disturbances and trespassing
—vagrancy
—drunkenness
—theft, fraud and insolvency
—violence
—sexual offences

On the whole, with a few exceptions, the picture is, not surprisingly, one of everyday delinquency, with rural offences, drunkenness and insulting the forces of order occurring most frequently. Statistically, and within our sample, murders are very rare. A few sentences to deportation for political crimes indicate the (predictably) small number of Parisian Communards in our sample, which is too national in scope to accord much importance to the disturbances—even major ones—affecting the capital.

At this stage, our analysis will consider delinquency as a whole. We hope at some later date to offer a more detailed breakdown of the material using the major categories of offences most frequently mentioned.[3] But if we were to draw any meaningful comparisons with other data it was absolutely essential to work initially on the largest possible number of cases (precisely because this "largest possible number" is not itself very great and we did not think it wise to break down an already reduced total at the very beginning of the survey). So out of a total of 11,918 conscripts, we have taken the 248 individuals (2.40 per cent) who have some mention of delinquency on their record cards.

In the first place we explored the relation between delinquency, as a whole, and three of the most obvious and accessible factors in this context provided by the documents: first, the *sector of production in which the conscript was employed* (agriculture or "non-agriculture"); second, substitution or replacement *(le remplacement)*[4] which, as we have already shown in the article in *Studi Storici* is, as one might expect, an index of a certain minimum financial security— or at least of *comparative non-poverty*; and lastly, *literacy* (see Tables I and Ia).

Table I[5]

Percentage of delinquents in the different categories of conscripts

Total

I (a)	Uneducated	3.40% (58 out of 1,706)	2.36% (173 out of 7,329)
(b)	Educated	2.05% (115 out of 5,623)	
II (a)	Non-agriculture	3.27% (118 out of 3,605)	2.36% (173 out of 7,329)
(b)	Agriculture	1.48% (55 out of 3,724)	

Table Ia

Percentage of delinquents in the different categories of conscripts (cont.)

Total

Not replaced	3.19% (187 out of 5,886)	
Replaced	0.54% (9 out of 1,670)	2.60% (196 out of 7,536)

Table Ia covers the same occupational categories as Table I, but does not include those who were themselves substitutes; on the other hand it does include not only the educated and the illiterate conscripts but also the fairly large number whose level of education was not recorded. That explains why the total numbers used in Table Ia (7,536) are higher than those in Table I (7,329).

In order to study these three sets of data, more conveniently, we have selected those conscripts who belong to the sectors of production and transport (essentially lower-class or poorly-paid categories:[6] men working in agriculture, artisan and industrial production, sea-going trades and various types of transport)[7] in all 7,536 young men not counting the substitutes (see Tables I and Ia). It is of course easy to predict where one will find the greatest delinquency: among the illiterate; among the non-agricultural occupations; and

Table II

Occupational categories	Replaced		Non-replaced		Substitutes	
	Delin-quents	Total	Delin-quents	Total	Delin-quents	Total
1. Farming; forestry	5	1032	43	2408	6	584
2. Resin-tappers Charcoal burners	0	5	1	16	0	2
3. Vine-growers gardeners	1	69	2	163	0	45
4. Agricultural labourers	0	26	12	172	2	38
5. General labourers	0	33	27	412	4	200
6. Servants	0	41	14	348	3	73
7. Household offices	0	2	0	6	0	1
8. Unskilled workers	0	9	4	64	1	69
9. Street and field trades	0	6	4	28	0	12
10. Sea-faring trades	0	1	11	237	1	22
11. Traditional transport	1	18	2	72	4	48
12. Building trades	0	75	17	392	4	186
13. Artisans, craft production, industry	2	291	35	1156	6	486
14. Large-scale industry	0	30	9	163	2	98
15. Textile workers	0	32	6	229	0	84
16. Total of "lower income groups"	9 0.54%	1670	187 3.19%	5866	33 1.69%	1948

(Translators' note.) For example, in category 1, farming-forestry, the French term *cultivateurs* properly refers to independent farmers, but conscripts who were actually farm-labourers sometimes called themselves *cultivateurs* too. Where the documents specify that the conscript was a farm labourer (a ploughboy, say) he is classified as category 4. Category 5, "general labourers", refers to men who may or may not have been employed on the land, while category 8, "unskilled workers", refers to those definitely *not* employed on the land, yet not classifiable under any later headings. The term *domestiques*, i.e. servants (category 6), could be used of farmhands, so it is distinguished from 7, where the occupation of the conscript has been specifically named as "concierge", "manservant" etc. Category 13 is a very large category covering most traditional trades where the scale of production is assumed to be small (carpentry, printing, china etc)—still the dominant mode of production in France at the time— while category 14, "large-scale industry", refers to "post-industrial revolution" types of industry, and can be presumed from the names of the new occupations (millhand, machine-minder, panel-beater, metal worker, gas refinery worker etc).

On the whole, most of the conscripts classified under the first six headings, could be considered to come from an agricultural environment, while the majority of those in the other categories probably did not.

among those who did not find substitutes (the "non-replaced"), since they were essentially recruited from among the poorer groups. It is therefore interesting to be able to evaluate the respective weight of these different factors. For percentages, see Table II.

Out of 7,536 conscripts, from the "popular" or "lower income groups" (as defined above, see note 7) the rate of delinquency among those who found no substitutes[8] was 3.19 per cent (187 out of a total of 5, 866 in this category); of those who did find substitutes (that is the most comfortably-off group, or to be precise, the least poor), only 0.54 per cent were delinquent (9 out of 1,670). The positive effects of the *substitution-wealth* phenomenon as an "antidelinquency factor" is borne out at the level of the particular social groups: for example, of those peasants *(cultivateurs)* who found substitutes (the better-off as a rule) only 5 were delinquents out of a total of 1,032 (0.48 per cent); while among peasant farmers who did not have substitutes, there were 43 delinquents out of a total of 2,408 individuals (1.79 per cent—the percentage has tripled). The phenomenon is particularly striking in the sub-group made up of those described variously as "agricultural labourers", "general labourers" "domestic servants" and "unskilled workers", groups 4, 5, 6 and 8 in Table II. Young men in this category who found substitutes (and were probably the sons of parents with small savings) provide *no* delinquents at all (in our sample at least: 0 out of 109), whereas of those young servicemen who really were proletarians in the full and original meaning of the word (that is those who both belong to these categories and were too poor to afford a replacement)[9] 57 (out of 996) had a mention of delinquency on their cards (5.7 per cent). Similarly in the sub-group "artisans and industrial workers",[10] groups 12, 13, 14 and 15 in the table, the conscripts who were replaced (and were often the sons of small employers or at any rate of moderately well-off workers) provide only 2 delinquents for 428 individuals (0.47 per cent) while of the 1,940 non-replaced servicemen in these categories (who are either genuine artisans with no money or typical industrial proletarians) 67 are delinquents (3.45 per cent—a percentage seven times higher).

To be poor or to have been born poor therefore meant that one was more likely to become delinquent one day. Various explanations of this phenomenon can of course be suggested, not necessarily conflicting ones: "class justice" probably does fall more severely on the offences of the poor, while being more indulgent towards those of the well-off. But on the other hand no one would dispute that if poverty does not exactly lead to crime, it does prepare the ground for it.[11]

A further distinguishing factor, relating to delinquency and non-delinquency, stems from the sector of production to which the conscript belongs: of the different categories—agriculture, artisan production, industry and transport—set out in Table III,[12] agricultural occupations provide significantly fewer delinquents than do the non-agricultural groups: the former have a delinquency rate of only 1.48 per cent (55 out of 3,724 individuals), the latter 3.27 per cent (118 delinquents out of a total of 3,605 conscripts)—that is twice as high. Perhaps the old sayings about rural innocence are not entirely unfounded. The difference really does appear to relate to the rural way of life, and not simply to the predictable differences between agricultural and non-agricultural occupational groups, differences which might be explained

Table III

Occupational categories	Illiterate: 0		Able to read and write: 2		Total	
	Delin- quents	Total	Delin- quents	Total	Delin- quents	Total
Total agricultural categories	22 2.09%	1052	33 1.24%	2672	55 1.48%	3724
Total lower-income categories excluding agricultural categories	⋅36 5.50%	654	82 2.78%	2951	118 3.27%	3605
Total lower-income categories	58 3.40%	1706	115 2.05%	5623	173 2.36%	7329

(0 and 2 were the code numbers used in the registers to denote: total illiteracy: 0, and the ability both to read *and* to write: 2.)

simply by inequalities of education and wealth between the two groups. This can be seen when groups of equal educational attainment and equal substitution rates are compared: the *agricultural categories* always have a lower delinquency rate than the others (see Table IV).

Only the *non-agricultural conscripts who found replacements* (last column) have a delinquency rate (0.56 per cent which is very low) anywhere near, indeed slightly higher than and actually extremely close to that of the *agricultural categories who also found replacements*. This finding confirms that in relation to delinquency, replacement (as a mark of non-poverty) is a variable so powerful as practically to eliminate delinquency at all levels, and to cancel out differences in environment (as between rural and non-rural groups for instance) whereas in all the other columns of Table IV, such differences are really quite significant.

The variable "education/illiteracy" is not negligible either when one seeks to distinguish levels of delinquency. But it is a very much less active variable in this respect than either "replacement" or "environment" (rural vs. non-rural). The figures speak for themselves (Table I): out of 1,706 illiterate conscripts,[13] 58 (that is 3.40 per cent) had

Table IV
Percentage of delinquents

	Illiterate	Educated	Substitutes	Non-replaced	Replaced
Agricultural categories	2.09% 22/1052	1.24% 33/2672	1.20% 8/669	2.10% 58/2759	0.53% 6/1132
Non-agricultural categories	5.50% 36/654	2.78% 82/2951	1.95% 25/1279	4.15% 129/3107	0.56% 3/538

been found "guilty" of one or more offences; among educated conscripts,[14] the delinquency rate is significantly lower: 115 out of 5,623, or 2.05 per cent. This is not an accidental difference, since it shows up in both the agricultural and non-agricultural groups as the following extrapolation from Table IV (Table IVa) shows:

Table IVa
Percentage of delinquents

	Agricultural occupations	Non-agricultural occupations
Among illiterate conscripts	2.09% 22/1052	5.50% 36/654
Among educated conscripts	1.24% 33/2672	2.78% 82/2951

The benefits of education and the Enlightenment are real then, and in the nineteenth century at least,[15] they helped to hold down delinquency rates. That being said, it would be wrong to exaggerate their importance. A close reading of Table I shows for instance that education ranks only third among the factors influencing delinquency, coming after replacement and environment (rural/non-rural). If one takes the three categories most susceptible to delinquency (the non-educated, the non-agricultural and the non-replaced, Tables I and Ia) one finds that each of them has a roughly comparable delinquency rate: 3.40 per cent (58 out of 1706) among the uneducated; 3.27 per cent (118 out of 3,605) among the non-agricultural; and 3.19 per cent (187 out of 5,866) among the non-replaced. But if in every category the negative criterion in question (*non*-educated, *non*-agricultural, *non*-replaced) is removed, one finds that the results obtained are very different depending on the factor selected: as between the non-educated and the educated, the delinquency rate drops only from 3.40 per cent to 2.05 per cent; between non-agricultural and agricultural categories i.e. the environment factor, it drops rather more—from 3.27 per cent to 1.48 per cent; but the most spectacular gap in the delinquency rate is that between the non-replaced and the replaced conscripts: 3.19 per cent as compared to 0.54 per cent. In other words, the poverty/non-poverty factor (of which replacement is an approximate but unquestionable expression) is far more important in determining the rate of delinquency than what might be called the alleviating circumstances provided by either a rural environment or improved literacy (the latter indeed coming a long way behind the other two factors).

The study of selected occupational groups confirms the leading role played by wealth and the secondary role played by literacy in reducing delinquency rates; if one takes

Table V

	Replaced and educated ("top dogs")	Non-replaced and illiterate ("under dogs")	Able both to read and to write	Able neither to read nor to write	Replaced	Non-replaced	Total (excluding substitutes)
"Forming-forest" category Delinquents							
—as a %	0.48%	2.42%	0.99%	1.91%	0.48%	1.79%	1.40%
—actual numbers	4	17	23	18	5	43	48
Total	832	702	2326	944	1032	2408	3440

(The total includes categories not in this table.)

peasants as a whole (farming/forestry category), delinquency is noticeably higher among those perpetual "underdogs", the "non-replaced illiterate": the group has a rate of 2.42 per cent.[16] It is much lower by contrast among the perpetual "top dogs", the "literate-replaced" (0.48 per cent—five times less proportionately than the previous group).[17] However if one tries to discriminate between the two factors (replacement and education) combined in this statistic, one finds that the former quite definitely overrules the latter since in the same agricultural category delinquents are twice as numerous (1.91 per cent) among the illiterate as a whole, (both replaced and non-replaced) as they are among the educated as a whole (0.99 per cent). But if one examines the replaced/non-replaced distinction, still among the agricultural conscripts, one discovers a far greater increase in the delinquency rate, which more than doubles, going to rather over three times higher: 1.79 per cent of the non-replaced have delinquency records, as against 0.48 per cent of the replaced. In this particular case (the conscripts of agricultural origin) as in the general finding for our total sample, non-replacement is clearly more important than illiteracy as a correlative of delinquency. Crime is more likely to be associated with poverty than with ignorance. We should not of course, forget that ignorance is often the daughter of poverty. All in all, one has only to look at the previously quoted percentages to see that the replacement/non-replacement alternative is a far clearer indicator of delinquency, at every occupational level, than is the variable education/illiteracy.

The same observation can be made of the composite category made up of agricultural labourers, general labourers, servants, household staff, unskilled workers, and street or field trades—all usually poor categories where delinquency is fairly frequent: the highest rate of delinquency is found among those who could not afford a substitute conscript[18] (61 delinquents out of 1,030 or 5.9 per cent) while it is lowest, indeed non-existent among those who could: no delinquents out of 117.

GEOGRAPHICAL MOBILITY

A second, very interesting set of data, relates to geographical mobility (our sources contain plenty of information on this question, whereas they can tell us little about social mobility).

There is no doubt that geographical mobility is affected by poverty. This is particularly clear among young men from agricultural occupations (Table VI, first line). Let us look first at the cases[19] where the *département* of *residence* of the young conscript is different from the *département* of his parents' *home* (which might imply for instance that the son had had to leave his family to seek a living as a wage-earner). Among the non-replaced conscripts (by definition the poorest or the least well-off, whichever one prefers) the percentage affected by this type of mobility is 12.21 per cent (337 out of 2,759).[20] Among those who were replaced, by contrast, the percentage of "mobile" individuals is easily three times as low—only 3.89 per cent (44 out of 1,132)—a very pronounced difference. On the one hand we have a stable and settled population of comfortably-off peasants; on the other, the poor who have been obliged, by their very poverty, to leave home.

In the lower-income non-agricultural groups however (Table VI, line 3) the difference is much less striking. These groups, occupied principally in the industrial and artisan sectors, are in any case far more mobile than the peasants: 18.57 per cent of these conscripts[21] (677 out of 3,645) are mobile by the definition adopted above (i.e. conscript's *département* of residence differs from that of parental home); that is twice the percentage of the total peasant group (both replaced and non-replaced) where only 9.79 per cent are mobile (381 out of 3,891).[22] And this mobility, this "urge to leave home" of the non-agricultural categories, affects the replaced conscripts (less mobile) almost—but not quite—as much as the non-replaced (more mobile). We do find a discrepancy between the two groups, but it is nowhere near as pronounced as in the peasant group. The replaced conscripts in the lower-income non-agricultural categories have a mobility rate of 15.06 per cent (81 out of 538); the non-replaced (poor) members of this category are *a little more* mobile,—the rate is 19.18 per cent (596 out of 3,107). One can see that the difference exists, and that it fits the pattern

TABLE VI

Département of residence of conscript different from that of parents

	Replaced		Non-replaced		Total	
	A Mobile	B Total	C Mobile	D Total	E	F
Total agricultural groups	44 3.89%	1132	337 12.21%	2.759	381 9.79%	3891
Total of group presumed of low income, including agricultural wage-earners	28 25.22%	111	242 24.15%	1002		
Total of non-agricultural, lower-income categories	81 15.06%	538	596 19.18%	3107	677 18.57%	3645
Total of moderately well-off categories	115 27.85%	413	131 31.57%	415	246 29.71%	828

we have already met, but it is very far from being the three-fold difference found among rural conscripts.

Finally, in the groups which we may call "moderately well-off" (Table VI, bottom line) mobility (measured as before) of all men (replaced + non-replaced) is extremely high: 29.71 per cent (246 out of 828). And there persists, as one might expect, even among these comparatively prosperous categories, a difference—though a slight one—in "favour" of the less well-off, the non-replaced, who here again prove to be more mobile than the well-off (replaced). The percentages of "mobile" conscripts are respectively 31.57 per cent (among the non-replaced) and 27.85 per cent (among the replaced). All in all, poverty is everywhere a motive for mobility; but this is particularly true among conscripts of rural origin, who are fundamentally stable if they have reached a minimum level of prosperity, but who have a propensity to leave home if they are the "non-replaced" (and presumably therefore poor).

★

Still on the question of mobility of this first type (residence versus parental home) one might wonder to what extent education (or illiteracy) is associated with this phenomenon.[23]

One thing can be established: the association as such is quite clear; and it operates in the same way as the poverty factor measured previously. The illiterate (who are very often the poor as well) move more than the educated. Among the agricultural groups, 14.26 per cent of the unlettered conscripts (i.e. zero literacy; can neither read nor write) have left home (150 out of 1,052); whereas the proportion falls to 8.83 per cent (236 out of 2,672) among the educated.

It will be noted (as we have already seen in connection with the factors affecting delinquency) that the difference attributable to lack of education is appreciably less marked than that linked with non-replacement, which continues to be the basic indicator of a "poverty culture". In the present case, the "education" variable is associated with differences in the percentages of conscripts who have left home, but these differences are not even as much as twofold, whereas

Table VII

	Educated: 2		Illiterate: 0	
	A Mobile	B Total	C Mobile	D Total
Total agricultural groups	236 8.83%	2672	150 14.26%	1052
Sub-total of lower-income workers (including agricultural labourers)	184 23.26%	791	91 27.74%	328
Total non-agricultural lower-income groups	545 18.47%	2950	146 22.32%	654

the criterion of replacement/non-replacement yields differences of up to three times as much.[24]

In the lower-income, non-agricultural groups,[25] mobility
is also more frequent among the illiterate than among the
educated. But the difference is not great: 22.32 per cent of
the illiterate are mobile (146 out of 654) whereas the figure
for the educated is 18.47 per cent (545 out of 2,950). The
same remark applies as in the preceding section (concerning
replacement):[26] since the non-agricultural groups are highly
mobile in any case, the differences attributable to illiteracy
are on the whole fairly minimal. But they do exist and always
reflect the same pattern: the less education one has, the
more likely one is to leave home.

It will also be noted that poverty, both cultural and
material, remains the basic factor affecting mobility, as is
indicated by the fact that the illiterate are the most likely
to migrate—whereas from a strictly "enlightenment" point
of view, without taking poverty into account, one might
on the contrary have tended to think that educated men
would be more "restless"—since education is supposed to
open up new horizons. The fact that at all levels the illiterate
nevertheless have the highest mobility rates, clearly indicates
that the propensity to leave home is prompted by belonging
the lowest and poorest category. Literacy by contrast does
not appear to have been a specific stimulus to migration.

We have furthermore tried (Table VIII) to combine for
one category at least (the farming/forestry occupations)[27]
the two criteria indicating deprivation (non-replacement
and illiteracy). As will be seen, the results show a high degree
of polarization: the better-off, educated peasants rarely
leave home (only 3.12 per cent live outside the *département*
of their parents' home); while the poor and ignorant (illiterate, non-replaced) are four times as mobile (the figure
for them is 13.11 per cent). If one separates the two factors
combined in this composite, one sees that it is poverty as
such, rather than ignorance as such, which is the crucial
factor in "moving on"; using the same criterion, residence
versus parental home, within the farming/forestry group,
one finds that the non-replaced conscripts are almost four
times as mobile as the replaced (11.17 per cent compared to

Table VIII
Farming-forestry

	Replaced educated	Non-replaced illiterate	Serving conscripts: educated	Serving conscripts: illiterate	Replaced	Non-replaced	Total (excluding substitutes for the replaced)
Mobile	3.12%	13.11%	7.5	12.9%	3.39%	11.17%	8.84%
	26	92	176	122	35	269	304
Total	832	702	2326	944	1032	2408	3440

3.39 per cent), whereas among the illiterate as compared to the educated, the difference in mobility is not even in the proportion of two to one (12.9 per cent to 7.55 per cent). It is indeed essentially poverty that drives men to migrate (Table VIII). If not actually starvation, it is at any rate hardship that drives the fox from his lair—and young men to seek their fortunes.

*

Another interesting factor to isolate is that of the mobility of the conscripts' parents (ascertainable if the birthplace of the conscript is different from the parents' place of residence[28] as registered twenty years later when the son is liable for national service and comes up before the draft board—the *conseil de révision*). *A priori*, one would expect that the "mobile parents", at least in lower-income categories, would be in general poorer and more "deprived", both culturally and materially, than the "settled parents". The data perfectly, or perhaps one should say cruelly, bears out this theoretical assumption (Table IX): the children of "mobile parents" in the farming/forestry category could muster only 21.15 per cent replaced conscripts out of the total of "non-replaced-

Table IX

	A Illiterate	B* Edu- cated: 1	C Edu- cated: 2	D Replaced	E Non- replaced
Farming-forestry					
1. (a) Mobile parents	318	18	422	165	615
(b) Settled parents	626	57	1904	867	1793
Agricultural labourers					
2. (a) Mobile parents	30	2	38	6	64
(b) Settled parents	38	3	91	20	108
General labourers					
3. (a) Mobile parents	44	3	84	3	127
(b) Settled parents	75	4	267	30	285
Servants					
4. (a) Mobile parents	52	6	75	14	132
(b) Settled parents	51	8	170	27	216
Household offices					
5. (a) Mobile parents	0	0	4	2	3
(b) Settled parents	0	0	3	0	3
Unskilled workers					
6. (a) Mobile parents	18	1	23	4	30
(b) Settled parents	20	0	36	5	34
Building trades					
7. (a) Mobile parents	24	1	111	16	120
(b) Settled parents	42	5	311	59	272
Artisan, craft industry					
8. (a) Mobile parents	65	3	355	66	398
(b) Settled parents	103	11	958	225	758
Large-scale industry					
9. (a) Mobile parents	22	1	65	10	67
(b) Settled parents	30	0	102	20	96
Textile workers					
10. (a) Mobile parents	20	2	44	7	59
(b) Settled parents	37	0	167	25	170
State employees					
11. (a) Mobile parents	0	1	18	16	7

(b) Settled parents	o	2	20	15	7

Other white-collar workers
12. (a) Mobile parents	1	o	96	58	44
(b) Settled parents	2	1	158	118	55

Liberal professions, arts
13. (a) Mobile parents	o	o	6	6	5
(b) Settled parents	1	1	10	6	6

Students
14. (a) Mobile parents	o	o	49	32	26
(b) Settled parents	o	o	115	65	64

Higher-status groups
15. (a) Mobile parents	1	o	6	6	2
(b) Settled parents	1	o	54	40	19

*"Educated: 1" means that the conscripts in question could read but not write, while "Educated: 2" refers to conscripts able both to read and to write.

Table IXa
Farming-forestry group

	Replaced, educated 2	Non-replaced illiterate
Mobile parents	116	241
Settled parents	716	461

plus-replaced" (165 replaced out of 780 "non-replaced-plus-replaced"), while the children of "settled parents", still in the farming-forestry category, could boast a much higher proportion of replaced servicemen: 867 replaced out of 2,660 "non-replaced-plus-replaced" or 32.59 per cent. As regards illiteracy, a similar pattern can be observed: the conscripts in the "farming-forest" group with mobile parents show an illiteracy rate of 41.95 per cent, while those in the same category with settled parents have an illiteracy rate of only 24.20 per cent.

On the whole, if we juxtapose, as we already have several times, the cumulative category of "deprived" conscripts (illiterate, non-replaced) and that of the "favoured" conscripts (replaced and classified as having maximum literacy, i.e. able both to read and to write) (see Table IXa) one finds that the mobile parents in the "farming-forestry" group have produced many more "deprived" children than the "settled parents". The sons of mobile parents in farming/forestry produce 241 "deprived" as against 116 "favoured" conscripts; the sons of settled parents produce 461 "deprived" as against 716 "favoured". The proportions are reversed when one turns from one group to the other.

One finds the same picture, though less dramatically, in the large group of unskilled or only slightly skilled wage earners:[29] 7.53 per cent of the sons of mobile parents found replacements, whereas 11.26 per cent of the sons of settled parents were replaced. Among these low-income workers, usually poor or in very modest circumstances, geographical instability seems therefore indeed to be an *additional* sign of poverty. This impression is even stronger if one uses literacy as a criterion: the conscripts from these unskilled or low-skilled occupations who are the sons of *mobile* parents show an illiteracy rate of 37.89 per cent; those in the same category whose parents are settled have a rate of only 24.02 per cent. So even in circumstances which we already know to be poor and relatively deprived, as in the case of these young workers with few or no skills, the fact that the parents have migrated gives an extra boost to the probability that their children will be illiterate.

Let us now take the category of conscripts who are workers or artisans listed as employed in industrial or craft production, and who are, in theory at least, according to the occupational category accorded them, skilled or at least semi-skilled.[30] Among those whose parents are mobile, 13.32 per cent are able to find replacements;[31] the situation is a good deal better, as one might expect, in those of the same category with settled families: 20.25 per cent of them are replaced.[32] So in industrial or craft production (where we know that the standard of living of the workers, whether the conscripts themselves or their parents, is generally far from affluent) geographical mobility of the parents is found once again to be associated with poor living standards (however one establishes the causal connection: poverty → migration or migration → poverty; for the present we are concerned only with the fact that the association exists).

As for illiteracy, the industrial-artisan categories are comparatively speaking more educated. Nevertheless, the presence of the "mobile-parents" factor as against a "settled family", here as in the preceding examples, introduces a clear form of discrimination: the "artisan-industry" conscripts whose parents are mobile have an illiteracy rate of 18.37 per cent.[33] Only 12 per cent of those in the same group whose parents are settled are illiterate—a distinct drop.[34] And as one can see, the difference falls into the same pattern as before.

In the category which brings together "medium to higher status" occupational groups,[35] the difference still, surprisingly, conforms to the same pattern; but it is much less marked than in the categories previously considered, since in this case one is studying (virtually by definition) groups of men characterized by a rather celebrated type of high geographical mobility which does not always, by any means, lead to socio-economic failure. At this level what one might call the "Rastignac phenomenon" is at its most evident.

Even so, in these more privileged categories while 58.42 per cent of those conscripts whose parents had changed residence were replaced,[36] the figure for those whose parents were settled was 61.77 per cent.[37] One might therefore suggest (not perhaps to anyone's astonishment, but all the same it is an interesting confirmation) that at every level and particularly of course in the lower strata, French society in the years 1848–68 tended to penalize geographical mobility and to reward the settled and the stay-at-home. At any rate that seems to be the case of our particular subjects, the "class of 1868".

*

The figures are presented in a slightly different way below, in order to demonstrate the connection between parental mobility and poverty of the sons (without of course suggesting that mobility causes poverty—although that might sometimes be true—but simply in order to point out that parental mobility and poverty of the next generation are both features located in the same socio-economic environment, that is the poverty of a given socio-economic group). Table X opposite clearly shows that at all levels (agricultural; non-agricultural; and even among the moderately or well-off groups) those conscripts who are replaced (those with some degree of prosperity) are much less likely to be the children of mobile parents than are the non-replaced and the substitutes. The two latter categories (both characterized by poverty or at any rate "non-wealth"), when compared with each other moreover, show generally comparable—and always high— proportions of children from mobile families (Table X).

The discrepancies between, on the one hand, levels of "non-wealth" and poverty (substitutes and non-replaced conscripts who have on average more mobile parents) and on the other hand levels of prosperity or non-poverty (replaced conscripts who on the whole have more settled parents) do not alter the fact that at *every* level, poor and not so poor, rich or not so rich, the rate of mobility increases when one turns from the agricultural groups to the groups of non-agricultural manual workers; and again when one moves to the "medium-status" groups.

*

The military archives also enable us to chart mobility rates *after* the term of service, when the conscript has returned to civilian life (for the whole period that he remains on the reserve: until the age of forty). We have called this pheno- menon *mobility-type 2*. This type of mobility appears to be much less influenced by initial poverty—the poverty of the young man and/or his parents—than was the type of mobility previously considered (mobility before the age of twenty).

True, the non-replaced peasants are more mobile than the replaced, from the point of view of mobility-2. In the farming/forestry group for instance, 20.22 per cent of the non-replaced were to move to another place of residence, while the figure for the replaced conscripts is 14.53 per cent. And the percentages for the total agricultural groups are respectively 20.77 per cent and 15.99 per cent. Among the

Table X
*Percentage of children of "mobile parents" in relation to total
conscripts in category in question*

	Substitutes %	Non-replaced %	Replaced %
I Agricultural workers	27.80	26.53	15.99
II Non-agricultural manual workers	32.37	33.47	24.35
I & II: Agric. + non-agric. groups	30.80	30.20	18.69
III Trade, food industry and "medium-status" groups	42.04	37.38	32.67
Total of I, II and III (without "higher-status" groups)	31.64	30.66	21.39

Table XI

	Replaced		Non-replaced	
	A Conscripts mobility 2	B Total	C Conscripts mobility 2	D Total
Farming/forestry	150 14.53%	1032	487 20.22%	2408
Total agricultural group	181 15.99%	1132	573 20.77%	2759
Sub-total of non-agricultural lower income groups	123 22.86%	538	786 25.30%	3107

non-agricultural lower-income groups (Table XI, bottom
line) there is also a greater tendency towards a change of
residence (mobility 2) among the non-replaced as compared
with the replaced (25.30 per cent against 22.86 per cent). But
these differences do not appear, and are even reversed, in
the group of lower-income workers (Table IXa below)

(25.45 per cent against 27.93 per cent); and again in the case of middle-income groups (Table XII below; 29.16 per cent against 36.32 per cent). Consequently in the latter instances there is no simple influence, traceable to initial poverty, at work on change of residence after the age of twenty: such a change has a much lower correlation with failure so to speak than the changes of residence by young men *before* they reached the age of twenty. The causes of these disparities may well be related to circumstances peculiar to the time: those parents of our conscripts who "tried moving" between

Table XIa
Concerning the data on mobility-2, and covering all wage earners of presumed lower income (agricultural and general labourers, servants and household occupations, unskilled workers).

Replaced		Non-replaced	
Young men with change of address after 1868	Total	Young men with change of address after 1868	Total
31 that is 27.92%	111	255 that is 25.45%	1002

Table XII
Data concerning mobility-2 covering "medium status groups"

	Replaced		Non-replaced	
	Change of address after 1868	Total	Change of address after 1868	Total
Food, trade (i.e. shopkeepers)	65	194	85	291
State employees	21	31	4	14
Other white collar workers	57	176	31	99
Liberal professions, administrative, artists etc.	7	12	1	11
Total	150 (i.e. 36.32%)	413	121 (i.e. 29.16%)	415

1848 and 1868 do not indeed seem to have achieved particularly successful results (if these are judged by their low
capacity to provide education or a substitute serviceman for
their offspring). Whereas by contrast the mobility of the
young men themselves after the age of twenty, that is after
1868, does not appear to be universally linked at all levels
with an initial handicap—indeed far from it. Our files here
seem to suggest certain contradictions which require analysis
of a wider range of documents if we are to explain them. Such
a study is not envisaged within this particular project, the
aim of which is deliberately restricted to the analysis of a
single major documentary source; so here we shall only note
the existence of this problem and move on.

These wage-earners are appreciably more mobile than the
farming/forestry groups. As for the negative effect of the
factor "replacement/wealth" as a brake on mobility, which
appears so clearly for the migrations previously considered,
it no longer appears to exist when one turns to mobility-2.

Here then it is the "rich" or at least the "not so poor" who
move the most.

Another element in the data suggests that mobility-2 is
reasonably independent of the initial handicap caused by
poverty (whereas other types of mobility were on the contrary
closely associated with it): mobility-2 does not seem to be

Table XIII

	A	B	C	D
	Education: 2		Education: 0	
	Mobility-2	Total	Mobility-2	Total
Total, agricultural group	479	2672	189	1052
	17.93%		17.96%	
Total low income non-agricultural group	697	2950	122	654
	23.63%		18.65%	
Total medium status groups	235	741	14	52
	31.71%		26.92%	

at all connected with illiteracy, at least for the important peasant group: of the young peasants who were illiterate, 17.96 per cent subsequently changed their address (Table XIII, line 5 columns C and D); for those who could read and write, the figure is 17.93 per cent (line 5, columns A and B). Illiteracy or education are not therefore responsible for any disparities in this case, whereas illiteracy was, when we considered other types of mobility, clearly an element, among other symptoms of deprivation, in the complex of poverty factors which contributed to the urge to leave home, and also to delinquency, among rural conscripts.

PHYSICAL STATURE

Having looked at the problems of delinquency and migration, we shall return to the conclusions of the article previously referred to[38] only on one point: that of height. Here we are in the presence of a variable where it increasingly appears that "cultural" factors (in the anthropological sense of the word: relating to *both* material *and* intellectual culture) are active alongside genetic factors. Among our conscripts, it is easy to see (Table XIV) that the illiterate are undoubtedly shorter in stature than those who have received schooling. The decisive thresholds are:

(a) below 1 metre 60: 20.31 per cent of the illiterate conscripts are under 1m60, whereas only 13.82 per cent of the conscripts with schooling are in this category.

(b) over 1 metre 70: the reverse is the case: only 15.32 per cent of the illiterate are as tall as this or taller, as compared to 22.50 per cent of the educated. We demonstrated in the article in *Studi Storici* that these physical differences do not essentially derive from the geographical origins of the illiterate conscripts (who were, it is true, recruited predominantly from the *départements* of the centre, south and west, where on the whole people are less tall), but that they were quite definitely associated with poverty itself (of which illiteracy is one sign among others); and also with length of schooling. Can it be that schooling, by limiting the amount of physical labour demanded of the young child, has a tendency to stimulate physical growth?

Table XIV
Effect of illiteracy on stature

	Illiterate		Educated : 2	
	%	Absolute number	%	Absolute number
Under 1m59	20.31	362	13.82	923
Between 1m60 and 1m64	35.52	633	31.61	2112
Between 1m65 and 1m69	28.84	514	32.08	2143
Over 1m70	15.32	273	22.50	1503
Total	100	1782	100	6681

In this respect, our earlier survey (in *Studi Storici*) was topical: it excluded large cities and used data basically relating to less wealthy regions in the centre, south and west of France, where both illiteracy and small stature are common; but the survey nevertheless revealed that even inside these relatively deprived regions, men who had received education were taller than their illiterate contemporaries. It appears then that where the region is identical, it is the standard of living or the way of life which is crucial here, rather than the geographical origin.

Similarly, to return now to the full-scale survey of all 11,819 conscripts on which the present article is based, the replaced servicemen are clearly taller than the non-replaced and the substitutes: we find 33.6 per cent of the replaced conscripts in the medium-tall category (between 1m65 and 1m70) and 26.7 per cent of them in the tallest category (over 1m70) (cf. Table XV.) The respective percentages are only 30.4 per cent and 18.9 per cent among the non-replaced and 30.9 per cent and 20.8 per cent among the substitutes. Conversely, below 1m65 and especially below 1m60, we find higher proportions of non-replaced and substitute conscripts than we do of replaced conscripts.

It may be asked which factor contributes most to "produce" short (or tall) men. Is it the *way* of life (agricultural or not)?

Table XV
Height and replacement (percentages to add up vertically)

	Substitutes	Non-replaced	Replaced
Under 1m59	15.6% 350/2234	17.2% 1083/6283	10.6% 242/2265
Between 1m60 and 1m64	32.4% 726/2234	33.3% 2096/6283	28.8% 653/2265
Between 1m65 and 1m69	30.9% 692/2234	30.4% 1913/6283	33.6% 763/2265
Over 1m70	20.8% 466/2234	18.9% 1191/6283	26.7% 607/2265

Despite the fact that the substitutes are, at least theoretically, "selected" from among the "taller" and in principle older men, they measure approximately the same as the non-replaced, evidence that these are both groups of young men whose socio-economic and cultural conditions of physical growth were roughly the same between birth and the age of 20. The replaced conscripts on the contrary are conspicuous by their taller stature.

Or is it the *standard* of living (poverty and low living standards reflected in illiteracy; or the contrary, prosperity)? Our tables provide a fairly clear answer: standard of living is more important than way of life. If for instance we take the two extreme groups defined by living standards: on one hand the non-replaced and illiterate (the worst-off group); and on the other the replaced and educated (the most privileged group), and follow their respective record on height through the various different sectors (agriculture, manual labourers outside farming, food trade and middle and upper income groups)[39] we find that the privileged (educated, replaced) (Column A, Table XVI) have only 9.83 per cent under 1m60 and 26.09 per cent over 1m69, among the farming-forestry category and that the percentages are not basically very different among the non-agricultural manual occupations (10.74 per cent and 28.65 per cent); among the group made up of all the young men from the food trade sector and the medium and higher categories (7.22 per cent and 28.87 per cent); and even among the young men listed as general unskilled labour (13.25 per cent and 30.12 per cent).

But if one turns, in each of these four categories, from the privileged group (educated-replaced) to the under-privileged (illiterate, non-replaced) (column B, Table XVI) the contrast is striking. And here too the disparity is visible in every category, whatever the environment, whether agricultural or not. So taking the farming-forestry "underprivileged", (illiterate, non-replaced) one finds 21.63 per cent of them in the shortest category (under 1m60.) and only 13.90 per cent in the tallest; for the non-agricultural manual workers the figures are 21.43 per cent and 15.18 per cent, and for the general and agricultural labourers, 23.82 per cent and 16.01 per cent.

It is therefore surely the standard of living (privileged

Table XVI

	A Replaced Educated: 2	B Non-replaced Education: 0
1. Farming/forestry		
1m59 and under	9.83% (81/824)	21.63% (151/698)
1m70 and over	26.09% (215/824)	13.90% (97/698)
2. Agricultural and general labourers, servants, unskilled workers.		
1m59 and under	13.25% (11/83)	23.82% (61/256)
1m70 and over	30.12% (25/83)	16.01% (41/256)
3. Building trades, traditional industry sector, large-scale and textile industries		
1m59 and under	10.74% (39/363)	21.43% (48/224)
1m70 and over	28.65% (104/363)	15.18% (34/224)
4. Medium and higher categories, food trade, State and other white-collar workers, teachers, professions, artists, students etc.		
1m59 and under	7.22% (34/471)	Statistically
1m70 and over	28.87% (136/471)	insignificant

versus under-privileged) rather than the way of life (rural versus non-rural) which in this case produces the contrast in physical anthropology.

Elsewhere, on the contrary, in the areas studied in the two earlier sections of the article, both complexes—standard of living and way of life—combined forces to influence the major data concerning delinquency and migration.

5

Changes in Parisian Rents from the End of the Middle Ages to the Eighteenth Century[1]

THE archives of corporate institutions have been, for generations of researchers, one of the fundamental sources for economic history. Whether they are universities, hospitals, cathedral chapters or factories, institutions do not die—or at least their longevity is out of all proportion to that of individuals. The shelves of records kept by institutions have therefore, as is well known, provided material for numerous studies of long-term developments in prices, rents, wages and tithes.

For all the proliferation of graphs, the subject of urban rents has remained one of the poor relations among quantitative historical studies based on corporate archives. The reasons for this neglect are simple: for one thing, economic historians, who have tended to be preoccupied by agricultural questions, were more interested at first in the leasing of land, and therefore concentrated on land rents in rural areas; ground rents in the towns before 1789 were disregarded. And in the second place, the difficulty of identifying buildings, and the problems caused by their falling into disrepair, often discouraged research into urban leases before it got off the ground, so to speak. Not only that, but the massive bulk of the documents seems to have inhibited historians, after the early investigation by the Marquis d'Avenel (whose results incidentally are not without value). And yet the question of shifts in urban rents over the long term is and was in itself a fascinating one; but so thorny that it has sometimes appeared to be quite insoluble.

It seems however that the time has come for a reappraisal of the problem. Modern techniques, in the age of computers, have brought about a revolution in historiography: they have made possible the exhaustive processing of vast quantities of data—quantities undreamed of by past historians, however eminent, who were the prisoners of their unsophisticated methods. It is precisely the case that any study of urban rents, because of the many pitfalls inherent in the subject, calls, if it is to be at all representative, for the examination of a substantial quantity of data drawn from as wide a documentary basis as possible. It is the analysis of a sufficiently large number of sources which makes it possible to construct several series of graphs, to correlate them with one another and to carry out the famous concordance tests which are necessary to establish the validity of any economic history of the *ancien régime*. The study with which this article is concerned was based on a corpus of over 20,000 leases or rental records, every one of which contains several interesting pieces of information. By using a computer, whenever this was called for, we have been able to process tens of thousands of items of data contained in the documentary sources; and from all the material thus classified, we have been able to discover series that have stood up to critical examination, showing a satisfactory degree of mutual compatibility.

Of the two authors of this study, one is a specialist in urban history with a particular interest in Paris; the other, as an economic historian, is concerned with long-term developments in the *conjoncture*, or overall economic situation. The study of urban rents lies at the meeting point of these two interests.

Taken as an indicator of the overall economic situation, rent fluctuations reflect a number of complex trends. It seems reasonable to suppose that they lie at the intersection of supply and demand. On the demand side, the essential factors, baldly stated, appear to stem from demography and purchasing power: when a town is growing and the number of its inhabitants increases, and when some at least of those inhabitants have rising real incomes, it is reasonable to expect that there will be pressure pushing *real* rents up in the town in question. But that of course depends on the supply of units of lodging; according to whether the number of houses or apartments being constructed is small or great, this upward trend may either shoot up dramatically or on the contrary be contained within more reasonable limits. A declining rent curve could be interpreted as denoting the reverse relationship of supply and demand.

Hence the usefulness of having a reliable rent-curve for a big city over several centuries. Such a curve cannot of course provide definite answers to any of the problems we have mentioned (demography, purchasing power, building rates). But it does give us a firmer foundation, in precise and detailed chronological terms, against which such questions can be set. It also offers a cross-reference for confirming or challenging information we already have from other sources on the paramount questions of population, income and house construction.

Plotting this graph becomes a fascinating activity when the city in question is Paris, and the surrounding region. Even today, when so much is known about trends in Antwerp, Beauvais or Seville, the economic activity of Paris under the *ancien régime* remains a mystery and its population an enigma—one which the burning of the archives has made quite impenetrable in some respects. In the circumstances, shedding some light on the history of rents, even from the modest perspective of institutional accounts, can help to disperse a little of the mist that shrouds the question. And we should remember that in this respect the data on Paris takes us beyond the city itself: once a pattern of rents within the capital has been established, the historian can make comparisons with rural ground-rents in the flatlands of the Ile-de-France; and with those of other, more distant places, in France and elsewhere, whenever such comparisons are permissible.

A brief word of methodological explanation is necessary concerning the problems of *deflation* and *conversion*. Our figures can be expressed in two forms: nominal (i.e. in *livres tournois*) and deflated (the equivalent in *setiers* or hectolitres of grain). Why the distinction?

It is an attempt of course to deal with the difficult problem of the depreciation of the money of account (the *livre tournois*). All our nominal curves, if left in *livres tournois*, seem to shoot literally off the page, when examined over three centuries. Such dizzy climbs cannot (or can hardly) be attributed to the housing market. It is always inflation, whether galloping or concealed, constantly depreciating the *livre tournois*, that keeps pushing up the curve of nominal letting prices.

This curve has therefore to be literally deflated—reduced in size—in order to yield some degree of comparability between centuries. To this end, the historian must select a stable unit of account to replace the *livre tournois*, one which will remain constant for the purposes of comparison and at the same time economically significant, over the whole period: from Joan of Arc to Necker.

Such a stable unit could be for instance a gramme of precious metal, gold or silver. From the point of view of stability, in spite of what some people have written, metal is certainly more satisfactory than the *livre tournois*. Its value is not immutable, but it is certainly less liable to collapse than the precarious unit which was the money of account in pre-revolutionary France. A rent-curve expressed in gold or silver would give us a very interesting reflection of reality.

However the most informative curve is one which expresses the average movement in rents from the fifteenth to the eighteenth century in terms of real goods and services, or if the term is preferred, of purchasing power. The curve thus constructed would actually correspond to a precise question of social history: given the social group composed of urban proprietors (whether individual or institutional), what changes in purchasing power, what deflated (i.e. real) income accrued to this group from the fluctuating receipts of successive leases of their properties between 1400 and 1780? In order to answer this question properly of course, we ought to have a weighted index both of prices and of wages in Paris from 1400 to 1800. And we are nowhere near that! But failing this, we can use as a 'deflater' the only continuous price series we do have for Paris for the whole period—obviously a crucial one—the price of wheat. We have therefore systematically 'deflated' our rents by dividing the nominal sum by the price of a *setier* of wheat, ironing out the short-term fluctuations in this price by using a moving three-year average. Thus we have from one triennial section to another, the equivalent in wheat of a rent originally expressed in nominal currency.

It would of course be a good thing if we could go further and deflate our nominal rents with the help of a weighted wage and price index for the capital, covering the three or four hundred years in question. Only when this is done will we have any proper idea of the progress of purchasing power among owners of urban property. Deflation using the price of wheat is only a preliminary and provisional step designed to attenuate somewhat the illusory bulges in the nominal curve. We propose in a later study to calculate the changing values of our rents over the centuries in terms of daily-wages on one hand and of grammes of silver on the other.

In conclusion, and without wishing to anticipate the publication of the detailed results, we can say that the average rent-curve, whether expressed in nominal or deflated values, displays over the very long term a steady upward tendency from the fifteenth to the eighteenth century. This rise, which forms a total contrast to the fall, followed by stagnation over several centuries, in real wages, is explained of course by the growth of the city itself and by the rising demand for lodgings (along with the ability to pay for them). But could it not also be caused in part by the gradually increasing height of Parisian buildings over the years? Many of the rents from buildings leased between approximately 1400 and 1800 concern houses as whole units: so the more storeys a house gradually acquires, and the more it is extended, by adding on rooms, into the courtyards and former gardens, the greater the surface area available for letting, and the greater the average value of the real rent coming in from the single building taken as a unit.

Looked at more closely and at slightly shorter intervals, our nominal diagram begins as expected with a predictable fall between 1420–1423 and 1440–1443. This is the "Joan of Arc depression" which coincides with the final traumas of the Hundred Years War. Then both nominally and in deflated terms there is an abrupt rise: the true Renaissance—first a recovery (1445–1455), followed by healthy growth (1455–1500). Next, from 1510 to 1560, accustomed as we are to the usual notion of "sixteenth-century expansion", we would expect to find a marked rise in rent. This is true of nominal values: the price revolution exerts an upward influence. But

LIVRES TOURNOIS

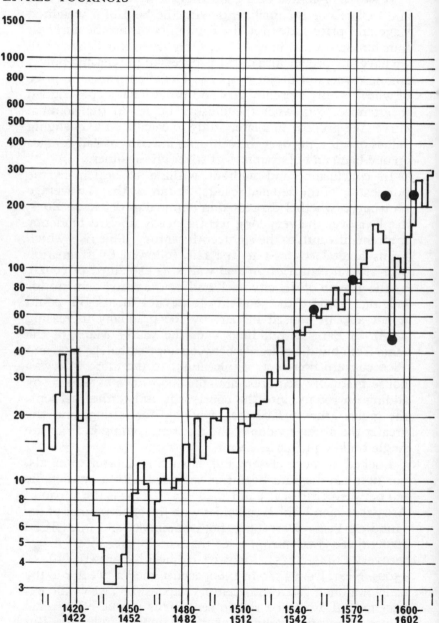

GRAPH I : Average nominal rent for the whole of Paris. The dots represent samples from the *Minutier central*.

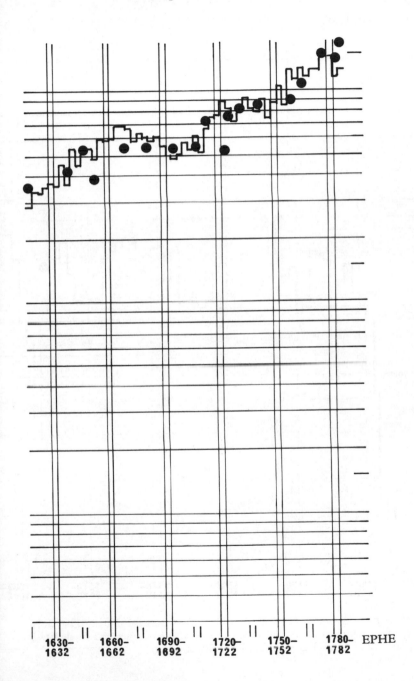

1630–   1660–   1690–   1720–   1750–   1780–   EPHE
1632   1662   1692   1722   1752   1782

SETIERS OF GRAIN

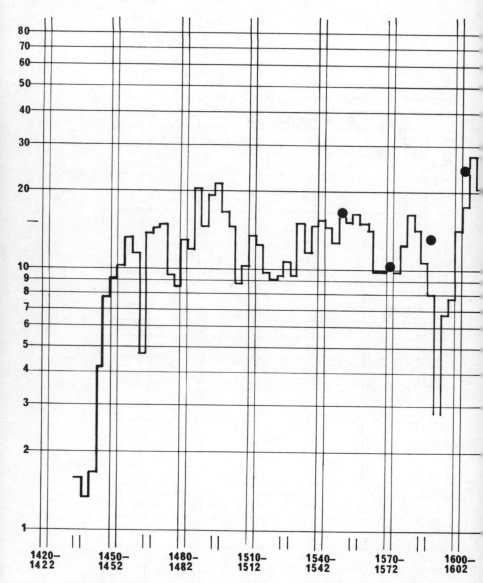

GRAPH 2: Average deflated rent for the whole of Paris. The dots represent samples from the *Minutier central* (also expressed in deflated terms). The vertical axis represents *setiers* of grain.

1630–	1660–	1690–	1720–	1750–	1780–
1632	1662	1692	1722	1752	1782

the curves expressed in deflated values give a less "growth-oriented" picture of the Parisian Renaissance. Real rents appear to have lagged behind or even to have declined from 1504–1506 to 1527–1530. This lag might be explained by the plentiful supply of lodgings, or perhaps more convincingly by a certain levelling-off or standstill in the ability to pay rent, i.e. actual demand (when one thinks for instance of the major crises and food shortages of the 1520s). Historians of Paris may one day be able to assess the relative value of these two hypotheses.

Between 1530 and 1560–63, while nominal rents continue their whirlwind ascent, deflated rents are characterized by a more modest rise: they merely recover their former value around a "high plateau" typical of the 1540s and 1550s; this brings them back approximately to the already quite high levels of the end of the fifteenth century.

Then come the wars of religion: from now on until the end of the series, we have the supplementary data provided by several samples from the records of leases from private landlords. The two series are in substantial agreement and thus enable us to have a clearer idea of the periodization of rents during the civil wars: a first "sticky patch" appears in about 1564–1575; on the nominal curve it is reflected merely by a slight slowdown in the rate of growth (so great are the inflationary pressures in this time of war and of shipments of precious metals from America). On the deflated curve, on the other hand, there is a perceptible downturn during these years.

A second crisis, naturally much more serious, coincides predictably with the siege and the preceding and subsequent events. This time both curves, the nominal and the deflated, mark the crisis with unusual unanimity. All the series— institutional records, private leases, nominal or deflated curves—agree in locating the lowest point of this depression in the three years 1591–1593 (indeed it would have been surprising if they had not!).

The impressive revival after the wars, in the early seventeenth century, marks the beginning of a new phase in the history of Paris: the upswing in rents, whether nominal or deflated, now tops all previous records, thus confirming the traditional picture, based on more qualitative evidence (of which the most recent *résumé* is to be found in Jean-Pierre Babelon's excellent book).

Until 1648, the institutional and private rent records corroborate each other satisfactorily, and in nominal terms reflect a steady upward trend throughout almost the entire first half of the seventeenth century; the deflated curves however reveal a certain levelling-off, noticeable between 1620 and 1648.

The impact of the Fronde emerges fairly distinctly, both in nominal and deflated values, after 1650. The sampling of private leases, based on a very extensive series of documents (448 leases in 1648; 383 in 1655; and 521 in 1669) encompasses this episode and clearly reveals its negative consequences: institutional rents on the other hand seem to have been less disturbed by the damage consequent upon the mid-century Paris rebellion.

The period 1657–1671 is characterized in nominal values by total recovery of the level reached immediately before the Fronde: the *Minutier* samplings clearly indicate this and the institutional rents go even further, since here the graph for the decade of the 1660s actually overtakes the pre-Fronde level. The purchasing power derived from these rents in the time of Colbert was obviously very high, since the 1660s and 1670s were characterized by a certain fall in the price of consumer goods, particularly wheat (see the deflated rent-curve). During the crucial period from 1672 to the end of the reign of Louis XIV, our nominal curves raise a few problems: the institutional rents appear to show a decline, followed by hints of revival after about 1699. But the samplings from the *Minutier* simply offer a picture of stagnation: their immobility between 1669 and 1710 is one of considerable length, unequalled by any other section of the Parisian graph. But some new samples are being taken from the four decades 1671–1710 and perhaps these will be able to introduce some relief to this curious picture of flat calm.

In deflated values, at the time of the great price explosions, after 1690 and again after 1709, the purchasing power of these nominally stable rents was somewhat curtailed. The eighteenth century marks a new rise which is found everywhere of course, both in nominal and deflated curves, in the institutions as well as in the *Minutier* samples. The institutional rents indicate that it begins in 1715. A sample from the *Minutier* for the same year suggests that it was already under way a little earlier than this, unless it began very suddenly: the average rent which was 542.52 *livres* in 1710 (sample), was 724.44 in 1715. By 1727 the revival is quite clear, after some sort of relapse, the limits of which are not yet clearly identified, revealed by the sample for 1723.[2] As for the graphs of rent by locality, they reveal differential developments and a clearly defined hierarchy, although this varies from age to age. In the present state of knowledge of the different areas of Paris, it will probably be difficult to account for the various fluctuations of these local diagrams.

In all, our study is based on a total of over 23,000 leases (or references to leases in the accounts) including both institutional and private rents. The overall trends, as identified by the institutional rent-curves and confirmed or qualified by the samples from the *Minutier*, constitute firsthand evidence on one of the basic developments in the economy of a great city.

APPENDIX

On the problem of concordance: as an example, in 1778, according to a sample from the central *Minutier* covering a total of 508 leases, both private and institutional, the average rent paid to private landlords was 1,524.25 *livres tournois* (calculated from 434 leases); the average rent paid on leases for property owned by institutions was 1,526.51 *livres tournois* (74 leases). As for the average rent paid on leases recorded in the institutional archives (the S series)—not in the *Minutier central*—it was 1,468.62 *livres tournois* for the period 1777–1779 (calculated from 100 leases). The difference between this figure and the first two mentioned is 3.75 per cent, which can be regarded as very satisfactory.

Table I

Arithmetical average of rents (from institutional sources)

Three-year periods	Average nominal rent in *livres tournois*	Average deflated rent (in *setiers* of grain)	Three-year periods	Average nominal rent in *livres tournois*	Average deflated rent (in *setiers* of grain)
1402/1404	13.75		1519/1521	22.95	9.18
1405/1407	18.00		1522/1524	23.60	9.40
1408/1410	14.00		1525/1527	32.21	10.63
1411/1413	25.00		1528/1530	28.02	9.37
1414/1416	38.75		1531/1533	45.73	14.99
1417/1419	25.62		1534/1536	33.60	11.69
1420/1422	40.97		1537/1539	38.07	14.91
1423/1425	18.75		1540/1542	51.14	15.45
1426/1428	30.71		1543/1545	48.92	14.51
1429/1431	10.07		1546/1548	53.54	12.90
1432/1434	6.80		1549/1551	64.24	16.77
1435/1437	4.70	1.60	1552/1554	59.58	15.16
1438/1440	3.16	1.33	1555/1557	65.03	16.17
1441/1443	3.15	1.68	1558/1560	68.43	15.03
1444/1446	3.89	4.18	1561/1563	81.91	14.14
1447/1449	5.44	7.77	1564/1566	64.43	9.79
1450/1452	6.77	9.15	1567/1569	77.30	9.84
1453/1455	8.71	10.2	1570/1572	80.09	10.20
1456/1458	12.00	13.3	1573/1575	85.83	9.72
1459/1461	9.61	11.4	1576/1578	108.13	12.37
1462/1464	3.40	4.7	1579/1581	126.53	16.15
1465/1467	8.00	13.8	1582/1584	168.39	14.23
1468/1470	10.23	14.4	1585/1587	157.26	10.86
1471/1473	12.66	14.8	1588/1590	137.80	8.09
1474/1476	9.15	9.4	1591/1593	48.00	2.67
1477/1479	10.10	8.5	1594/1596	114.16	6.68
1480/1482	14.79	13.0	1597/1599	99.10	7.77
1483/1485	12.25	12.0	1600/1602	148.76	14.16
1486/1488	19.30	20.3	1603/1605	168.39	17.81
1489/1491	12.81	14.72	1606/1608	269.77	27.12
1492/1494	15.87	19.12	1609/1611	205.89	20.58
1495/1497	19.50	21.19	1612/1614	286.85	27.64
1498/1500	19.16	16.66	1615/1617	296.27	28.71
1501/1503	21.84	14.85	1618/1620	289.70	25.47
1504/1506	13.60	8.77	1621/1623	340.63	26.00
1507/1509	13.54	10.18	1624/1626	337.51	25.42
1510/1512	18.50	13.60	1627/1629	357.60	24.06
1513/1515	18.09	12.39	1630/1632	371.84	26.04
1516/1518	20.29	9.61	1633/1635	362.34	25.90

Table I *(Contd.)*

Three-year periods	Average nominal rent in *livres tournois*	Average deflated rent (in *setiers* of grain)	Three-year periods	Average nominal rent in *livres tournois*	Average deflated rent (in *setiers* of grain)
1636/1638	454.33	35.60	1711/1713	514.60	23.80
1639/1641	369.18	25.93	1714/1716	664.08	35.67
1642/1644	538.39	36.88	1717/1719	753.76	42.38
1645/1647	452.34	24.86	1720/1722	773.49	38.43
1648/1650	546.54	28.14	1723/1725	893.85	42.14
1651/1653	539.63	27.63	1726/1728	821.13	39.84
1654/1656	486.57	27.18	1729/1731	720.50	44.39
1657/1659	601.97	32.32	1732/1734	835.55	55.70
1660/1662	586.24	30.00	1735/1737	923.04	51.02
1663/1665	604.50	33.08	1738/1740	822.65	43.64
1666/1668	683.76	50.01	1741/1743	804.34	42.51
1669/1671	686.70	59.66	1744/1746	906.83	49.90
1672/1674	662.10	54.99	1747/1749	741.96	42.34
1675/1677	585.84	43.07	1750/1752	874.34	46.80
1678/1680	635.39	43.37	1753/1755	1050.91	54.22
1681/1683	612.01	41.91	1756/1758	850.34	46.44
1684/1686	589.32	46.55	1759/1761	1246.34	69.78
1687/1689	615.76	45.34	1762/1764	1135.48	57.69
1690/1692	557.28	35.61	1765/1767	1286.14	54.52
1693/1695	500.73	26.15	1768/1770	1177.28	43.17
1696/1698	481.96	23.41	1771/1773	1262.23	43.59
1699/1701	508.82	30.67	1774/1776	1252.20	48.67
1702/1704	572.30	40.34	1777/1779	1468.62	64.70
1705/1707	530.01	31.93	1780/1782	1434.62	65.81
1708/1710	615.58	29.90	1783/1785	1196.03	54.74
			1786/1788	1281.04	58.63

Table II
Samplings from the Minutier central

Date	Average nominal rent (in *livres tournois*)	Average deflated rent	Date	Average nominal rent (in *livres tournois*)	Average deflated rent
1550	63.72	16.64	1697	531.00	25.79
1572	91.53	10.48	1710	542.52	26.34
1588	226.19	13.29	1715	724.44	38.90
1593	46.28	2.58	1723	536.00	25.27
1604	229.00	24.23	1727	760.40	36.89
1620	356.32	31.34	1734	818.35	54.55
1640	430.40	30.22	1743	842.10	44.50
1648	531.57	27.37	1760	909.00	50.89
1655	393.75	22.00	1766	1090.00	46.20
1669	546.78	47.45	1778	1480.00	65.19
1682	547.83	37.52	1784	1408.00	64.43
			1788	1697.65	77.69

PART TWO

THE HISTORIAN IN THE COUNTRYSIDE: NEW DIRECTIONS IN RURAL HISTORY

6

Rural Civilization[1]

ANY attempt to define rural civilization must begin with a set of contrasts. To talk of the countryside assumes that there are cities; to talk of peasants assumes that there are townspeople. Rural civilization is a seamless fabric which unites a certain number of cellular groups—villages, parishes, rural communities. Depending on their circumstances, such groups may be surrounded or dominated by powers and/or social and economic forces outside, or superior to, the cells in question. Among such powers and forces, which may coexist with, or succeed, each other, we might number feudalism, the towns, states, trade and industry, capitalism, bureaucracies (whether party or state) etc. Every village, as Mendras has pointed out, is thus enclosed both within a surrounding society (other villages) and by an over-arching or dominant society (city-dwellers, feudal powers, capitalists, bureaucrats, priests or policemen).

HISTORY

In the first place, rural civilization is the product of a particular history (and in this respect we shall concern ourselves principally with the case of Western Europe and in particular with that of France, which is both useful and convenient because it is well known). This history is *stratigraphic*: the specific contribution it receives from every century or group of centuries, and from every millennium, is not wiped out but merely overlaid, or at worst eroded or damaged, by the contribution of subsequent centuries. One has therefore, even before it becomes possible to understand their structural arrangement, to read the sum of these contributions as if they were laid bare by a geological section— from the bottom up if one is a historian; from the top down if

79

one is a geographer or an anthropologist. The case of the West European peasantry is extremely informative in this respect: its societies are constructions of great complexity. During their phase of maximum expansion (fourteenth to nineteenth century) they were making use of legacies both ancient and recent, representing almost ten millennia. In Provence for example, the local domestication of the wild sheep, which began very early indeed, could be said to have been achieved by about 6000 B.C. The peoples of the "Cardian" culture, and after them the Chasseans, who were responsible for these sheepbreeding innovations, were to die out as such, but their contribution to agriculture was to remain embedded for ever in the great province of southern France. Cultures may pass, but cultural legacies remain.

After about 2000 B.C. and especially during the Iron Age (from about 500 B.C. until the time of the Roman Empire), a new wave of innovations took permanent root in western rural civilization. Varieties of oats and above all rye, which was for so long to give its characteristic colour and texture to the black bread eaten by European peasants, completed the available range of cereals, which had previously consisted only of wheat and barley. Spring corn—the distant forerunner of triennial rotation which was later to become immensely popular—was also making its first timid appearance. Along with it came broad beans, peas, lentils and other pulses: they were a source of vegetable protein for humans and, by contributing nitrogen from the atmosphere, they also enriched the soil. It was during this second half of the last millennium B.C. that vines and the art of grafting were brought by the inhabitants of Rhodes to the Mediterranean shores of what is now France: the Hellenic origins of grafting techniques are preserved in the French dialect word *enter* (German *impfen*)—to graft, which comes from the Greek *emphuteuëin*. Grafting also made it possible to produce massive quantities of chestnuts and walnuts, a source of carbohydrates and fats for the common people. The vine was a vital newcomer: it offered many people a chance to drink a liquid comparatively free of microbes (wine), in which alcohol had an antiseptic function. In this way, the ravages of many epidemics, which would otherwise have been spread by drinking water, were limited. (Other civilizations achieved similar results by different methods: the very widespread habit of drinking tea in China since antiquity meant drinking boiled, and therefore sterile, water.) At all events, from the first century A.D., the culture of the grape, now thoroughly acclimatized, spread throughout Gaul: it was to become one of the essential foundations of local rural civilizations; soon it was no longer using the Greek and Italian stocks of vines, but its own plants, domesticated or hybridized on the spot by a few gifted vine-growers. The *pinot* stock was to be found on the Rhône-Saône axis or in the Côtes du Rhône/Burgundy; and the *cabernet* along the Bayonne-Bordeaux-Muscadet line. A complementary invention, the *cask*, first produced from the wooded slopes of Lower Dauphiné, paved the way for twenty centuries of national wine-production.

THE HORSE, THE KNIGHT ON HORSEBACK AND HIS
ASCENDANCY OVER THE RURAL POPULATION

Another cultural wave influenced—and indeed violently traumatized country life: the arrival of the domesticated horse from the east. Between 1500 and 500 B.C., it became established fairly widely throughout western Europe. That is not to say that the horse immediately and directly transformed agricultural techniques themselves: the age of the horse-drawn plough came much later (the thirteenth and even in some places the eighteenth century).

But the "noble beast" was associated with a new social distinction: in its way it marked the appearance of a group of aristocrats, living off contributions levied from the peasants, and of course riding on horseback (as the names *chevaliers*, *équites* suggest); they went to war in chariots or mounted on chargers. The small agricultural communities of the Neolithic Age, before the discovery of metals, had remained comparatively egalitarian, and Jean-Jacques Rousseau would probably have liked these super-archaic populations, whose unpretentious tombs and ornaments indicated an endearing absence of social hierarchies. But with the Bronze and Iron Ages, and the simultaneous introduction of the horse—

which was, incidentally, only one symptom among others in this respect—things changed radically. A group of leaders now appeared and detached itself from the peasant mass. This group was rich in the treasures that a civilization of metals and trade was already beginning to accumulate. And it also had the military and property-owning prestige derived from possession of the horse (we might note in passing that the last domestic creature to be inherited by the peasantry of western Europe—long after the horse—was the American turkey. The social "spin-off" from this farmyard fowl was of course insignificant compared with that from the horse).

From now on, at any rate, using methods and techniques which varied greatly according to ethnic groups, regions and mentalities, a group of *Rulers*, who were for long years to be identified with the "men on horseback", presented western rural civilization with a *fait accompli*: the peasants, or the great majority of them, now begin to figure in the documents, or in the findings of excavations, as the community of the *Ruled*. And ruled they were to remain in many places for at least fifteen or twenty centuries—until the French Revolution or even later. Marc Bloch very justly points out that as long ago as the first century B.C., Caesar found the mass of the rural population of Gaul subjected, by ties of dependence or indebtedness, to a group of *équites* (knights) and landowners. Earlier texts by Greek geographers and the archaeological discoveries of which the treasure of the Lady of Vix is merely the best-known, confirm that Caesar was describing a situation which in fact dated from long before. In later years, the modes of domination were to vary considerably, and scholars who have studied the early or classical Middle Ages, Guy Fourquin for example, point out quite correctly that each successive type of peasant alienation is quite original and distinct from the system of oppression which precedes or follows it. The Ruler with the long moustache who directs and dominates his *clientèles* during the Celtic and pre-Roman era, is a very different master from the slave-owning lord of the *villa* of Gallo-Roman times. The *villa* in question, in a province like Gaul, in any case represents only a form of colonization brought from outside, superimposed on the indigenous society and affecting only a minority of the rural population. As for the regime of the *colonus*, a very ancient institution but one about which there is clear textual evidence only from about the fourth century A.D., this already meant in practice a fairly well developed type of *seigneurie*: the *colonus*—in other words the peasant— is indeed attached to the soil by legal and mystical-cum-folk ties which make him virtually a dependent of his noble masters. The *colonus*, say the documents, "is like a member of the earth". Other forms of land-based power appeared in the following centuries: the early medieval *seigneurie*, with bondage and *corvée*; the classic medieval *seigneurie*, less restrictive than that which preceded it. In spite of some significant differences between them, these last two types of manorial power both posit a triangular relationship between Peasant (P), Land (L) and *Seigneur* (S). P is more or less attached to L; P is dominated by S to whom he owes respect, dues and/or *corvée* labour. S has outright or perhaps merely pre-eminent rights of property over L—and some- times over P too. Let us therefore conclude this section by putting the case for a long-term perspective—a millennium or even longer—on this question. Marc Bloch, in the out- standing chapter he wrote in 1942 for the *Cambridge Economic History of Europe*, which can in a sense be taken as his intellectual testament, underlined the unquestionable conti- nuity which, through a chronologically unbroken chain of institutions, linked the petty local chieftains of Gaul, with their flowing locks, and the feudal lords of the Middle Ages. Both were possessed of rights of command and taxation, and that mysterious faculty of racial fecundity which was for so long to fill the honest folk of the forest clearings with awe. And if one looks at the question from the point of view of the underlings, the successive generations of peasants, whether one was a client of the first, a slave or *colonus* of the second, a serf of the third, or a mere dues-paying dependent of the last variety of masters of the land, one was always, for all the variety of circumstances, living through the permanent experience of being one of the Ruled. And in the compressed chronology required for this article [in the *Encyclopaedia Universalis*] that is what matters in the end.

THE OX AND THE PLOUGH

Nevertheless, the history of rural civilization cannot be reduced (far from it) to the dialectic between the Master on horseback and the Serf on foot. The most cursory glance at our slice through the strata of time would immediately notice another important innovation: the plough, a device for turning over the ground, together with the draft ox without which the technique of ploughing is inconceivable. Imported from the Middle East, the plough and the ox became widespread in Gaul (after some earlier but obscure local experiments here and there in the course of the last millennium B.C. The earliest type of plough (the *araire*), a symmetrical implement, differs from the asymmetrical plough with mould-board which was to succeed it in later centuries. Despite its fairly modest performance, the early plough was the key to agricultural surpluses which ensured the maintenance of the chieftain class. It also contributed to the population increase, by making it possible for a greater number of mouths to be fed by an hour's human labour (an hour's ploughing in this case).

The innovations which are recorded as having taken place after the beginning of the first millennium A.D., roughly speaking, are less sensational than those which preceded them. But they nevertheless survive, quite visibly, in our historical section. We can pass quickly over the contribution of the Gallo-Roman period: it can be defined as a colonization venture, imported from outside and superimposed on the native reality. It was often associated with local, but Romanized aristocrats. It left behind an impressive scattering of villas, some of which have survived, either in the form of large estates or transformed into villages. In the areas where penetration was greatest (the southern half of France) the legacy of this period has been impressed upon the landscape in the permanent lines of a grid type of land division— the geometric turn of mind of the surveyors of the first century A.D. was responsible for the vast chequer-board of *centuriations*, some of which can still be seen in Languedoc in the outlines of field and lane. Another lasting legacy lies in the fairly substantial population increase characteristic of the Gallo-Roman period, and in the establishment of human settlement on the plateaux, which became great cereal-producing areas. This new settlement called, in the short run, for a kind of technology—associated with high productivity but wasteful of cereals—which did not long survive the Roman Empire: I am thinking in particular of the famous Gallic sickle.

The real agricultural revolution—the big one—came later, between the fifth and the thirteenth centuries. This was the result of a series of inventions or makeshifts which spread in a variety of ways. Some of the technical secrets that characterized all these changes came from as far away as Asia, from China or India; others came simply from Central Europe. To take the new medieval plough for instance (the *charrue*) with wheels, coulter and mould-board: the last-named and most essential feature, for turning the ground, seems to have appeared among the Germanic peoples, while the wheels and coulter simply came from Cisalpine Gaul and classical Italy. The "triple alliance"—(wheels-coulter-mould-board) had been accomplished by the second half of the first millennium A.D. As for stable-harness, the stirrup, the horseshoe and horse-collar came from China, East Europe or Rhineland Gaul, giving rise in the west, after the eighth to ninth century of our era, to a new synthesis of equestrian skills: from this were later derived both medieval chivalry in the full sense of the term and the powerful horse-drawn plough used by northern farmers in the thirteenth century (cf the work of R. Fossier). The water mill, of eastern origin, but to be found in the west by Roman times, was already in widespread use in the great demesnes of the Carolingian era. And it continued to spread well after the year 1000, accompanied by the windmill, a newcomer of the Gothic age: these revolutionary procedures for the manufacture of flour eliminated a bottleneck in the sequence of tasks between growing the grain and making bread: before the mills, grain was ground extremely slowly, by women and slaves using pestle and mortar. So the mill meant increased production of wheat and rye, since the grain could now be ground faster and more easily in large quantities.

The adoption and general use of these innovations (plough,

mill and harness) would have been impossible if they had not been carried forward, after the year 1000, on a powerful current of human and economic fertility; of rising population and the greater availability of silver and iron—all of which was facilitated by the breakdown of the old oppressive system of the feudal domain, farmed by compulsory labour, that had flourished in Carolingian times. A sort of spontaneous agrarian reform, combined with the great forest-clearings of the eleventh and twelfth centuries, enabled the peasants to multiply in number and to adopt new methods: from now on in the north of the Paris basin, twelfth- and thirteenth-century farmers could afford the luxury of harnessing their horses (shod in the new fashion), with the modern horse-collar, to the new type of plough. We should not, for all that, exaggerate the extent of the agricultural revolution in the early and classic Middle Ages (ninth and twelfth century respectively); although it was certainly the midwife of new agrarian structures which were to leave lasting marks on our landscape, it is nothing in comparison with what can only be called the 'green revolution' taking place in China during the same period (eleventh to twelfth century) under the guidance of the Chinese agronomists: they imported early-maturing rice from Indochina, selected it by empirical cross-breeding, and ensured that it was widely planted by issuing pamphlets and government propaganda to the remotest parts of the Celestial Empire. Can one seriously imagine Hugh Capet doing anything of the kind?

But our attempt to uncover the strata of rural civilization cannot be reduced to an easily compiled catalogue of great inventions. It obliges us to consider the successive waves of settlement which gradually established human habitation on a massive scale, destined to last and to root itself in the densely-populated countryside of western Europe, until the numbers of people (in rural areas) reached the peak recorded in the eighteenth and nineteenth centuries.

This settlement took place in a series of "great leaps forward". In this category, one tends to think in particular of the massive forest clearings of the eleventh century; this is perhaps too simple a view. As we have seen, in Gaul under the Roman Empire, there had already been a considerable expansion in the number of inhabitants and of those farming on the cereal-growing plateaux. Less well known, but very spectacular nevertheless, is the population growth in the Merovingian period. In the age of the "do-nothing kings" *(les rois fainéants)*—whose non-activity was perhaps a guarantee of non-intervention and therefore of non-harmful activity!—thousands of villages, farms, hamlets and tiny settlements were established in what is now northern France and western Germany. It was then that the countryside took on, at least in part, its new appearance, one of clearings still surrounded by forests. The following period however, the Carolingian, was for a time to succeed in restraining this powerful upsurge of the peasant population. Did Charlemagne's contemporaries, in some early version of Malthusianism, practise the infanticide of female children, in the villages, to prevent an excessive increase in the number of potentially fertile wombs? Such a hypothesis is not altogether implausible, to judge by the unbalanced sex ratio (i.e. a shortage of women) especially among the poorest categories, recorded in ninth-century documents. The year 1000 and the following centuries witnessed a new population rise, familiar to historians, in both town and country. Thus there gradually came into being the France of 17 to 20 million inhabitants and the north-west Europe (France, Germany and Britain) of some 40 million (figures applicable to present-day frontiers) which are both attested by the beginning of the fourteenth century. Of these millions, at least 85 per cent were peasants.

But again, rural civilization is so much more than—and so much else besides—a combination of population growth and newly-ploughed fields. It suggests perhaps most of all the image so familiar, at least in the west, of the *village* built around its *church* and *graveyard*. The image—not of course fixed for all eternity—is in fact fairly recent in origin: it was only in the course of the last third or quarter of the first millennium A.D. that people began to bury the bodies of their dead together on a site near the church—a crucial sign of the first real Christianization of the countryside which was now at last thoroughly accomplished. As for the peasant or village community, it must have existed in one form or another for a very long time—probably since the prehistoric age. But it only took on this classic form as it gradually, during the twelfth and thirteenth centuries, achieved its own identity: as against the lord of the manor in the first place—and often in opposition to him; then a little later as against the monarchical state—and often in cooperation with it. The peasant community, which is often—but not always—identified with the parish, provided kings with a convenient unit for their local and fiscal levies: from this community they derived the taxes which, from about the fourteenth century in particular, they had increasingly begun to levy. This function—acting as a source of fiscal revenue—brought the peasant community much anxiety and hardship, but it also gave it a new importance. From now on it was, more than the nobility, recognized by the king as a valid partner in a dialogue—and the more so in that the distribution of power within the classic village was—apart from its regrettable male chauvinism—more democratic than in our own time. There was no question, that is, of conferring the monopoly of decision-making upon a select municipal council. Power within the community belonged (until the French Revolution) to the assembled heads of households—to whom on these occasions were added a number of widows whose personal misfortune gave them rights within local politics which would normally have been exercised by their late husbands.

*

From the fourteenth century until the beginning of the eighteenth century, then on during the period 1720–1860 (even 1720–1913 in the case of France) it becomes possible to observe rural civilization *in vitro*—in laboratory conditions, as it were—if one does not actually dare to talk of it as being "in repose". It is true that there are some massive and disastrous fluctuations (I am thinking in particular of the period 1340–1450 in the west, and of 1630–1660 in Germany and even in France). But between 1300 and 1700 the time of major advances seems to be over. The pioneers of forest clearing reached some sort of limit in about 1300, which was certainly extended subsequently, but not very much and then only in the eighteenth and nineteenth centuries. The remaining patches of green woodland were not now to be greatly reduced by large-scale clearing operations. And the rural populations had now stabilized. They still fluctuated somewhat, it is true, but they were not to rise above the level first reached in 1300–1310 until 1720–1730. So during its "classical period", rural civilization, having expanded to its maximum so to speak, and now hemmed in and somewhat set in its ways, before its progressive disintegration with the coming of industrial and post-industrial society, lends itself conveniently to structural observation and functional description.

Rural civilization in, let us say, the seventeenth century then (but this century presents many characteristics already discernible at the end of the Middle Ages and which persist into the eighteenth) should be regarded, first and foremost, from the viewpoint of demography. This matters far more than, say, woodcarving or costume, popular literature or any other folk tradition that might come to mind when one hears the words "rural civilization".

The demography in question is one of balance, or at any rate it tends (not always successfully) towards a degree of balance. (This remark is really only true of the west: in China on the contrary, peasant societies seem to have been endowed with faculties of population expansion that make the mind reel. Of course we do not, for obvious reasons, have the parish registers for the Middle Empire that would help to pass judgment on the Chinese case.)[2]

On the question of the cellular structure of rural settlement, one should also at this point mention the problems of the family or "domestic unit" (H. Mendras). As a general rule, in the northern regions of West European peasant society, the rural family is *nuclear*, that is to say centred essentially on the married couple, whether small farmers or day-labourers. The couple has an average of two surviving children, and sometimes, if the mortality rate of the period is not too high or the household is not too poor, the couple may also have under their roof an elderly parent or a servant-girl or man. In the homes of rich farmers, who are in any

case only a tiny minority of all heads of family, one may
of course find several servants who are part of the "household". Whatever its appendages and with all its possible
variations, the nuclear family as the dominant model after
the thirteenth century (cf. R. Fossier) is found in the northern
half of France, in England, the Low Countries and in short
in the major areas where peasant society is most highly
developed (or least under-developed by present-day
standards). In the southern half of France, and in Mediterranean countries in general, while the nuclear family
certainly retains its numerical predominance, representing
the majority of all families, it loses the virtual monopoly
it has in the north. It coexists in the south with various
kinds of extended family which, in times of crisis (fourteenth
to fifteenth century) or even in much later times (seventeenth
to eighteenth century) may account for important minorities
of the total rural population (up to 30 or 40 per cent).
The extended family, of which there may be several kinds,
unites under a single roof the previously-mentioned couple,
their children, plus:

a) one or more of the couple's parents, grandmother or
grandfather as case may be; this is the vertically extended
family;

b) or one or several brothers, sisters or cousins, married
or single; if married, accompanied by spouse and children—
the horizontally extended family.

The combination of (a) and (b) within a single extended
family is extremely rare. But the chronological transition
from (a) to (b) is quite conceivable.

What about the leadership of the extended family? In
the south of France, where more is known about the question
thanks to the work of Jean Hilaire, the *paterfamilias* is the
head of the extended family. In the Basque country there
are even fairly perceptible traces of surviving matriarchal
patterns; while in the north of the Massif Central (Auvergne,
Nivernais) the extended families still to be found in the
eighteenth century are organized on lines neither patriarchal
nor paternalist, but very close to the Yugoslavian *zadruga*:
this pattern supposes:

1. intra-family collaboration between three, four or five

married couples, united by sibling or cousinhood ties.

2. the choice of a *master* and *mistress*, not married to one another, who correspond respectively to the *domacin* and *domacina* of the Yugoslavian *zadruga*.

3. the common ownership of property, autarky, and even "intra-zadruga" endogamy, if one can use this convenient tautology.

The last extended families of the Auvergne and the Nivernais to be constructed on this pattern provided Restif de la Bretonne with his first models for building a type of socialism that was to be both utopian and dynastic.

One cannot talk about families without talking about inheritance customs and the circulation of goods by the laws of succession. These specific questions have been magnificently discussed in Jean Yver's book *Géographie coutumière de la France* and in two articles by the same writer.

Yver's book gives an overall view, by province or group of provinces, of inheritance customs in the France of the *très ancien régime* and in regions or settlements on its borders. So I will mention just one or two points. To take northern France first: here among populations with very solid ethnic traditions (Normandy, Flanders), the equal distribution of goods is the rule: the property of the family is shared in equal parts among all the children (or as it may be among all heirs having an entitlement by virtue of their position in the dynasty) when the succession is opened following the death, whether of the father of the house or of some other person. This custom encourages the subdivision of land: and in this sense it is both archaic (linked to the ethnic group, Flemish or Norman) and modernist (egalitarian). In the south, by contrast, and notably under Roman law, the sovereign power of the *paterfamilias* is paramount: he is entitled to bestow his land, undivided, on one of his sons— not necessarily the eldest—in order to maintain the estate intact. More fundamentally, both in the south and also, in particular, in fairly large areas of the north, one would have found the following idea strongly held and very widespread (especially after the reform of customary law): that the land of a family or a household should not be divided, but passed on from one married couple living in any given house to another married couple. Inheritance was thus considered to pass from father to one son, or if there were no sons, from father-in-law to one son-in-law—to the *exclusion of other married children*, who would merely receive a marriage settlement.

In other words, there were basically two systems: one of successional division, according to the structure of the family; and the other where the inheritance was preferably indivisible and the succession passed from the old couple to the young couple. One system (the Flemish or Norman) set more store by consanguinity; the other set more by marriage.

But in the end, in the sixteenth century, the demographic pressure became too strong: although "ethnographic" distinctions of the kind mentioned were not totally eliminated, there was a general trend in the direction of division of inheritance and land partition, especially in the Paris region and even in the south of France. In the long run, this tendency worked against the stability of the rural world.

*

The economic structures of rural civilization were based on the coexistence of a subsistence economy, represented by the peasant smallholding, and a surplus economy (one at least of *alimentary* surplus, since as regards *monetary* surplus, the smallholding in question also provided its share of it); the second (surplus) category was composed chiefly of medium-sized or large holdings, usually owned by nobles, clerics or the urban bourgeoisie. Such landowners would sometimes farm their estates directly, in person, but more often through the intermediary of tenant-farmers or sharecroppers.

This schema of course admits of many exceptions, which complement or qualify it but never invalidate it entirely. Tithes and other levies took grain from smallholdings and eventually directed it towards urban consumers; the little plots belonging to vinegrowers and gardeners were not intended to contribute to peasant self-sufficiency but were more likely to supply markets in town. And when one turns to the produce of large estates, one finds that it was not always their grain that travelled most frequently to the market of the nearby town. Wheat grown by rich farmers was very often (at least in backward areas) eaten by the master's household. Or else it was bought (when they could afford it) by the daylabourers of the neighbouring village, whose tiny "properties" were too small to feed a family—unless, that is, it was eaten on the spot, by rats or weevils in the barn. In fact in peripheral regions (the Cotentin for instance) large estates were much more likely to sell livestock than grain; four-footed creatures—cattle, calves and pigs—could take themselves more easily along the bumpy roads to town than cartloads of grain.

If one seeks to locate it within time and overall trends, the agricultural economy of rural civilization may equally well be considered from the point of view of its balance mechanisms—the feedback processes which, whenever the system is accidentally or temporarily upset, enable it to be brought back to the position of stability towards which its own structures naturally incline it. There are some very considerable examples, lasting over several centuries, of rural civilizations departing a long way from this "position of equilibrium", to return to it gradually later on.

Take for example the series of consecutive catastrophes—epidemics of plague, the Hundred Years War and the accompanying or subsequent famines—which, compounding each other like so many Hiroshimas, began, especially after 1348, to destroy the contrived architecture of rural economy and demography as it had become established in the west since the thirteenth century and the Gothic period. Essentially composed of peasants, the "French" population (estimated according to present-day frontiers) was probably in excess of 17 million in 1320–1330. It had fallen to under 10 million (and perhaps even lower still) by 1440. Whereupon there appear within the rural economy certain mechanisms which, by 1460–1480, gradually appear to be compensating for the past: in a society where there were now fewer people, the plots of land owned by the remaining peasants expanded—because they swallowed up the smallholdings of those who had died, as property was concentrated, by patterns of succession, in the hands of a single heir. Those who farmed their now much-enlarged properties could live better: one man's misfortune turned into another's salvation. And generally, where once there had been villages, now deserted by depopulation, the forests began to grow again in about 1450; or grazing replaced cereal-growing. As a result, the peasants had plenty of game, wood for fuel or building, and grassland for pasturing their flocks. Moreover, still in the period around 1450, labour was in short supply and there was much land to be cleared: marginal productivity of labour (that is the productivity of the last man to be hired) was therefore very high and agricultural wages rose accordingly. In any case, the concept of a rural wage was not, as it happens, necessarily linked to the circulation of money. In an economy which often remains virtually "natural", it may refer to payment in kind, or to the share of a crop received by farmhands or seasonal labourers. While high wages prevailed in the period after 1460, it seems that the demand for land expressed by the few remaining farmers was low; consequently the rents that noblemen and large landowners could charge were extremely depressed. For the peasants these were good times: they were neither being fleeced nor flayed by the landowners and could afford a very comfortable standard of living.

But alas, this agreeable state of affairs, which reached its peak in about 1480, had an annoying and logical tendency to go into reverse: for the combination of good wages, high income from the land, larger holdings, high consumption of bread, meat, wood and game meant by definition a very respectable standard of living—and therefore, in all probability, lower mortality, a higher birth rate (in a traditional type of society) and in the end a rise in the population. Inevitably, mechanisms which are the reverse of those already described swing into action—the feedback becomes a backlash. In the sixteenth century, as the rural population increases once more, individual peasant holdings shrink alarmingly, until the countryside is reduced to "patchwork farming" again. Real wages decline, and the empoverishment of the rural workers begins to take place—affecting both payments received in kind and money wages. At the same time, as the demographic wave swells, the demand for land grows once

more. The *proprietary class*, the rural Establishment so to
speak (the landed gentry, the tithe-exacting clergy and the
tax-levying state) is in a position to increase its demands,
since the peasants of whom there are now simply too many,
have no choice. Threatened on one hand by land division for
demographic reasons, under attack on the other by the
property accumulators, labouring under the burden of
taxes of various and increasing kinds levied by those who
control the land, by about 1550–1660 the peasant smallholder
no longer knows which way to turn. The standard of living of
the mass of peasant-farmers declines, poverty becomes
widespread, and a pattern of famine and epidemic—and of
late marriage in order to minimize the hardships of poverty—
becomes established. Mortality increases, birth rates fall,
and the demographic upswing is finally stifled in the late
sixteenth and seventeenth centuries by the feedback mechanisms already described. Schooled by perpetual suffering and
self-discipline, rural civilization thus showed itself capable
of attaining the zero population growth which was eventually
to become in our own time the dream (hard to achieve)
of population experts all over the world, who now look
back with nostalgia on the days of balance. At the cost of
acute hardships and deprivation, this civilization showed
that it carried within itself the energy necessary for its self-
stabilization.

To turn to something rather different, rural civilization
also had to cope with the problems of power, politics, resistance and revolt. It had its own cells of political socialization
(the community of inhabitants) and even of military socialization (the group made up of the unmarried young men of
the village, organized into a traditional local association
which might, when called upon, help to provide the foot-
soldiers of a rural army). However the essential centres of
decision-making and tax-gathering (state, Church, town,
seigneurie) were all, to a greater or less extent, beyond the
control of the peasantry. The result was friction and conflict;
and also the outbreak—fairly frequent in traditional
societies—of peasant rebellions and wars; they can be
compared to strikes and workers' insurrections in industrial
societies. Agrarian uprisings did not aim at the complete

takeover of power—such utopian dreams were cherished only by a handful of millenarians who were far less influential in rural areas than they were among urban populations. More prosaically, rural rebels sought above all to recover for the village some part of the power vested in the society that surrounded it, and, by so doing, to relieve or even abolish some of that society's exactions from the peasantry.

Rural revolts were rarely the doing of the poorest categories among the inhabitants of parish or village communities; though one does find—usually, it is true, in that particular type of rural civilization which is already thoroughly penetrated by capitalism—a number of well-defined class-struggles between the rich *laboureurs* (well-off peasants) and poor *manouvriers* (day-labourers): the (isolated) episode of the *flour war* in the countryside round Paris in 1775 is a typical example. But essentially, peasant risings, if they are at all significant, concern the solid kernel of the village, the comparatively well-off (since everything is comparative): in other words secure smallholders, small to middling peasant-farmers and sometimes wealthy farmers (where there were any). Striking evidence on this question is provided in the statistics published long ago by Pirenne concerning the peasant wars in Flanders in the early fourteenth century: most of those rebels who were taken red-handed, carrying arms, were owner-occupiers of small, often medium and sometimes even large farms. They owned upwards of one hectare—and sometimes a good deal more. Eric Wolf, who has studied "twentieth-century peasant wars" in China, Russia, Vietnam, Cuba and Algeria, has reached very similar conclusions.

The best-known, though not necessarily the most frequent type of agrarian revolt in traditional rural civilization is the *anti-seigniorial* rebellion. In the eleventh century for instance, the peasants of Normandy "by twenty, by fifty and by the hundred" launched a powerful conspiracy against the nobles and seigneurs who were exploiting them, they said, by levies and by excessive *corvées*; they had taken from the peasants the common lands, woods, streams and heaths and had established their own domains and grazing lands instead. This rising ended in tragedy: the rebellious Norman peasants were massacred. The *Jacques* rebellion of 1358, in the Paris region, was led, it seems, by the more prosperous peasants—and they massacred the nobility. The German peasants in 1525 banded together in their communities or *Gemeinde*, and waged their struggle on several fronts: they opposed both the power of the nobles who were oppressing them, and the Church which they accused of being unfaithful to the Gospel (this was during the Reformation); similarly in France in the Paris basin and in Languedoc) rural taxpayers refused to pay tithes to the clergy in 1560. In 1789, in a situation certainly very different from those just mentioned, the peasant masses, stimulated ideologically by the smattering of culture dispensed by the parish primary school, rediscovered and cultivated their ancient hostility to *seigneuries* and the aristocracy; this combined effectively with the "anti-privilege" grievances of the urban masses.

Rebellion against the nobility is not however the most typical element in peasant protests—far from it. Over a very long period, from the fifteenth to the eighteenth century, the peasants of what is now France, for instance, directed most of their "militant" activity—such as it was—against the state and its agents, whose function was to collect taxes; on the rebound so to speak, they found themselves in conflict with the royal army used by the government to suppress the revolts. Aggression of this type is quite logical: in an essentially peasant society, the state is one of the cornerstones—perhaps even the essential element—of the non-peasant or "over-arching" part of that society. This dichotomy (peasant/non-peasant, dominant/dominated, over-arching/under-going) may therefore be reflected in struggles against the state.

Several rather remarkable anti-fiscal or anti-state rebellions have been studied recently by Mousnier, Porchnev, Foisil and Bercé. The *Nu-pieds* (or "barefoot rebels") of Normandy, peasants of the *bocage* who rose up in 1639, were acting in solidarity with the salt-burners who boiled sea-water in their cauldrons on the beaches of the Mont-Saint-Michel. The burners sold their salt cheaply to the villagers—while Richelieu wanted to have the cauldrons smashed, so as to force the Norman villagers to buy the expensive salt sold by the state salt-farmers. The Barefoot rising of 1639, which originated in the little village communities of peasants in the *bocage*, was led by parish priests and curates, by petty nobles, indebted aristocrats and needy lawyers. So this rebellion had its *own* clergy, aristocracy and third estate, and was directed against official society and the (fiscal) power elite in the name of a counter-society in miniature—rural-based and ready to challenge authority. The Barefoot rebels demanded a reduction in taxes and a return to the golden age symbolized by the names of Henri IV and Louis XII, two kings whose fiscal greed was only moderate. And lastly they demanded the autonomy or even the independence of Normandy. In the Périgord, the *nouveaux croquants* of 1637 were led by La Mothe la Forêt, a petty noble of mystical and regimental tendencies. They wanted a de-bureaucratized society where village representatives would come to pay their modest and informal fiscal contributions to the king in person, as he sat under his oak tree. The payment would be made directly, *hand to hand*, without any intermediary levy to line the pockets of the grasping tax-farmer.

Finally, mention should be made of peasant revolts against the *towns*—which were accused of forcing prices up by black market practices; of harbouring tax-gatherers and other extortioners; of being the haven of land-grabbers who bought up the poor peasants' smallholdings; and the repair of brigands who from time to time launched sorties and raids against defenceless hamlets, from behind the shelter of the city walls.

> *You'll die in your cities*
> *You'll rot on your backs*
> *Like bugs and beetles*
> *you lousy jacks*

sang the peasants of the Vendée in 1793, against the *Blues* or *Republicans* who lived in the towns. And the first *Croquants* of the Limousin-Périgord, two hundred years earlier in 1593, might have sung the same kind of refrain against their enemies and exploiters who lived in the towns: against Périgueux and Bergerac, which were hated by the *Croquants* as if they were Sodom and Gomorrah. In a general way, when facing its potential enemies of all kinds—*seigneurie*, state, town, higher clergy—the village was quite capable of fighting alternately—or even simultaneously—on several fronts; if necessary it could practise a "multi-purpose strategy".

Leadership of these rural revolts caused some problems, for the village all too often spent its time contemplating its own navel—that is for most members of the community the parish pump was the centre of their little universe. So when these country folk had to deal with the outside world, they tended to call upon leaders from among the natural mediators between themselves and the unfamiliar forces of the surrounding society—the petty *notables*, parish priests and even, when they were not in direct conflict with the peasants, the local nobles.

RELIGION, CULTURE AND FOLKLORE IN RURAL CIVILIZATION

In the case of peasant societies in western Europe, rural religion essentially means a form of Christianity, interpreted according to the ways of local folklore. In theory, by the heyday of rural civilization (thirteenth to eighteenth centuries) the most flagrant elements of paganism had long since been eradicated from peasant religious practices: the animistic worship of trees, stones, plants and creatures had disappeared. Set in wooden statues, the moonstones had become black Madonnas. Christian missionaries were until quite late on (the seventh century) burning idols representing mythical monsters and chopping down tree-gods. Legions of Christian saints peremptorily occupied the sites of sacred springs and woods, giving personal and human form to the old paganism of folklore. They could not root it out entirely: St. Medard or St. Swithun controls the rain; Saint Barbara protects from storms. And hundreds of miracle-working saints conveniently posted at every curative spring keep watch over the respective organs, from head to foot, of the invalids coming to be cured. The Church did indeed—especially after the Council of Trent (1545 and after)—rather half-heartedly remind villagers that the saints and even the Virgin were able merely to intercede with the Trinity. But to the peasants who prayed to St. Joseph or St. Anthony, such casuistry meant nothing: from their point of view, the saint quite definitely had personal powers—he did not have to go through the Almighty in order to grant small favours on earth. In this sense, the saint remained a minor rural deity—even a tourist attraction (if one thinks of pilgrimages). This is still very close to paganism. It was in any case not wise to take issue too violently with this imperfect but credible and effective theology devised by villages *ad usum rustici*: during the Reformation, Huguenot ministers often tried in France to evangelize the countryside and smash statues of the Virgin Mary: on many occasions they had to take to their heels and were lucky to escape being massacred by the enraged parishioners. Similarly, the second attempt to eliminate the old ways from rural Christianity, on the part of the Jansenist priests of the early eighteenth century, often ended in disaster for the Church. In seeking to eliminate the worship of saints and to put an end to the cult of the dead (evident for so long in the custom of burying the dead under the floors of churches) Catholicism finally found itself digging its own grave: it was to alienate the very many peasants for whom religion without folklore was inconceivable.

But the scope of folklore goes far beyond the terrain of cults and sanctuaries. It also finds concrete expression in a thriving *oral culture*—represented for example by the *folk tale*, stored in the memory of the professional story-tellers who learn their tales by heart. When they grow old, they pass on their lore to a younger man with a good memory who will, in turn, as he grows old, hand on the torch to someone younger. Thus is transmitted, from the mists of time, a store of folk wisdom, both narrative and normative, which circulates, is transformed, taken apart and put together again, travelling from Gibraltar to the Urals and back—or even further, through the wilds of Eurasia. From this point of view, rural France was, until the nineteenth century, only one province among others in a very wide world. In France, folk tales found their way into print and thanks to the writing of Perrault even came to be considered great literature. In Russia, Vladimir Propp, who has made a detailed study of this genre, at once literary and popular, has suggested that the extremely rigid and rule-bound structure of the folk tale might reflect some very ancient religion of the journey of the dead and the transmigration of souls towards the beyond. Without necessarily going as far as that, we might note that the first two stories (nos. 1 and 2 both from the Reynard cycle) collected by Aarne and Thompson in their vast and systematic classification of folk tales in the nineteenth and twentieth centuries, were also the first two that came spontaneously to the lips of the peasant storyteller whom Noël du Fail (in about 1540) depicted in one of his novellas as active at the very end of the fourteenth century: testifying to the impressively unchanging character of rural folklore over the centuries. The constant transformations and renewals that affect the folk tale frequently seem to represent a perpetual turning back on itself, like a snake biting its own tail. And it is certainly true that in the legendary store of tales that circulate within rural civilization, there is a quasireligious—but non-Christian—conception of fertilityfecundity: the immense popularity of the Melusine theme (the creature with the body of a woman and the tail of a serpent) is significant in this respect. Melusine, who inhabits wells and springs, is both the earth mother of great dynasties, peasant and noble, and the guardian of the forest: after a fruitful union with a mortal, she knows when to give the word for trees to be cut and land to be cleared; she guarantees the fruitfulness of the harvest and the prosperity of the *house* (in both senses of the word: lineage and building). She symbolizes a cult of the powers of reproduction in which the interests of agriculture and the family, and sexual obsessions relating to the phallic mother, are inextricably mixed. We should not deduce from this however that the folklore of rural civilization is purely archaic and therefore politically conservative; in fact it contains elements that are distinctly subversive and possibly revolutionary. Melusine herself in certain regions is stoned by the peasants in her own well for being a wicked mistress towards them. And peasant legends are full of stories about the wicked landlord who exploits or deceives his tenants and underlings. If he should perjure himself, swearing he has always dealt honestly with his people, he is immediately struck by a thunder-bolt and transformed into a black dog or a wolf—doomed for ever to be an ancestor-totem for his descendants. On stormy nights, he will return in his beastly form to haunt the family hearth.

Space does not allow us to discuss at any length the *material civilization* of the village: at the end of the Middle Ages and even in the classical period (seventeenth century) it was still very meagre. The peasants were dressed, for example, in patched clothes, bought second-hand from townspeople; their furniture consisted chiefly of a few chests, prudently locked against thieves. But later, in the eighteenth and nineteenth centuries, this "material culture" was to flower during the phase of economic and demographic expansion of rural civilization: the big Normandy cupboard would from now on represent, in the rustic household, a Cartesian conception of order; and regional costumes—like the Breton coiffe in particular—would be evidence of the acculturation of the village tailors, influenced both by the fashions of the old court and the bourgeoisie and by the republican ideas coming out of Paris.

Folk culture also concerns the distribution of roles and powers within the peasant community. The group formed by the unmarried young men is distinguished from that of the married men: sometimes the two categories confront each other in fiercely fought games of *soule* (a ball game which is an ancestor, or an "uncle" at least of modern rugby). This segregation of the young bachelors confirms a bipolarization which is sometimes found, unexpectedly, even in the official stratification of social categories (cf. P. Chéreau). The distinction made between active citizens (electors) and passive citizens (non-electors) at the time of the French Revolution often reflects, at least in the village, a *de facto* differentiation between age-groups, rather than a true separation into social classes. If one also bears in mind the rather more discrete existence of separate groups of married women and young girls, one finds that the peasant community may be quartered, like coat of arms, into four sectors of membership, according to age and sex; (and on top of this, complicating the pattern even further, are social differences between rich and poor, farmers and labourers etc.).

In some of our provinces, there were actually equivalents of the Polynesian "men's houses": barrack rooms, clubs or cafés, which were the context for a specifically masculine sphere of social behaviour.

Another feature of folklore—rural *witchcraft*—raises slightly different problems. It was exacerbated from the sixteenth century by the Reformation and Counter-Reformation, which, when they purged religion of its most magical aspects, divested the priest of his functions as a medium and turned him into a mere employee of the Church. The Reformation and Counter-Reformation, by dint of much neo-theological fulmination against sin and against Satan, were actually attributing increasing importance to the Evil One. By the same token, they conferred considerable status on the village witch and witchcraft in the sixteenth and seventeenth centuries. Endowed with maleficent powers, the efficacy of which was contested by very few people at the time, the witch was in a position to make her adversaries— often those in high places—suffer and pay up. The witch thus represents the revenge of the beggarwoman against the rich, and of woman against the "phallocracy" of a male-dominated society.

*

Stable, stabilized and balanced, rural civilization was nevertheless open to change. How much, depended upon the region. In France, where historical and statistical studies have already provided us with a fairly clear picture, we can distinguish as early as the eighteenth century and *a fortiori* in about 1830, two types of zone (and this dichotomy would very likely be found, with variations, among the other 'nations' of Western Europe). In the north-east part of what was the old kingdom of France—north-east of what has, for the sake of simplicity, if not of accuracy, been christened the Saint-Malo–Geneva line, are the human settlements living on the rich soil of the rolling openfields. Here the people have been marked, to a greater or lesser extent, since the end of the seventeenth century, by the increase in literacy provided by parish or local elementary schools, both of which progressed on the whole steadily from the Renaissance to the Revolution and from the Revolution to the time of Jules Ferry. The rural population in these areas, better educated than elsewhere, presents, from the eighteenth century on, a greater diversity of trade and occupation than the country people of the poor west (Brittany), centre (Massif Central), or south (Pyrenees), whose populations had for long centuries been essentially engaged in subsistence farming (with exceptions in wine-growing areas). The "loam-footed" men of the north-east had more wheelwrights, blacksmiths, farriers, workers in wood, leather and iron, more school-masters too, than their western, central and southern counter-parts. Better fed moreover than the rest of the French peasantry, the more "developed" peasants who lived north of the Saint-Malo/Geneva line were actually a few centi-metres taller than the national average. This difference in height—very pronounced in comparison to the small, rickety and often unhealthy men south of the line—has little or nothing to do with genetics. It is to be explained by the better food (more meat and cereals) and also possibly by the greater school-attendance in the north, which may have rescued country children from back-breaking physical labour. The men of the "north-east half" were also better integrated into national life. They were more willing both to pay taxes and to sacrifice their blood. From Joan of Arc to Captain Coignet, they have been more prepared to give their lives on the field of battle for the mystical person of king or emperor than the men of Occitania: the latter, cut off by their dialect, had little love for a northern France which in turn had small regard for them, and sometimes took the opportunity of showing their resentment. Yet another difference is that in the north-east, good roads, built by the monarchy or the local authorities, using peasant forced labour, after the eighteenth century, criss-cross this more developed part of rural France: thus providing encourage-ment for the grain trade and helping to defeat subsistence crises. Thanks to the roads, the successful cereal-growing economy of the rich flatlands was able to fulfil its potential— a much higher one than that of the cold slopes of the Massif Central, where the people had to be content with rye and chestnut bread.

The reasons for the agricultural superiority of the north-east go back a long way. Much the same could be said about the Netherlands, Belgium, West Germany, southern England and northern Italy. After about the twelfth-thirteenth century, such regions as north-east France, to confine our-selves to this example, generally adopted the plough and harrow, triennial crop-rotation, oats and horse-drawn vehicles. Grain yields in Picardy and around Paris reached fifteen to twenty hectolitres per hectare—and eight or ten units of grain harvested for every one sown—from the end of the Middle Ages and throughout the modern period. From the very first then—and with many centuries' advance—they were already reaching the high grain yield per hectare which England, with her "agricultural revolution" was only to attain with some difficulty towards the end of the seventeenth century and in the eighteenth. In the Nether-lands, the "green revolution" took place in the fifteenth century. Taking advantage of a buoyant demography and raised buying power, a high demand in the towns for meat and milk and the possibilities of substitution afforded by grain imported from the Baltic, the Flemish peasants of the Memling-Breughel period—who had not read any treatises on agriculture—put their agricultural revolution into practice, instead of merely dreaming of it. They flung themselves boldly into farming hops, flax, hemp, clover, buckwheat and temporary grasslands. As a result, fallow fields—so long to remain a feature of the French countryside—disappeared in Flanders under a wide range of crops; and herds of cattle, producing milk, butter and cheese, appeared in large numbers on smallholdings. The manure they produced helped increase vegetable yields, which in turn meant that more land could be given over to grazing (and thus to more manure) since it follows that if fields improve their yield, there is no need to keep expanding their size. The vicious circle of old-style farming: low wheat yields → too large areas of arable → lack of grazing → lack of stock → lack of manure → low wheat yields thus gave way, in the regions of what is now Belgium and the Netherlands, to a "virtuous" circle—the self-same pattern that was to contribute to the "spiral"-type development of the Dutch economy until the seventeenth century. This agricultural revolution in the Dutch style, later propagated as far afield as England (in the seventeenth and eighteenth centuries) and in France (in the eighteenth and nineteenth centuries) would finally make it possible to feed the urban and rural populations, which would be far more numerous than in the past. It would facilitate the take-off of the world economy during and following the Age of Enlightenment.

In terms of landscape, the contrast between, on the one hand, the early-developing regions of north-east France and more generally of the temperate zones of north-western Europe, and on the other, the under-developed rural regions of the Mediterranean south, the Massif Central and the far west of the Breton peninsula, does not always present the same pattern. In France, the oases of modernity, or of rural modernization, are to be found in the rich soil of the wide openfields of the north-east, with their flat rolling plains, their large villages, where the houses cluster together, separated by the large estates of capitalist farmers. Conversely, the *bocage* (enclosed fields) in western and central France and the irregular fields of the south are often associated with archaic farming patterns, the survival of share-cropping and smallholdings still worked by oxen and primitive ploughs until about 1850. In England, the picture is completely different. The British equivalent of the *bocage*, the enclosures, were both the foundation and the guarantee of the modern agricultural revolution of the seventeenth and eighteenth centuries: they encouraged—to the advantage of those large landowners and rich farmers who were prepared to experiment—a spirit of agrarian individualism and enterprise. The archaism of the French *bocage* is the opposite of the modernity of the English enclosure.

However, very ancient differences between the more developed and less developed regions (within the context of traditional rural civilization) are observable in terms of mentalities as well—indeed quite simply in individual or collective behaviour. In the Mediterranean region in general (the peninsulas and especially the islands) and in the very far south of France, the pattern of crime in rural areas continued, until the eighteenth century, to be typical of ancient times: directed against persons. The record seems to have been held in Corsica at the end of the seventeenth century—the annual figure for death by homicide was 0.7 victims per 100 inhabitants. (By way of comparison, in one of the most notorious areas for violent crime in 1971–1972— the 28th precinct of Manhattan-Harlem in New York—the homicide rate was only 0.2 victims per 100 inhabitants, that is barely a third of the Corsican figure). Death by murder in rural Corsica in the seventeenth century actually reached levels comparable to the mass slaughter of Frenchmen in the First World War. It seems that population figures for the island paradise in the age of Louis XIV were seasonally adjusted by assassination. In the relatively developed country-side of northern France, by contrast, the homicide rate noticeably declines between the sixteenth and eighteenth century. The peasant's aggressive instincts were either turned upon himself (suicide was more frequent in the north than in the south) or else was sublimated into offences against property—larceny, theft, fraud. But in any case, the *overall* crime rate goes down in the eighteenth century, in Normandy for example. It looks as if agricultural society, as it was developing in the Age of Enlightenment, was becoming more capable of controlling the emotions of its members. In this respect, such a society might be able to teach our own industrial or post-industrial society, with its tendencies to ultra-violence, a thing or two.

*

But the distance from the Capitol to the Tarpeian Rock is not very great. Between the fourteenth and the early eighteenth century, after passing through some massive upheavals and without any spectacular growth, rural civiliza-tion had in a sense become settled in its poverty and folklore, in economic and demographic stagnation in the very long term—triumphing over even the most serious, negative and long-lasting fluctuations. But after about 1720–1730, every-thing changed; throughout western Europe, this same rural civilization was seized—without however losing its distinc-tive characteristics—by a frenzy of growth. For over a century, the peasant population increased and flourished *in situ*, while still providing people for the expanding towns. At the same time, the demographic structures of rural society began to look more modern in the eighteenth century. Mortality declined with the spread of medical care, better living standards and levels of personal hygiene and child care rather less abysmal than in the past. Faced with rising numbers, and fearing that they might have to face increased poverty, the peasants tried to stem the tide with flimsy defences. They were initiated in France for instance, especially after 1800, to the essentially masculine secrets of *coitus interruptus*; these were widely circulated among young peasants and conscripts through conversations in taverns and barracks; those who had learned of this contraceptive practice introduced it in their conjugal relations. Economic growth, notably in agriculture and cereal production, also took place in the eighteenth and nineteenth centuries: it met the challenge of the new mouths to be fed; and it also succeeded in raising slightly the average per capita ration in both town and country. This agricultural growth was effected in the first place simply by clearing new ground and by an intensification of labour, both human and animal. Then, beginning at dates which vary from place to place (in general in the nineteenth century, though sometimes in the eighteenth, in continental Europe), a true agricultural revolution takes place: grain is now selected (Vilmorin); and stockbreeding becomes selective (this development lay behind one of the currents of thought which would later lead to Darwinism). Forage crops (rich in nitrates) now entirely replaced fallow land. The adoption of the new perfected ploughs was a first step that was eventually to lead to the spread of the McCormick harvester—and much later again the tractor. In France these two types of machine were to be introduced in large numbers only in the early and mid-twentieth century respectively.

Culturally, peasant horizons were extended during the phase of expansion. I have already referred to the striking development of regional costume (though this was mostly worn on high days and holidays); and the amount and quality of household furniture owned by the peasant family also substantially increased in the eighteenth and nineteenth centuries. As for culture in the intellectual sense, the old oral traditions now tended to coexist more and more alongside an increasing corpus of popular literature, printed by the *Bibliothèque Bleue* (the Blue Library) of Troyes, in the eighteenth century for example. This series of books conveyed to those peasants who could read (and who would then read out loud to others on long winter evenings) a culture which was urban in origin and *medieval* in character, and was now, thanks to mass publication, reaching the villages —three or four centuries late! Peasant political culture also underwent considerable change in the eighteenth century: it encouraged peasants to assert themselves. Now, more forcefully than in the past, they were disposed to attack the *seigneurie*, that cornerstone of the "eternal order of the fields", an order indeed in which many rural people no longer believed or put their faith. The peasant Revolution of 1789 and the following years would spring fully armed from this new state of mind, which was frequent among the literate elite who had attended the parish schools. The primary schools of the nineteenth century would only accentuate this anti-aristocratic and anticlerical orientation which could be encountered from now on in certain country regions.

Since 1915–1920 however, we have witnessed the slow death or at any rate decline of "rural civilization" as it has been described here. Its zenith coincided exactly with the peak of population growth in the countryside in the mid-nineteenth century. Its decline began with particular rapidity after 1915–1920; for the 1914 war wiped out the young adult male population of whole villages; and more "effective" still was the industrial (and agricultural) technology which drove labour out of the fields and into the cities. Simultaneously, the mass media of press, radio and television replaced the old folklore of the countryman with the more dazzling folklore of the cartoon strip and urban violence. Farmers want refrigerators now, not fairy stories.

We should not—of course—regret these intrusions, for it would be absurd to claim that rural civilization was an idyllic state (built as it was, as we must recognize, on the poverty of the largest number). But rural civilization has not yet lain down and died, either gracefully or ungracefully.

It still survives, to a greater or lesser degree, even today, in the overdeveloped society of the western world, in its own marginal, unspectacular way. It may not have said its last word yet.

BIBLIOGRAPHY

AARNE, Antti, *The types of the folktale : a classification and bibliography*, translated and enlarged by Stith Thompson, Helsinki, 1961.

BLOCH, Marc, See *The Cambridge Economic History*, Vol. I, *The agrarian life of the middle ages*, ed. M.M. Postan, for the chapter by Marc Bloch referred to in this article.

BERCÉ, Yves-Marie, *Histoire des croquants : étude des soulèvements populaires au XVIIe siècle dans le sud-ouest de la France*, Geneva, 1974.

— *Croquants et Nu-pieds : les soulèvements paysans en France du XVIe au XIXe siècle*, introduction by Yves-Marie Bercé, Paris, 1974. (Collection "Archives".)

FOISIL, Madeleine, *La Révolte des Nu-pieds et les révoltes normandes de 1639*, Paris, 1970 (Series "Recherches" no. 57, published by P.U.F. for the Faculté de Lettres et Sciences Humaines de Paris-Sorbonne).

FOSSIER, R., *Histoire sociale de l'Occident médiéval*, 2nd edn. Paris, Armand Colin, 1973.

FOURQUIN, Guy, *Seigneurie et Féodalité*, Paris 1970; English translation by I. and A. Sells, *Lordship and Feudalism in the middle ages*, London, Allen & Unwin, 1976.

HILAIRE, Jean, *Histoire des institutions publiques et des faits sociaux (11e–19e siècles)*, Paris, Dalloz, 1976. (3rd edn.)

— *Régime des biens entre époux dans la région de Montpellier, 13e–16e siècles*, 1958.

MENDRAS, Henri, See the many publications on rural society by Henri Mendras, for example his recent *Sociétés paysannes*, Paris, Armand Colin (Collection "U"), 1976, where the concepts mentioned in this article are explained.

MOUSNIER, Roland, *Fureurs paysannes*, Paris, 1967; English translation by Brian Pearce, *Peasant uprisings in seventeenth-century France, Russia and China*, London, Allen & Unwin, (Great Revolutions series), 1971.

PIRENNE, Henri, See the many publications by Henri Pirenne on mediaeval Europe; on the particular issue raised in this article see *Le soulèvement de la Flandre maritime de 1323–1328, documents inédits publiés avec une introduction par Henri Pirenne*, 1900.

PORCHNEV or PORSHNEV, Boris F., *Les soulèvements populaires en France de 1623 à 1648*, Paris, SEVPEN, 1963.

PROPP, Vladimir, *Morphology of the folktale*, 2nd edn., Austin, Texas, 1968.

RÉTIF or RESTIF DE LA BRETONNE, Nicolas, *La vie de mon père*, Paris, Garnier edn., 1970.

WOLF, Eric, *Peasant wars of the twentieth century*, New York, 1969.

YVER, Jean, *Essai de géographie coutuière : égalité entre héritiers et exclusion des enfants dotés*, Paris, 1965.

7

The "Event" and the "Long Term" in Social History: the Case of the Chouan Uprising[1]

PRESENT-DAY historiography, with its preference for the quantifiable, the statistical and the structural, has been obliged to suppress in order to survive, which is a pity. In the last few decades it has virtually condemned to death the narrative history of events and the individual biography. Such genres, not unworthy of attention and sometimes quite justifiable—though perhaps too inclined, in the interests of narrative pace, to leap from massacre to boudoir or from bedchamber to anteroom—still survive today in our cultural supermarkets, thanks to the multiplicator effect of the mass media. The Muse of history herself nowadays disdains these "long sequences of simple and uncomplicated events" so beloved of historians of the old school. As we all know, she has turned towards the study of structures, the persistent patterns of the "long term", and the collection of data amenable to serial or quantitative analysis.

In France these preferences, now firmly established, first appeared in the work of Bloch, Febvre and their friends, disciples or successors in the *Annales* school of history. Fernand Braudel, when he was writing *The Mediterranean*, relegated the events of war and diplomacy to the final section: the heart of his book is essentially the archaeology of a sea—with its strata of millennial or merely secular temporality. Ernest Labrousse's first book encompasses, in its broad sweep, the entire history of prices in the eighteenth century: his raw material consists of figures; his normal timespan is about a hundred years; the shortest period he considers (detailed in a second book) is the *intercycle* (a decade and a half); this does not leave much room for events. Such abstinence from the recording of events—entirely justified within the author's perspective—is also to be found in J.

Marczewski's more recent studies of growth. In another
area of research, Pierre Goubert in his book on the Beauvaisis
has resurrected the countless parish registers, gathering
dust in church and village archives, and through them has
brought back to life the demographic *ancien régime* of
seventeenth and eighteenth-century France, with its impressive numbers of pregnancies, early deaths and late marriages.
In the course of this exhaustive analysis, Goubert certainly
encountered events: famines for example, or at the very
least serious food shortages—a typical hazard for populations
of the good old days. But such "events" are mentioned by
Goubert only in order to stress what surrounds them, to
place them within a recurrent structure which regularly
brings round, by virtue of a universally applicable concept,
the inevitable "subsistence crisis"—itself accompanied by
a series of typical, negative and quantifiable characteristics:
high cereal prices; high mortality rates among the poor
through malnutrition and among the rich through epidemics;
a decline in the number of marriages, which are postponed
until better days; the temporary barrenness of women who
are normally fertile, whether as a result of amenorrhea
caused by famine or for other reasons.

What is known as "structural" or "total" or "systematic"
history has even attempted, quite legitimately, to relate to
its own norms events which might appear to be extremely irreducible, so extraordinary, dramatic and disastrous are they—the Black Death of 1348 for example, which
exterminated a third (and in many places half) of the population in western Europe. Viewed from a great distance,
from an international or intercontinental vantage point, this
pandemic loses its teratological character and can be reduced
to a predictable episode in the overall process which was
taking place between the fourteenth and sixteenth centuries,
and which might be termed the bacteriological unification of
the planet. This unification was itself conditioned by such
global phenomena, from the eleventh century on, as the
population expansion of the three great masses of human
settlement (China, Europe and Amerindia), and the inevitable
establishment of communications between these masses,
as a result of the opening up of land and sea routes, whether

for commerce or for conquest. Typical of this "opening up" were for instance the integration of Eurasia following the creation of the Mongol and world empire of Genghis Khan; the establishment by the Genoese of a silk-route through this empire—thus providing a short-cut for viruses between Central Asia and the Crimea; and the westward expeditions of the following era, with the discovery (again by a Genoese) and penetration of America. All of which was of course greatly to increase the probability of massive waves of microbe infection being carried from east to west: first the Black Death, which was imported from Central Asia to Europe via the Crimean port of Caffa; and then, even more serious but comparable in principle, the extermination of the American Indian populations by the action of bacilli carried by the Spanish settlers between 1500 and 1700. The most disastrous epidemics, viewed in this planetary perspective, appear as no more than the logical consequence of the unplanned expansion of the number of people in the world, of trade, military expeditions and colonization. They are no longer regarded as unique events. And they are "digested" by global history.

History of the all-embracing kind then, which concerns itself whenever possible with the quantitative and structural, attempts to transcend the event, to absorb or recycle it, so to speak. That does not imply any claim to suppress time itself: even the most logically composed structures (in rural history for instance, where these things are less complicated than elsewhere) have their phases of disequilibrium, their swings and cycles, their moments of reversal or restoration and their secular pendulum movements which can be regarded as the very stuff of today's historical narratives.

Such victories at the frontiers of knowledge, won by the historians of the last half-century, are irreversible; but they would be even more satisfactory if history really was entirely logical, intelligible and predictable from start to finish; if the event or chance happening could be exorcized once and for all, thus eliminating that aleatory element which, to the historian, is like an irritating piece of grit inside his brand-new discovery! Total exorcism is of course inconceivable. A trend or a structure can quite easily be unmasked. All that is required is a little patience, a great deal of work and plenty of imagination. But the aleatory transition from one structure to another, the *mutation*, often remains, in history as in biology, the most perplexing zone, where chance appears to play a large part. Once one has reached this zone, factors which are often mysterious delineate the poles of necessity within the field of possibilities: once they have surfaced, their existence is obvious—but a moment before their appearance, they were as unpredictable as they were unprecedented.

In fact, certain schools of historians or individual researchers have tried in their various ways to resolve this awkward problem, to tame the event, so to speak, even when it appears to represent a point of rupture. They have set out to give it its specific weight in quantitative and structural history. The American writers of the "new economic history", for example, have proceeded by way of the "counterfactual hypothesis" (that is one which posits an alternative, imaginary course of history). Taking some of the most outstanding events in American history, they have challenged classic (and sometimes hackneyed) interpretations of them: was the purpose and result of the War of Independence, waged by the thirteen colonies, really to counter the intolerable losses caused to the New World economy by English tariffs and monopolies on the import of tea or the export of tobacco? Did the building of the railroads in the nineteenth century really launch or stimulate the economic growth of the USA? Did the New Deal actually do anything to remedy the problems caused by the depression of the 1930s? Using such questions as their starting-point, American historians such as Fogel, North and their colleagues have invented a fictional history in which none of these events occurred—one in which there was no War of Independence, no railroad, no New Deal. Then with the aid of the most sophisticated econometric techniques, they have calculated the effect on sales of tobacco in the eighteenth century, on economic growth up to 1880, or the revival of trade between 1930 and 1940 of these imaginary situations. In other words (using a method whose promising possibilities do not have to be spelt out) they have, in order to calculate the impact of a given event on the trend of

American economic development, postulated the non-existence of the event and attempted to estimate the difference thus introduced. The results of their calculations (was this something premeditated by the representatives of the new economic history?) was not, I may say, encouraging for those who might have been hoping for a new lease of life for *l'histoire événementielle*. In the three cases I have mentioned, the prefabricated non-occurrence of the event in question did not, it seems, lead to any radical modification in the growth rate of the economy concerned. Take the case of the railroads for instance: if they had never been built, and if instead more traditional means of transport (carts and the extra canals which would have been dug) had been used, the loss in overall growth in the American economy would only have been of about the order of five per cent—that is to say virtually negligible. And it appears from similar research projects that the American economy could have managed very well without the shock treatment administered by the War of Independence or the radical thinking supposedly introduced by the New Deal.

The approach adopted by these young American economic historians however, although technically extremely sophisticated, is in some ways rather lacking in subtlety. It amounts to taking as a point of reference the famous events that are part of the "1066 and all that" of the American people (the War of Independence, the epic of the railroads, the New Deal and so on) and then moving on in time towards the totality which these events may or may not have influenced. A different and more complex heuristic approach (and one which would restore to the event its proper status, even in quantitative and structural history) might be imagined: to move in the opposite direction, back through time, starting from a given structure, the existence of which is well attested and empirically evident, but the origins of which are shrouded in mystery, and to look for the initial traumatic event which may have acted as a catalyst for its emergence. The event itself would then have to be relocated, always bearing in mind its aleatory features, within the structures prevailing at the time of its occurrence. This indeed is the approach adopted by Paul Bois in his book, *Paysans de l'Ouest (Peasants of the*

West), an important one precisely for this kind of problem. The recent paperback edition of this work in France should make it more easily available to interested readers, who will now have a chance to judge for themselves, on the evidence presented, the *structure-event-structure* procedure adopted by the author.[2] It seems to me, at any rate, to possess sufficient exemplary significance to justify presenting it here at some length. In conclusion, I shall make brief reference to similar attempts by other writers who are also concerned to restore the *event*, however unique, to its proper place within a kind of history which is nevertheless committed to being systematic.

The point of departure for the reflections of the author of *Paysans de l'Ouest* was André Siegfried's famous and important book *Tableau politique de la France de l'Ouest (A political survey of western France)*. Siegfried, the inventor of "electoral geography", had noted the preponderance, among the peasant populations of the Armorican *massif*, of right-wing, clerical and anti-republican political parties. According to him, such preponderance was to be explained by the survival "of a still lively tradition of the *ancien régime*, hierarchical, catholic and conservative, as opposed to the republican or democratic tradition, which is anticlerical, egalitarian and progressive". Western France was, to use the terminology of the July Monarchy, a bastion of "Resistance" to "Movement". The problem thus raised by the political attitudes of the French "far west" was to prove of lasting interest, since the west has remained, long after Siegfried's book and practically up to the Gaullist years, a stronghold of political and social conservatism. And yet, it seems that while Siegfried's description of the phenomenon is illuminating, by the same token the explanation he gives (by relating this political and mental superstructure to local and social infrastructures specific to the contemporary west) is not very convincing, that is if one follows Paul Bois's dissection of it. Can one really explain the conservatism of these regions by the system of land tenure? The trouble is that land tenure throughout the Armorican *massif* does not invariably display the feudal and paternalistic character attributed to it by Siegfried—far from it indeed. Should one therefore invoke the predominant pattern of farming, based, again according to Siegfried, on sharecropping, a system thought to be productive of socio-political backwardness? This is a semantic illusion, Bois replies. Sharecropping is only a marginal phenomenon in western France: most of the so-called sharecroppers (*métayers*) in these provinces are in fact tenant-farmers (*fermiers*) and have quite modern rental arrangements. As for the clergy, who in Siegfried's time supported the right, they certainly have a good deal of influence in the west, but this is not as universal as has been suggested. Holy water often, but not always, mixes well with cider. Is it not in any case a tautology to explain the political clericalism of a region in the 1900s by its religious clericalism? In short, neither feudalism, nor sharecropping, nor even the Church will do, says Bois, as explanatory factors sufficient to account for the political attitudes of western France. Indeed André Siegfried himself eventually realized the shortcomings of his own system, and was led *in extremis*, in order to explain the stubbornly reactionary character of the *bocage*, to call upon the mysteries of ethnic identity!

The most useful contribution to the debate, and one which would help us out of the Siegfriedian impasse, would be a monograph on a single limited region: by concentrating on a "micro-region" the historian can go over it with a fine toothcomb and identify the factors that really count.

And this Bois has done. His chosen constituency is the *département* of the Sarthe. This does indeed provide a clear example of the contrast between the Right (in the majority) solidly entrenched in the western *cantons* of the department; and the Left (in the minority, but holding its own) which has local strongholds in the south-east. Here, still loyal to their forefathers and to their local tradition, the descendants or successors (all farming, or at any rate country people) of the peasants and weavers who voted *"Montagnard"* in 1849, were still, in the 1960s, giving a high percentage of their votes to the communist party.

Needless to say, the twofold division of the Sarthe (east/west or left/right) while confirming Siegfried's analysis as to the existence of an entrenched conservatism, fails to bear out his interpretation of the phenomenon. The electoral map of this department (of which Le Mans is the chief town) reveals no correlation, positive or negative, with the distribution of large estates. So Siegfried's formula, whereby a conservative vote is associated with big landowners and the rural paternalism they invariably generate, is not supported by the evidence. Similarly, if one looks at the same factor from a diachronic perspective, the decline of the large estates in the Sarthe, which is recorded after 1850, did not lead to a parallel decline in conservatism: the democratization of land ownership did not in itself lead to the democratization of political life. More generally, the social and ecological differences of the present day, so beloved of American-style political scientists with their delight in correlations, only play a minor role, if they have any effect at all, in the differentiation of the political and mental fabric: in the Sarthe of the twentieth century, the conservative voters of the west and the left-wing supporters of the south-east are all brought up in the same countryside—their boots are coated with the same mud. The only distinction of any significance—and one to which we shall return—is that per capita income in the west of the department is higher than that in the south-east, in so far as the easterners have a less fertile soil to work on.

As for the religious factor, at first sight this clearly appears to be fundamental. The west of the department, as a "bastion of the Right", remained "strongly Christian" for a long time. For years the villages here were inhabited by passionately devout women and pious laymen. Every Sunday, the parish church and the local café (where the family would gather after mass to drink coffee, with a drop of something stronger) would be packed. Whereas the south-east, the stronghold of the left, could be considered by 1920—or indeed by 1856— as a region "disaffected" from the Church, where the men, and following their example, the women, had given up going to church or taking the sacraments, except on special occasions (births, marriages and deaths). Only here too, one should exercise prudence, since the true significance, for political purposes, of the religious factor, is something of a problem. In our own time, the west of the Sarthe, hitherto Catholic and given to high levels of religious observance, is in turn tending, without any great fuss or fanaticism, to detach itself quietly from the Church. Yet it remains, in spite of this, and notwithstanding the gradual decline in importance of its priests and the disappearance of the clerical party as such, politically conservative and even reactionary, just as in the past.

It is impossible in the end then, in this region of contrasts (two-thirds of the Sarthe favours the Right, one-third the Left) to explain the present *by* the present, or to elucidate contemporary political choices by underlying social or religious structures. Even an all-out statistical assault on the phenomena actually observable today would take one nowhere towards an explanation—the computer would probably seize up.

One is therefore obliged, it seems, to turn to the past. And more particularly in the Sarthe, where the west backed the Chouans and the south-east was "Blue" (Republican), one cannot avoid reference to the major *event* which split the area in two—the Chouan rebellion. By means of a regressive analysis, Paul Bois has come to the conclusion that the great peasant war really was the key event, the matrix in which the long-lasting political attitudes that so impressed Siegfried, have their origins.

Such analysis must begin—given our French tradition of electoral geography—with the map. And we do indeed find that the rural rising of 1793–1799 (with further echoes in 1813, 1815 and 1832) exactly corresponds in geographical distribution, to the western regions of the Sarthe which were to vote "White" in the nineteenth and twentieth centuries. It affords a striking example of multisecular fidelity, eventually to reap its reward in the form of Gaullism, when the elected representatives of this stubborn land finally tasted the sweets of power after generations in the political wilderness.

But if one is to demonstrate conclusively that there is a link between the *long term* and the single *event*, one must prove satisfactorily that the *Chouannerie* was not itself simply the result of political, spiritual and ideological attitudes already implanted in the region in question and dating from long before the Revolution. Unless this can be established, the entire argument becomes circular: it merely brings us up once more against a very ancient set of political and mental structures going back hundreds of years, despite the apparent interruption caused by the "event" of the Chouan rising. Nothing at all would have been explained; the whole question would simply have been pushed further into the past, before 1789, and the problem of the origins of present-day political attitudes would remain unsolved.

It is at this point in the argument that we come to what seems to me the most remarkable part of Bois's demonstration —remarkable that is, to those who are closely concerned with the problem of the event-structure relationship. A meticulous process of identifying the *terminus a quo* has in fact made it possible for Bois to show that the *"ancien régime"* and "conservative" cast of mind which was to characterize the western regions of the Sarthe from 1793 to 1799, and thereafter until the 1970s, *had not yet been formed* in 1789.

This brings an abrupt change of focus. From its "macro-chronology" of 175 years, the book moves into a "micro-history" compressed into a couple of two-year periods and concentrating on certain crucial happenings: "the events".

The identification process referred to above was carried out by Paul Bois by means of the 1789 *cahiers de doléances* (registers of grievances). As hardly needs saying, these documents, when properly handled, can provide capital evidence on peasant attitudes in the 1780s.

For the sake of convenience, the argument from the *cahiers* employs a counterfactual hypothesis: if the Left-Right opposition, with battle-lines clearly drawn up, lasting from 1793 to the 1970s, had its origins in some political or mental division dating from before 1789, one would expect to find in the west of the Sarthe (among the "Whites") an extremely moderate set of *cahiers de doléances*, offering little challenge to "feudal" oppression; one would expect the south-east by contrast to produce very aggressive *cahiers*, pouring out denunciations of the nobility and in particular the clergy; in short that each side would display its "true colours" for the centuries to come. But this hypothesis, while impeccably logical, is not borne out at all by the evidence. Where, in 1789, is the "red zone", as it would be called today—anti-feudal, anti-seigniorial and above all anti-tithe (since until 1789 tithes represent the heaviest burden by which the peasants were oppressed)? Lo and behold, this turns out to be the *west* of the department—the home of the future Chouans! It was so hostile to tithes that one might almost think it the land of "priest-eaters" (in fact on this particular point, it was nothing of the sort: protests against tithes were not directed against the parish priest, who was usually respected, but against those much higher up, the great tithe-leviers, that is the higher clergy, the abbots of monasteries and the prelates whose income from the land the peasants considered to be excessive).

By contrast the south-east, the home of the future republicans, the "Blues" of 1793, ancestors of the "Reds" of 1848 and 1946, seems—another paradox—to have been extremely moderate in 1789, to judge by the mild demands advanced in the *cahiers* in respect of seigneurs, feudalism and tithes.

The hypothesis which Bois, as an "event-structure" historian, had intuitively sensed was therefore vindicated: in 1789 the lines of battle were not yet fixed; by 1793 when the Chouan revolt began, they were. And fixed they remained for five generations. The event was a two-step process so to speak: first the short initial period when passions were roused and sides taken (1789–1793); then a war of subversion, a seven-year tragedy (1793–1799)—which irreversibly fixed the stark choice made by the peasants after the first four years of revolution

Thanks to the Sarthe documents, we can follow quite closely, thus making it more comprehensible, the course of this initial stage, during which attitudes were adopted. A few "soundings" taken at intervals can illuminate the quickly-succeeding phases.

The first phase is identified with the first elections: those of 1790 and 1791. They were much more democratic and thus more indicative of the peasant consciousness than has generally been supposed. For the system of "passive citizens" excluded from voting only a small number of the very poor, of vagabonds and servants (and if the latter had voted they would in any case have been influenced by the not very democratic attitudes of their masters). It emerges that the elections of 1790–1791, which really were therefore both free and valid, even by the sometimes exacting standards of the twentieth century, reveal not only a pronounced anti-noble and anti-clerical tendency, tallying with the *cahiers* of the Sarthe in 1789; but also—and it is here that the first hint of the future Chouannerie can be glimpsed—they express a radical determination to drive the bourgeois of the big towns (Le Mans in this case) from their official positions. In other words, the decisive event which is the common factor throughout is the emergence of class-consciousness among the peasants, whose aggressive feelings, originally directed against feudal oppression, were very soon to be turned against the local bourgeoisie. (If the Sarthois were out of step, it was really only because they were ahead of their time.) First anti-*seigneur*, and later, because of the "events", anti-town, this attitude of all-round hostility as it crystallized among the country people, had two distinct sides. At the time of the referendum of 21st July 1793, asking for approval of the Constitution of Year I, this transfer of hostility and reorientation of rural consciousness was already, or very nearly, a *fait accompli*. The rich peasants of the west Sarthe, who had grain to *sell*, refused to accept the devalued *assignat* currency in exchange for their cereals. And one of the symptoms of their bad temper and growing animosity towards the Republic was their massive abstention when the referendum was held. By thus expressing their attitude, they were finding a way of protesting simultaneously against the persecution of the "good priests" and against the call-up of young peasants who were being sent to their deaths on the frontiers. By contrast, the poor farmers of the east and south-east of the Sarthe, who needed to *buy* grain, threw themselves into a campaign of demonstrations calling for price-controls, aimed at holding the price of cereals in particular to a minimum, thus aligning themselves with the *sans-culottes* of the towns, who were natural supporters of the Republic. From now on (1793) the ideological split between the two poles of the Sarthe department is fixed in its main lines: the west, originally anti-feudal, but now going over entirely to the Chouannerie, is on the point of conflict with the south-east, which remains loyal to the Republic. The two camps are in position: in the space of a few years, the passing event has produced a lasting mentality—a short-term phenomenon has produced a long-term structure.

But this short-term phenomenon, the flash in the pan so to speak, is not merely the cause of future political structures. It also refers back to an already pre-existent infrastructure. This is one of the original features of Bois's book: he works back from the peasant ideology and identity of today to the event which everyone thought was dead and buried because it lay so far back in the past; then from that event itself, he sets out to inquire even further into the pre-revolutionary economy and society, searching for the original sources, ones which while they do not predetermine a still very uncertain future, nevertheless provide a range of possibilities, a magnetic field as it were, within which the aleatory events of 1790–1793 would have freedom to operate.

What was the scope of the magnetic field in the *bocage* around Le Mans before the Revolution? To take land ownership first: the nobles and other privileged persons did not (contrary to what one might have expected) exert in what was to be the department of the "Sarthe" (both east and west) a preponderant influence before 1789, not even in the region which was later to turn Chouan—indeed less here than anywhere else! In fact they had already left their family seats; they lived in the towns, often a long way off. As for seigniorial dues, apart from the tithes they were insignificant. The bonds of exploitation could perhaps be symbolically represented by the following percentage: only seven per cent of the peasants were dependent on the nobility in the sense that they farmed a noble's land. So there were not many country folk who could be incited to rise up in favour of the aristocracy for reasons dictated purely and simply by a client relationship.

Far more significant than land-ownership by the nobility was that of the bourgeoisie—which accounted for 51 per cent of the land! The bourgeoisie had already become the potential target of the frustrations of the mass of peasants, even before the episodes of the Revolution and counter-revolution. This would be particularly true of the west of the Sarthe, where the energetic and hardworking peasant farmers, who had become rich (unlike the poor devils on the sandy soil in the south-east, who had not the remotest hope of owning land) had definite ideas about taking over the cultivable areas—giving the land to those who worked it, at the expense of the bourgeois who had appropriated it for themselves. We shall see how hopes of this kind were to be dashed.

Sociologically, the archaic institution of sharecropping was unknown in the region even before 1789. The peasant population of the Maine was in fact predominantly composed of tenant-farmers. In this French *bocage*, as in England in the modernizing period after the enclosures, there was to be found a stratum of rural society whose legal and social status, on the whole a modern one, certainly did not encourage backward-looking attitudes. Moreover, this rural population was not irremediably divided, as was sometimes the case in the openfields of north-eastern France, into rich peasants and poor labourers, deliberately and sometimes physically opposed to each other. Peasant society in the future Sarthe before 1789, particularly in the west, formed a morally homo-geneous whole: tenant-farmers, *bordagers* (more humble tenants) and day-labourers were united by the ties of kinship; by internal clientele relationships; and by rubbing shoulders every day in the same village. It is easy to imagine how this "mass of rustics" was able, at different times, to present a united class front, in 1789 against tithes; and in 1790–1799, with increasing bitterness, *against* the bourgeoisie of the towns and thus, indirectly, *in favour of* the refractory clergy.

There already did exist, however, before 1789, a real source of differentiation within peasant society, one which prepared the way for the geographical division between Chouan and non-Chouan regions: this lay in the geographically deter-mined difference of incomes, already referred to. The dynamic farmers of the western Sarthe, sellers of grain and future Chouans, enjoyed a surplus of hemp and cereals from their rich soil—and had a per capita income fifty per cent higher than that of their less fortunate counterparts in the south-east. Because of the poor quality of their land, the latter were obliged to buy their grain, and thus were more likely to feel solidarity with the consumers who lived in the towns. Moreover the south-east and east were the home of large numbers of woodcutters and especially of weavers, who were moved by their own occupational motivations and demands (the need for subsistence foods, already mentioned; the fact that they were purchasers of grain and hemp; hostility to the tentative straitjacket which the *ancien régime* sought to impose on the textile industry; willingness, for all kinds of reasons, to accept the leadership of the urban merchants). All of which drove those who made their living from wood and cloth to make common cause with the *bourgeois* or popular masses in the towns, against the stock farmers, against the hemp producers, and above all against the big cereal growers of the west, who were accused of making the hungry consumers "sing for their supper".

There were therefore, as Paul Bois writes, "two different populations in the *bocage*": the westerners, sitting comfortably on their sacks of grain and forming a block hostile to the cities (whether the latter were dominated, as was still the case in 1789, by elites either noble or with pretentions to nobility; or, as in later years, by one or another fraction of the bourgeoisie or the "non-privileged" in *ancien régime* terms). And on the other side of the anthropological frontier, were the other people, those of the south-eastern Sarthe, poorer and more open to urban influence; not at all inclined to be revolutionary in 1789 in opposition to "feudal" oppression, but in the years to come, by contrast, showing themselves ready to throw in their lot with the towns against the "pure-blooded" peasantry of the west.

The study of these very ancient structures, underlying the traumatic event, finally allows Paul Bois, once he has finally reconstructed them, to return to the event itself: after the patient investigations described here, it becomes possible to provide an extremely detailed characterization of the event, thus illuminating its role in creating political and mental structures which were to predominate in the Sarthe long after 1793.

To say what this event—the Chouannerie—really was, in all its ramifications (whether immediate or long-term), means in the first place saying what it was not. The Chouannerie did not of course, as everyone knows, originate with the aristocracy. Neither was it—and on this point Paul Bois has something new to say—the result of a clerical initiative, engineered by priests who had refused to take the oath. A careful analysis of the refractory clergy in fact indicates that the majority of priests (proportionately more numerous in the west than in the south-east) who refused the oath, made up their minds to do so—apart from a handful of individuals of great personal courage—less from personal conviction than as a result of pressure from the rural environment: the peasants in the west Sarthe were precisely those who refused to countenance their spiritual guide, the cultural leader of their Sunday gatherings "going over to the enemy" and betraying the countryside on behalf of the town.

The cement that bound together the Chouannerie, as is attested by the slogans of the rebels themselves, was the union "of the country people against the townsfolk"; more precisely of peasants against the "bourgeois", who are designated and hated by name. This hatred is directed against "that lot in the town", the "bourgeois villains", the "Blues"; the national guardsmen who come from their homes in the town to the villages, in order to loot, to drink the peasants' wine with impunity, and to tear the clothes off their daughters' backs in order to wrench the scapularies from their necks.

This anti-town fervour had been diagnosed very early on by an Angevin aristocrat, Count Walsh de Serrant; as early as the elections to the Estates General, "he had organized a sort of electoral campaign against the bourgeois candidates, by trying to arouse the wrath of the country people against them".

This aversion, the origins of which lie in the very composition of the *bocage* itself, was to find its greatest justification in the *revolutionary events*. For the 1789 Revolution, in spite of its promising beginnings, had succeeded in rubbing the "peasant class" up the wrong way. It had brought this "class", which inhabited the west of the Sarthe and in general western France, nothing but a long series of disappointments. The first of these was agrarian: dues payable to secular lords, the burden of which was insignificant, were of course, abolished along with the *ancien régime*, but tithes, which *were* heavy, simply reverted to the owner of the land and were thus payable by the tenant-farmer, that is the peasant, for whom the night of 4th August thus came to look like a bad joke. Then there was disappointment over tax: the land tax which replaced the *taille* was paradoxically made heavier than the old tax by the new authorities, in order to compensate for the suppression of the *gabelle*. And this was also, like tithes, charged to the tenant farmer, who paid it to the state on behalf of his landlord. Added to these were fiduciary and military disappointments: the inflation of the *assignats* and the call-up of country lads to fight in the Revolutionary Wars. Perhaps worst of all was the disappointment over land, which centred on the problem of the *Biens nationaux* (National Property): the efficient farmers of the south-east had had their eyes on the wealth of the Church since 1789 (as their *cahiers* prove). They were to see their hopes thwarted. The urban bourgeoisie, better equipped financially than even the richer tenant-farmers, snapped up, for high prices, the lands of the clergy, which were often the most fertile in the locality and extremely tempting. The frustration of the farming people of the west began to be vented thereafter in a number of bitter and vengeful pronouncements: "let the people who have bought up the *biens nationaux* be the first to go off to the wars on the frontier (the future Chouans were in effect saying). Then they can defend their precious Revolution, since it has given them all the best land. The sons of the peasants cannot see why they should get themselves killed for an ungrateful Republic."

So in the western Sarthe there was a remarkably powerful interaction between event and structure, of which the outcome was to be the Chouannerie, itself in turn the source of a chain of consequences lasting many years. A regional peasant community, closely integrated and already possessing an unusual degree of autonomy, had taken the full shock of an unforeseeable train of frustrations. The vital years of the Revolution were consequently experienced by these country people in their native region as a stroke of fate, an external phenomenon, coming from the towns, the shock waves from some remote disaster. They had the sensation that they were entering into collision with a causal sequence quite independent of their own system, and one which was unwarrantably interfering with their normal destiny.

In the less fertile south-east of the department on the other hand (the eternal contrast yet again), the parties were on a more friendly footing. The bourgeois of the towns were not greatly tempted by the poor land owned by the local clergy, and did not flock to buy it up. The peasants and petit-bourgeois of the local villages were thus able to acquire the clergy's holdings with little trouble. The new rural proprietors, now *notables* in their own parishes, provided so many recruits to the revolutionary cause: their experience made them sympathetic to the new regime and made them available as counter-Chouans in the short run and supporters of the republican party in the long run.

We have come to the last link in the chain: we have followed Paul Bois in his journey from present-day ideology to the traumatic event which gave it its origins; then from this event to the pre-existing conditions which, if they did not altogether determine it, certainly coloured and informed it; from these conditions, we returned to the event in order to make a better estimate of its significance through our increased knowledge. A final question remains unanswered: why was the Chouan rebellion, despite its military defeat, such a resounding success in terms of long-term cultural survival? Why, in short, did this event—and no other—have the rare privilege both of shaping the future and of providing an impetus that lasted for years? How and why did it manage to acquire the solidity of a structure?

Bois's answer, a rather expeditious one perhaps, to this question can be summed up in a few simple propositions: let us say to start with that the west was politically virgin soil: on the eve of Revolution, political consciousness hardly existed at all (except perhaps among the weavers) and had to be built up from scratch. The pre-Chouan and Chouan periods (three or four years of maturation from 1790 to 1793, and six or seven years of terrible ordeals, 1793 to 1799) created this political consciousness, moving in to occupy terrain which thereafter became extremely difficult for rival ideologies to reclaim (a comparison can be made with the Cévennes, a region which was to remain Protestant even in the nineteenth and twentieth centuries, quite simply because, for reasons which later lost their relevance, it had elected to become Protestant in 1560).

In the western Sarthe, in addition, the socio-economic infrastructure was to remain for a long time, until 1860 or even 1900 or so, much the same as under the *ancien régime*; this base accordingly favoured the retention of a political and mental superstructure of Chouan tendencies. On such favourably-disposed terrain, the phenomena often encountered in such circumstances were set in motion: stabilization, consolidation—and takeovers by other forces: peasant consciousness, which had been so original and so isolated in the early days, soon needed allies. So it allowed itself to be taken in hand by the lobbies composed of the local nobility and, especially, the clergy, lobbies which alone had the inestimable "merit" in the eyes of the Chouan activists, of having come to the insurgents' aid, if only at the eleventh hour, when it was most crucial. As a result, a number of "homeostatic" processes occurred: the Chouan or ex-Chouan culture, paradoxically identified with the royalist and conservative Right, gradually came to be associated, almost as a point of honour, with all kinds of other structures, ancient and modern, of the *bocage*, with which it finally became identified, body and soul: from the Sunday drinking and social gatherings after mass to the ecclesiastical and noble tradition of leadership originating in the second period which eventually infiltrated even the agricultural trade unions. "Reproductive" mechanisms, inculcating traditions relating to the heroic sagas of the west were also at work, at the extremely effective level of family indoctrination and of peasant education and folklore. In short, the political and mental structures of the west of France in the nineteenth century, which amounted quite simply to preserving the original event in aspic, keeping the Chouans in the deep freeze so to speak, were from now on *there*, like Mount Everest, ineradicably and irremovably fixed, until our own times. The Chouan event had acted as a contingent catalyst, as a bridge between the socio-economic structures of the *ancien régime* and the politico-cultural structures of the present day. The decline and progressive collapse of the former did not bring about *ipso facto* the disappearance of the latter. The physical and biological reality of the *bocage* is now being destroyed by bulldozers. But the spiritual identity of the *bocage*, rooted in its people's minds since the days of the Chouans, is proving more resistant than woods and hedges.

The author of *Paysans de l'Ouest* has thus been able to reveal, in what is almost a textbook demonstration, how the *event* can be a means of innovation, an accidental transition as it were—governed by remote factors, and with delayed action in time—from one *structure* to another; in this case from the old infrastructure to the modern superstructure. The discrepancies in time, which naturally thwarted any attempt at analysis lacking in sufficient historical depth, had always defeated previous studies of the west—even the most sophisticated, such as Siegfried's. The only escape from this frustrating impasse turned out to be an appeal to history, using the event–structure mode.

But Paul Bois's successful inquiry is not alone of its kind. Quite independently, other attempts of similar nature, more ambitious in scope if less complete in their analysis, have recently appeared. Perhaps they indicate a new trend in historiography. So they deserve a mention here, in conclusion, since this article is concerned with some of the same problems. One such example is the essay by Jean Baechler on "Les origines du système capitaliste" (*Archives européennes de sociologie*, 1968, 2). The (medieval) origins of capitalism are conceived of by Baechler, similarly, as the effect of chance operating on a given situation: as an accidental "malfunctioning" that occurred in the tenth and eleventh centuries in a society whose technology was flourishing, but whose fabric had been dissolved by sectional anarchy. Such an exceptional situation thus offered a golden opportunity, at the end of the High Middle Ages, to the individual small cells of the society: that is the barons and their fiefs; but also, from the very start, to the towns and merchants, in short the "exceptional" individuals—the *bourgeois*. Thus, he argues, chance encouraged the formation of a logical structure, capitalism, which was from the very beginning endowed with what he calls irrepressible and cancerous energy. This structure and this energy which had always been contained within the range of possibilities open to humanity in the last two millennia, would, once they appeared, sweep all before them; they would cover and contaminate the whole planet within ten centuries, growing and flourishing without encountering any serious obstacles, if we are to believe Jean Baechler, like the catfish that colonize waterways. Unlike the *Paysans de l'Ouest*, the "Origines du capitalisme" is more suggestive than definitive, more brilliantly intuitive than truly rigorous and wholly convincing. Indeed this is what Baechler intended it to be: provocative and provisional by virtue of being incomplete. His article, like Bois's book, seems to me to constitute an important step towards investigating the possibilities open to the historian of reflecting on the encounter between event and structure, accident and necessity.

8

In Normandy's Woods and Fields[1]

TAKE one nobleman and his *seigneurie*, consider his rich and varied experience, his wealth of contacts with villages and markets, the life of the gentry and the life of the country people, and one has a picture that is hard to rival, in its living immediacy, of an agricultural society in its heyday, in mid-sixteenth century. Several such noblemen have left us their family diary (the *livre de raison*) or their daily notebook. Gilles de Gouberville is one of them: and among this little collection of diarists, he is undoubtedly one of the best informed and most perceptive in his daily jottings. His journal is a goldmine for historical anthropology, an irreplaceable document, well worth a few pages of commentary.

Born under Francois I, into a family of genuine rural nobility, Gilles de Gouberville reaches his thirtieth year early in the reign of Henri II, and his fortieth as the Wars of Religion are beginning. A landowner who farms his own estate, having opted as we shall see for cereals, livestock, game and cider-apples, he has his farmhands ("*la garsaille de céans*" as he unceremoniously calls them, "our bunch") work a huge estate at Mesnil-en-Val, a good hour's walking distance from Cherbourg and from the sea. His land is in the heart of the *bocage*, criss-crossed with hedges and partly covered by the original forests which settlement has not yet entirely cleared. Geographically this is Armorica, which means that the soil is poor and stony; exposed rock shatters the fragile ploughs which Master Clément Ingouf, the local blacksmith, a clumsy and boastful man, "repairs", only to have them broken again the next time. Local technology is not exactly advanced: the ploughs in question, "made in Saint-Lô", are very light (a man can carry one on his shoulder) and are in any case pulled by oxen, as is often the way in the *bocage*.

He may not be very well equipped, but Gouberville is nevertheless an enlightened farmer, firmly in the mainstream

133

of his day; he watches in person over his labourers' work with the keen eye of the master; he knows enough to change his seed-corn (unfortunately in return for bad seed from his neighbour) when his own grain has become too coarse. True, like everyone else, he practises triennial rotation— wheat–mixed fodder–fallow—with long intervals (again in the Armorican fashion) during which the land is rested for several years, allowing gorse bushes (nourishing for the soil) to grow again in the fields temporarily out of cultivation; but at least he is aware, as were many of his contemporaries, that rotation can be improved by sowing peas on the fallow of the third year; peas both enrich the earth and are a source of protein for humans. Moreover, Gouberville, who has an enquiring mind, experiments with all kinds of fertilizer on his land: among them sea-sand, compost with a base of pond mud, the remains of burnt gorse and scrub (the ash is good for his turnip field), lime from the lime-burners' kiln, seaweed from the beach, rotted compost from musty dungheaps, and animal manure brought from the pastures of the *outfield* and spread on the *infield* or cultivated land. So our agriculturalist is quite efficient and, for his time, not particularly superstitious. He does not appear to suffer (except, for some reason, to do with the cultivation of osiers) from that obsession with the so-called "days of the good moon" which so plagued the vinegrowers of the Languedoc during the same period. His furthest venture in this direction is that, having bought and been much impressed by one of Nostradamus's books in 1557, he follows the prophet's advice when deciding the date of seedtime in 1558. The indifferent results do not seem to have encouraged him to repeat the experiment.

The paradox is that this wealthy landowner, active, willing to experiment and by no means stupid, should end up producing grain that neither costs him nor brings him in very much money: the cost of cereal-growing is low, since harvest—the one time when the farmer needs to hire extra workers—is taken care of, in this climate of truly Carolingian archaism, by the virtually unpaid obligatory labour of the villagers—the *corvée*. But then the proceeds from selling the harvest are extremely low as well: indeed Gouberville only puts very small amounts of grain up for sale. His corn,

which rarely finds its way to market, is mostly consumed
at home, by himself, or by his farm labourers, relations and
dependents—when it is not simply eaten by weevils in the
barn or by fieldmice on the stalk. Or else corn is given to
the farmhands as payment, or part-payment, in kind.
Gouberville after all lives in western France: this is the
self-sufficient *bocage*—where there are few large towns and
the land is not fertile. If the farmer of this region has any
contact with the money economy it is more likely to be
through animal-farming and four-legged goods than through
large sales of vegetable produce.

Gouberville himself is no exception to this western tradition, and his stock farming is notable for its quantity, if the
quality sometimes leaves a little to be desired. The manor
at Mesnil-en-Val is surrounded with outbuildings, all of
very ancient construction: there is a shed for oxen, a stable
for horses, another for mares and a fourth which serves to
shelter his cattle in winter. There is a dairy too, but it is not
made much of, for Gouberville and his household eat little
cheese, buy their butter in town, cook with lard and prefer
cider to milk. The golden rule of this kind of stock-farming
seems to be: stick to draft animals and sell meat on the hoof.

Rather limited by comparison with Normandy today,
this animal farming is also very primitive in its methods.
It manages to do without much stabling for instance, even
in the winter cowshed mentioned above. Many of the cows
have bells, as they still do in Switzerland and the French
Alps today, and may stray far from the manor into the great
forest of Brix—so typical, in its way, of the vast woodlands
still covering northern France in the sixteenth century. To
find cows or pigs of which all trace has been lost for a month
perhaps, or even a whole year, enormous cattle-round-ups
through the forest have to be organized, using the villagers
to do the searching—a *corvée* for which the reward is a jug
of wine. The disadvantages of this kind of free-range stock-
farming over such a wide area can easily be imagined.
Calves become separated from their mothers and may go
for three days at a time without milk; others grow up un-
castrated and turn into bulls so wild that it takes up to seven
men to master them. Stray cows escape from the woods and

charge through the main street overturning the cloth-merchants' stalls. It goes without saying that in the very same Cotentin where three centuries later some inventive peasant geniuses were to create the famous Normandy breed of cattle, there was no attempt at selective breeding. The mentality of the cattle-farmers of the sixteenth century remained resolutely marked by *laissez-faire* on this point.

So in Gouberville's day, the animals bred totally at random without the option of a mate of pure (or what passed as "pure") blood. The only exceptions to this "rule", or rather absence of rules, were mares (and bitches). Mares were sent long distances to be mated with stallions from the Caux. As with the breeding, so with the feeding: neither was very sophisticated (acorns for the pigs, pasture and hay for the other animals). Clover was not to be grown in this region until the seventeenth or even eighteenth century.

But such as it was with all its inadequacies, stock-farming supplied the essential connection between squires like Gouberville and the money economy.

Top of the list of sources of income for instance, was pork and everything connected with its production. We find Gouberville selling pannage *(la paisson)* or the right to graze acorns in his forests to the villagers at extremely high rates (up to 50 *livres* a year, that is more than he gets for his grain on the market). And his own well-fed pigs, with a six-inch covering of fat on their backs, are killed in winter and sold for good sums of money (fetching a total income of 60 to 80 *livres* a year); they are salted and sent as far away as Paris. His bullocks, cows and sheep on the hoof, by contrast, only go to the local markets, but these are very active ones, supplying the network of fairs linking the little towns and villages of the Cotentin. The squire and his retainers, followed by the beasts they are bringing to market, are regular visitors to these fairs: it is an opportunity to chat and drink with the minor gentry and the local peasants—and to bring home an annual total of a few dozen *livres tournois* if business is good. Wool travels further afield than livestock; before the Civil Wars which dislocated trade circuits, merchants from Paris would come as far as Lower Normandy to buy wool and send it to Rouen or even to the capital.

So animal husbandry was better integrated than cereal-farming with the monetary economy. Hunting, on the other hand, had a special place within a much more archaic and symbolic set of relationships, one in which gift and counter-gift were of significance. Whether he is trying to sway a judge or to seduce a lady, Gouberville's unvarying tactic can be summed up in the simple motto: "Say it with meat." So we find him presenting the successive ladies who occupy his thoughts sometimes with a plump kid or a leg of beef, more often with an offering of game: rabbits, hares, venison pasties—all accepted by their wealthy recipients as if they were hothouse flowers. The young men in the household of this Norman squire—his father's illegitimate sons, or visiting adolescents from neighbouring noble families—are quite as energetic and they too are great hunters. Even the peasants, in spite of the landlord's prohibitions—which are not very strictly enforced—hunt without scruple. There is remarkably little to show for all this activity: it can take three or four hunters all day to catch a hare. But that is all the more reason for the bewildering number of methods used to catch wild things in this little corner of the Cotentin. There are always the crossbow and arquebus of course, but the hunters may also try their luck (sometimes needing one of these two weapons as well) with the *juc*, a snare set for woodpigeons when they settle to roost at the *jucher*; or with nets, used to trap starlings by the dozen; they may go tracking *(la traque)*, following the prints left on fresh snow, in wood or over marsh by the wild boar or the hare; foxcubs and young rabbits are dug up from their earths; for birds there are limed twigs or the *yraigne* (a net in the shape of a spider's web, used to catch blackbirds); foxes are trapped; ferrets with filed teeth are kept ready for use in dry beech logs; or there is "English" hunting with hawk and setter imported from over the Channel; wolves are ambushed with arquebuses; or surrounded by hallooing beaters *(la huée)*, a manoeuvre requiring the cooperation of all the men from several villages.

Within this arsenal of methods and weapons of all kinds, closer perhaps to the hunting habits of primitive man than to the organized slaughter allowed by today's firearms, a social hierarchy can be discerned. Leaving aside the small-time professional and specialized hunters—like the mole-catcher who festoons the hedgerows with strings of captured moles—among the peasants, the essential techniques remain medieval and cost little. They are based on the crossbow, a simple weapon which can be made in the village and used to bring down any size of game—duck, deer or even the small teal. The weapon of the aristocracy and the clergy on the other hand, spreading by 1550 to many manors and presbyteries, is the arquebus. This is a heavy implement (it takes two men to operate it) and an expensive one. Whereas a bowstring costs only three sous, the barrel of an arquebus can cost as much as a cow (five or six *livres*). At that kind of price, it is obviously wise to do the same as Gouberville and his friends and manufacture one's own powder by burning charcoal and scraping saltpetre. Finally, moving out of Gouberville's class altogether, beyond the purses of the minor gentry who kill deer or wolves for their own pleasure, is that sporting activity *par excellence* of the higher aristocracy: the organized staghunt. In twenty years, Gilles joins only one party of this kind (and he leaves it in disgust when a stag puts out the eye of one of his greyhounds).

Understandably so, for a good hunter depends on a good dog, as Gouberville and those like him very well know; and their passionate attachment to hunting makes them inspired dog-breeders, displaying a solicitude for canine genetics which they are far from exhibiting towards their other stock—horses excepted. (But then horses too are a possession of emotional value; selection is a sign of affection.) The kennel-master of the Cotentin, then, participates in the established north–south breeding network: he buys dogs from England and in turn sends dogs to Bordeaux. If necessary, he sends bitches for mating to some quite distant region to obtain the best results. The pups are put out to nurse and a female is spayed only after judicious consideration. If one of his dogs has its side gashed by a wild boar, he sews it up again himself, as carefully as he would a pair of breeches. Should his dogs be stolen, he takes steps to have the thief excommunicated, no less, by means of monitory letters read out in thundering tones from the pulpit by his friend the parish priest. A dog is a treasured companion. If one lends it, it is only in cases of extreme emergency—for example to help out a young neighbour who finds himself under a pressing obligation to kill a few hares to celebrate his betrothal.

A modest cereal-grower and a run-of-the-mill stock-farmer, but a knowledgeable breeder of dogs and horses, Gouberville in one area reveals himself to be an enthusiastic innovator: on the subject of apples and ciders. Both as an active practitioner and as a representative, he sheds some light on many details of one of the most striking changes to affect the countryside of western France in the sixteenth century or so.

Here as before, Gouberville's talents as an innovator are not the result of market demand. His ciders, with very few exceptions, are not intended for sale. They stay at home to quench the thirst of master, family and workers on the manor; or they simply circulate as gifts, liberally distributed to friends, relatives, invalids or visiting guests. The very idea of selling the juice of his apples hardly seems to have crossed the mind of this country gentleman. His motives, all extremely honourable as we shall see, lie almost entirely outside the market. His general philosophy is best summed up as "cider is good for you". And indeed how could anyone fail to subscribe to this, one wonders, if one takes the trouble to read the prescriptions and medical treatises written by reputable doctors in Normandy in the modern period. "Cider", writes one of the learned gentlemen of the University[2] in the early seventeenth century, "is restorative of the roots of humour and humidity". It keeps the belly "soft and relaxed"; by "the benignity of its vapours" it induces a pleasant sleep. It not only undoubtedly prevents the harvester from "becoming over-heated in his labours", but also restrains the man of business from becoming "choleric in his occupations". It is thus both the friend of the peasant classes and the comforter of the middle classes, since it maintains a man in the requisite "modesty" and "measure" (*médiocrité*). More precisely, cider is good for gout, gravel and nephritis; it is particularly recommended, like coddled eggs or chicken broth, for invalids, especially if they have become dehydrated by fever or exhausted by purging. Armed with these sage precepts, the medical practitioners therefore prescribe cider by the jugful to their patients, who ask for nothing better— and indeed they get the very best: mature cider for women in childbed, or to cure a fever; unblended cider for pleurisy; new cider for a wound in the groin. An entire pharmacopoeia of remedies based on alcohol seems to have operated in Gouberville's region in about 1560, for the treatment of country folk in sickness. Cider is not of course the only curative drink: the rich take a bottle of Bordeaux for their health, or a little claret wine, perhaps a *vin rosé* from Orleans. And beer is not despised either: one invalid drinks *48 litres* of it as a "detoxicating agent" during his treatment. But cider, because it can be produced locally, has the clear advantage of being cheap; it does not, like beer, encroach upon the precious cereal stocks. And it grows on trees so to speak, since apples flourish everywhere in the hedgerows, or, like vines, thrive on soil too poor for other crops; cider, the miracle-worker, is always there in times of need for all ranks in peasant society.

We may smile perhaps at this popular fancy for the manufacture of alcoholic drinks in the sixteenth century, whether wine or cider. We should be quite wrong. For even setting aside the list just mentioned of secondary and not entirely serious justifications, the increase in cider-growing in Renaissance Normandy, like that of vine-growing in the Paris region, had very solid foundations: drinking wines and ciders of low alcoholic content, and drinking them in massive quantities (the daily consumption by some of the manual labourers of the Languedoc in about 1500–1560 might be as much as two litres of wine a day) meant that one was absorbing a few low-grade calories (of alcoholic origin), which was all to the good. But first and foremost, it meant one was drinking a comparatively sterile liquid, a good deal less dangerous, that is to say, than the polluted liquids to which water-drinkers were virtually condemned, when one thinks of the countless sources of bacteria (manure, sewage, run-off from flax-steeping, waste waters contaminated by mass epidemics) which might, in Normandy, a land of schist and granite, pollute the surface waters supplying the brooks, pools, streams, wells and even springs. In such circumstances, cider provided one of the most agreeable forms of insurance against death and disease. A team of historians from Normandy has demonstrated, with the aid of graphs, that mortality during epidemics in the region in the age of Louis XIV, fluctuated in direct relationship with the high price or scarcity of cider (along with other factors).[3] The connection is perfectly logical: high cider prices mean that, among the poor, drinkers of water will be more numerous, more thirsty and more vulnerable to infection. So with their simple-minded but in the end perfectly lucid peasant intuition, Gouberville and his fellow-villagers were absolutely right: they planted and grafted apple-trees to their hearts' content, in the interests of their households, thus contributing both to a real growth of the economy and to an improvement in public health. After all, of what significance were the problems of a few inveterate local drunkards and a certain number of "pot-bellied boozers" as our diarist calls them, compared with the thousands of lives saved every year by the increased opportunity for more people to avoid drinking water, or at least to drink as little of it as possible? It was only later, when the discovery of the techniques of distillation reached the non-wine-growing regions of western France, and when there was a rise in these country regions in the consumption of apple-based spirits, that the negative aspects of cider-production were, in the nineteenth century, to outweigh the positive qualities which had prevailed for so long and contributed to the prosperity of the western provinces.

Gouberville was thus encouraged in his experiments with apples by the general and justified confidence in cider expressed by his contemporaries and compatriots. But quite apart from the warm encouragement he received from an entire folk culture, his personal motives were quite clear and straightforward: without any thought of gain, as his private journal testifies, Gouberville liked to give himself up to the pure pleasure of finding out, of creating and experimenting. This gentleman who would not for all the world set his own hand to the plough does not scorn to spend hours pruning and grafting his apple trees. "Spent a good three hours all alone, pruning" (21 April 1562). He experiments just to see what will happen: he tries to graft in April for example: "We took a cutting (from an apple tree) and came to graft it in the garden by the barn as an experiment to see if it will take, since it is now mid-April" (15 April 1554). The journal of the lord of Gouberville thus offers us a sight rarely to be found in documents: a practitioner of old-style selective husbandry at work. After sluicing down the cider mash from his own manor and elsewhere in the neighbourhood, to wash out the thousands of pips, *Maître* Gilles plants them under a litter of bracken leaves, and rears a whole seed bed of little trees or *surets* which he then distributes free, by the cartload, to his friends. When the proper time comes, he leads his gardeners out and grafts the remaining shoots with his own hands, using scissors, saw or double-bladed knife. So obsessed with apples is this lord of the manor that there are no peach or fig-trees, no raspberry canes or currant bushes in his garden, but he has in his orchard twenty-nine different varieties of apple tree, sent for from Rouen, from the Basque country or from Lower Normandy. The final result of this activity, strictly non-commercial but rather part of an effort to increase self-sufficiency within the manor and to improve the estate, is a transformation of the landscape, a change in the face of the countryside which from now on will be dotted with apple trees. The familiar apple blossom spread over the fields of Normandy in the sixteenth century, thanks to the many initiatives of Gouberville and many like him throughout the province.

This rural world—a strange mixture of the archaic and the forward-looking, where squires can do much as they please—is typically, though not of course in its entirety, a self-sufficient society. Not that Gouberville is unaware of the significance of trade and money; he scrupulously notes in his journal for instance the successive devaluations of the *livre tournois*. But all the same, in this century when silver from the Americas is supposed to have trickled into all the most commercial sectors of the economy, a man of substance like our country squire finds himself not short of money (his nest is after all rather well-feathered) but simply short of ready cash. One is always coming across telling sentences in the journal to the effect: "bought some cloth in Cherbourg; did not pay for it as I had no money. Will pay on Monday." Needless to say, the notion of a purse to hold his money seems to be quite unknown to this Norman *châtelain*. He puts all his sous and other small change in his handkerchief and ties it up by the four corners (then naturally loses the handkerchief or has it stolen on several occasions). As for his workers, he often pays them only after a long delay, "for want of (ready) money", as usual, or perhaps simply to keep them on tenterhooks. When he actually does pay them, more often than not it is in kind: a bushel of seed-corn, a measure of oats, a heifer or a pair of shoes, all to be deducted from their wages. Another sign that precious metals were in short supply, in spite of the recent shipments from the New World, is that the lord and his household all eat off pewter; at Mesnil-en-Val there is no silver on the dresser.

In this rustic corner of the Cotentin, old-fashioned yet flourishing, the autarkic society is recognizable too by the underdeveloped division of labour. For want of proper premises or workshops, stocks of raw materials and capital (even in small amounts), or indeed of a regular clientele, such artisans as there are in the countryside (and even these operate only on a part-time basis) take on "piece work" only now and then. They come for instance, when offered the chance, to set up shop in the manor of a rich customer like Gouberville, who provides them with materials and offers them a commission substantial enough to make it worth their while to move in. So one after another they pass through the Gouberville manor: the linen-weaver who comes to make the few dozen lengths of cloth ordered by the master; the local saddler-cum-cartwright (actually a tenant-farmer most of his working life) who is brought in to make Gouberville's yokes and harnesses. Another day it will be the tailor who arrives to make new clothes for the entire household, or the blacksmith who is asked to sharpen all the tools kept for carpentry before returning them to the manor workshop. And if for instance someone is needed "to cut rungs and uprights for a new ladder", the master will simply ask one of the servants who is good with his hands. Like Adalbert de

Corbie or the gentle *abbé* Irminon, our subject is possessed
with a positively Carolingian ideal of autarky, which impels
him to produce—or to have produced—on the spot anything
he may require, preferably without any money changing
hands. By the same token, the idea of making money is
itself so profoundly foreign to him that it is perhaps under-
standable that he should sometimes be reluctant to spend
those coins that he had finally managed to tie up in his
handkerchief.

Nowhere perhaps is the measure of this self-sufficient
society so readily grasped as when one looks for a moment
beyond the *terra firma* which is the natural habitat of our
gentleman farmer. Gouberville does occasionally catch a
glimpse of the sea, which is so close by; and thus enables
us to grasp the full extent of his self-sufficient parochialism.
However wide the view, this landlubber's eye seems to notice
(in the pages of his journal at least) only a few little boats
(barques) carrying logs or bacon, and bound for Rouen or
perhaps Paris. A boat like this, when not in use is simply
beached on the sand; it holds the equivalent of two ox-carts—
no more. As for the peasant-fishermen of the Cotentin coast,
some of whom are *Maître* Gilles's tenants, they are always in
a hurry to return from their herring-fishing expeditions to
get on with more serious matters—looking after the cows,
cutting the corn, laying down apple juice. There are exceptions of course to this seaside ultraprovincialism. Just once,
for instance, Gouberville, while taking a glass of cider at
Barfleur *chez Gillette la Blonde*, sees malaguetta pepper and
elephants' tusks from Africa laid out on the beach. Another
time, his faithful Cantepie has thoughts of joining a more or
less imaginary expedition to Peru. In fact, Cantepie soon
thinks better of this and is only too happy to be known in
the village for the rest of his days as "the man who nearly
went to Peru". The one maritime "expedition" Gouberville
and his lads were ever to take part in was—all the way to the
channel island of Alderney. The little party, on the pretext
of some quarrel with the English, went off and forcibly
seized some of the islanders' cattle and mares, without
paying of course; and brought them back on to the mainland
—to the manor at Mesnil. A gentleman may after all turn

pirate, even on this small scale, without losing his dignity. All the same, such exploits, Homeric no doubt, do not exactly amount to trade, large or small. And accordingly the extremely scanty references, to be found in a journal covering not far off twenty years, indicate the almost non-existent contact between a traditional society and the major currents of seaborne trade which, when economic histories are written, occupies (perhaps unwarrantably) the centre of the stage. This parochial mentality, this stubborn deafness to the outside world, is quite unmistakable in the diary, despite the fact that Gouberville and his household live so near Cherbourg, which could hardly, after all, be called a minor seaport. This rural society then seems to be up to its knees in mud most of the time; the economic world it recognizes is the network of local markets or self-sufficiency within the village. True, the smallest capillaries of the great trade routes do succeed in reaching even these remote estates tucked away in the Cotentin, and can act as a stimulus or inspiration out of all proportion to the tiny volume of goods that actually circulates. Purchases of printed books, say, or spices, by Gouberville and people like him, gradually come to influence tastes both literary and culinary. Sales of wool and bacon to Paris bring a little money into the region. All these taken together however amount to hardly more than a homeopathic dose. To tell the truth, it is only when Gouberville turns his back on the empty seas and looks closely at his own micro-society, of manor and village, that he really has something positive to convey to us.

For Gouberville, a noble by birth and the overlord of much land, stands both at the pinnacle and at the centre of a social microcosm, composed, in concentric circles around him, by the people of his family household, his parish and his *seigneurie*.

In the household of this confirmed old bachelor, who by definition (and exceptionally for someone in his position) has not established a conjugal unit, the "family" means the sibling group of illegitimate sons and daughters of his own father, that is the natural brothers and sisters of our diarist, several of whom, notably Simonet and Guillemette, continue to live under his roof for many years. Never for a moment does the lord of Mesnil waver in the affection he bears these relatives of inferior status, with whom he has lived since childhood. This affection is a reflection of respect rendered to all the achievements of his father, even the least "respectable" of them. "Item" writes Gilles de Gouberville in one of his wills, "since I am sick in my bed, wounded with one or several arquebus shots, and knowing nothing to be more certain than death and nothing more uncertain than the time of its coming . . . I give a hundred *sous* of rent annually to each of the bastard children of my late father, that is to Simonet, Hernouf, Jacques, Novel, Jean the younger, and to Guillemette . . ." The original group, the bastard children of his father, was soon to see the family circle expand to take in the natural children fathered by Gilles himself, and born to a dearly-loved mistress whom, for reasons of rank he was forbidden to marry. "Our family", *la famille de céans*, was not entirely composed of natural children though. It also included at a lower level fourteen servants, that is the valet Lajoie, nine other menservants and four maidservants, who were engaged upon everyday farm or household tasks. One has the curious impression of a large-scale agricultural enterprise which made use of a proletariat without, however accumulating profits or setting great store by money.

It is true that the upkeep of this throng of servants does not cost the master much; after half a century of wage decline, their pay is low: six *livres* a year with board for the farm-labourer who sees to the cart and plough; whereas in the Languedoc at about the same time, despite the poverty of the region, the carter gets his 15 *livres* a year, and he too is fed and lodged.

To be sure, in addition to the wages in money, plus board and lodging, Gilles also gives each of his servants some item of clothing every year: a shirt or a pair of shoes (worth 15 *sous*) or linen. But none of this amounts to very much. Some wages are so low as to be virtually non-existent. A goat-herd for instance gets 50 *sous* a year plus a pair of shoes. Pierrot, the little boy who is taken on to look after the sheep, and who when he sleeps out at night with only the flock for company, can see the eyes of the wolves glinting dangerously around him, receives twenty *sous* a year and a pair of shoes, plus a lamb. The women's wages paid by the master are also much lower than those in the south of France. A seamstress making shirts earns six *deniers* a day when she works in the Norman manor, whereas the lowest-paid female farm workers around Béziers or Montpellier would receive ten *deniers* a day in about 1560. There is the same wage-differential between south and north, or rather south and west, when one looks at the payment of the artisans who occasionally come to ply their trade at Mesnil-en-Val: a master mason is paid two *sous* a day as against five *sous* in the Montpellier-Béziers region at the same period. The study of wage-zones in France as far back into the *ancien régime* as this has yet to be undertaken. But many indications suggest that the south, where money was more plentiful and demographic pressure less acute, was favoured with more substantial, or perhaps we should say less depressed wages[4] than the north-western region of Armorica, which was poor and already over-populated, with a consequent surplus of labour.

Could one of the reasons for this poverty in Lower Normandy be the total absence of militancy among the workers? In over a decade of minutely-recorded entries, Gouberville does not mention a single case, individual or concerted, of opposition to his person, from his servants. And yet the master, who in "everyday" life abhors violence and the arts of war, does not hesitate to dispense to the entire male population of the household, without distinction of rank, from the young noble on a visit to gain experience or the bastard brother, to the farmhand or hired lad, corporal punishments which he considers appropriate: he has a range corresponding to the age or rank of the culprit, from a thrashing to a box on the ears, a kick up the backside or a spanking (but he never strikes a woman, not even a servant). These signs of displeasure are apparently received by the offenders with the necessary deference. They are not met with any physical riposte which would compromise the master's prestige. The only retaliation open to discontented servants is absenteeism, at which the serving-women have become particularly adept. One of the maidservants, Jeanne Botte, disappears several times without leave. Then in order to make up for her absence, she returns to the manor with a lady-friend dressed in red (who will probably spend the night with the master and will be sent off home by him the next day with a couple of *sous* and a pound of flax as recompense). And Jeanne Botte is back in "the family fold"—until the next time.

So we should not paint too black a picture of the proletarian condition in the Cotentin during the sixteenth century: the workers at Gouberville are wearing shoes in a region where their great-grandsons of similar status would still mostly be wearing clogs, several centuries later. They eat in the same room as the master, at a table near his, and their diet appears to be well provided with meat (indeed their board seems to be the principal element in their wages). We should note too that they have opportunities to save in a small way. Very often, they are given no choice: instead of the money he owes them, the Master gives "in lieu of wages" perhaps a foal to one servant, a heifer to another, to a third a mare out to grass in the forest, which the recipient will have to catch for himself, a couple of bull-calves, etc.

Enabled to save on a modest scale then, voluntarily or involuntarily, the farm labourers, like men of other categories or estates, also have their own specific social gatherings, such, for instance, as the hiring-fair when servants offer their services to prospective employers once a year, near the feast of Saint Mary Magdalen (18th–26th July). Every small town or large village in Normandy in about 1560 had its hiring-fair, a sort of cross between a slave-market and a village carnival. Watched by the local notables, and their good ladies, by the landowners and the parish priests, those who aspired to be taken on as farm labourers would compete against each other in a programme of games and prize fights. These rustic trials of strength had an entertainment value—but they also enabled the judicious employer to pick out the strong men, those who would be most useful in the fields.

Domestic labourers, who were always present and visible to the master's eye, were clearly distinguished from that inferior social category which occupied the very lowest rung in Norman society: the vermin-ridden world of beggars and tramps, in other words the poor in the statutory sense of the word. As if they were transparent, invisible in normal times to a gentleman's gaze, such people are noted by

Gouberville's pen only on very clearly defined occasions:
at the burial of an important personage for instance, the
poor turn up in hundreds to receive the *donnée* or traditional
alms-giving (and indeed when they are too slow in dispersing
after the funeral they are chased off with sticks). This attitude
to the poor appears too in another anecdote: one day Gouberville comes home even more covered in fleas than usual, so
much so that his faithful servants, gathered together about
his person, take an unconscionable time to rid his skin and
his clothes of the vermin. An explanation is soon found: the
master has had the imprudence to sit down on a tree stump
which a few hours earlier had been used as a seat by "one of
the poor". Bringing disorder on one occasion and parasites
on another, the poor are thus placed in the category of
suspicious persons—to all intents outside the pale. The
farm servant on the other hand (apart from cases of prolonged unemployment or disgrace, of which there were
certainly plenty) is considered to be a man within the pale,
even if he is in rags. For the time of his hire, which is punctu-
ated by orders, cuffs, mugs of cider and exhortations to
duty, the farmhand is, from the point of view of his noble
overlord, one of the family.

Outside this closed inner circle of residents at the manor
comes the second circle, a rather wider one: the parish. And
here (at least in the particular instance of Lower Normandy
society) we find combined certain institutions which were,
at the same period in other regions of France, the south for
example, kept rigorously apart. These institutions are, on
one hand, the parish as a religious unit centred on the church,
and on the other, the community of inhabitants as such. In
the case of Gouberville, the honest peasants confound the
two, without meaning any harm, and for the greater profit
of the landlord, if not of the priest. The assemblies of villagers meeting for the purpose of assessing liability for the
royal taxes, or of knocking down to the highest bidder (in a
sort of ancestor-cannibalism) the apples that grow in the
churchyard orchard, take place, quite straightforwardly in
the church after Mass on Sundays. *Maître* Gilles, who knows
his village, lets the assembled parishioners become locked
in "squabbles and arguments" among themselves as to which

of them will pay how much in taxes—then at the psychological moment, he walks into the church, calms the hubbub ... and has a straw man of his own appointed as official tax-assessor or auctioneer. On the whole, the lord of the manor, who is more of a coaxer and a tactician than a tyrant, manipulates the assembly of underlings without difficulty; it is all the easier for him since he is on good terms with the better-off peasants of the parish (to whose families he may pay gracious visits, sometimes even recruiting his lady-loves from their womenfolk). As for the priests in charge of the parish church, they are no obstacle to this kind of rule: the parish priest is an absentee who only visits his flock once a year; and his curate is an insignificant individual who between hearing confessions (he comes up to the house to purify the sins of the Master and his household), is employed at the manor on minor domestic chores, like chopping wood or raking dung from the cowsheds. There is no chance that this humble servant of God will in any way resist the wishes of the lord of the manor: not until the Wars of Religion did organized resistance, of urban origin and ultra-Catholic moreover, reach the village to disturb the easy-going rule of *"Not'maître"* ("t'Master")—who then indeed and with some reason came under suspicion of having Calvinist sympathies.

The third circle, farther flung and less clearly defined than the parish is the *seigneurie* (from which the nobility of the *seigneur* in question is institutionally distinct but socially inseparable). The *seigneuries* of Gouberville for example include several villages from whom the lord receives *cens* (quit-rent) and where he has the right to requisition men for *corvée* labour. They do not bring him in very much: a few *sous* for a *cens*; a few *livres tournois* for the tenancy or "hiring-out" of scattered parcels of land (which are part of the manorial demesne but which are too far away to be useful and are ceded on temporary leases to a tenant-farmer). Three important items stand out however in the otherwise fairly light and lightly-managed economy of the *seigneurie* of Gouberville: first there is the demesne or *réserve* itself—in other words the master's own land which is farmed directly; as we have seen, it runs at a financial loss, but it accounts for large-scale movements both of produce and labour. Secondly, there is the mill—the object of tender devotion and well worthwhile repairs which are carried out by *Maître* Gilles: the landlord's charges for the mill alone bring him 331 bushels of wheat a year, that is far more than any other single source of income, whether seigniorial dues or rent. And yes, the third large item in the *seigneurie* is the *corvée* or compulsory labour: the wheat harvest is always and hay-making sometimes carried out for our landlord, as in the days of the old emperor Charlemagne himself, by villagers liable for service, the *corvéables*. In fact these services seem to be rendered if not exactly joyfully, then at least in a spirit of traditional consensus: they begin, as harvest-time approaches, with a summons to those concerned, issued by the parish priests from the pulpit, thus expressing the alliance between manor and altar; and they end, on the fine evenings of harvest home, with suppers, drinking and dancing until midnight in the huge barn at Mesnil-en-Val. Perhaps the festivities make the labourers (who do not appear to know that this unpaid labour disappeared long ago everywhere else) forget the unusual character of the tasks they are fulfilling. And as coda to this list, Gouberville has one more seigniorial right up his sleeve—a more classic one this time, which costs him little and benefits him more than somewhat: the *droit du colombier* or the pigeon loft. The master's pigeons are allowed to peck the grain from the fields of the peasants, and when it has passed through the birds' digestive systems, it returns as useful fertilizer to the master's ploughed fields.

If we leave aside on one hand the estate itself, the directly farmed *réserve* which is not specifically seigniorial in any case (and which was to survive unchallenged with varying degrees of prosperity until our own times); and on the other the largest items mentioned (the mill and harvest labour: ridiculously anachronistic but not excessively onerous), it then appears that apart from these two areas, a *seigneurie* of the type exercised by Gouberville did not really grind the faces of its subjects. It was in any case quite well accepted by them; after all the lord rendered them unquestionable services in return. His "*réserve*" had little to do with the outside world of trade: it offered employment and subsistence to the local people, thus providing a source of security for the village. The squire himself, in the absence of any real leadership of peasant origin, acted as a local, almost a tribal chieftain.[5] He adjudicated quarrels, dispensed justice in minor matters, etc. A convincing indication of this acceptance, whether willing or enforced, is the remarkable infrequency or even total absence (at least in this part of the Cotentin) of resistance to the *seigneur*.[6] This lack of opposition is striking enough in the history of popular revolts of the period, which are directed much more against taxes than against nobles. It is even more remarkable when, by examining a "slice of life" like Gilles's journal, one is able to compare the exception (opposition to the master) and the rule (everyday resignation to the existing order). There is only one case of conflict, and that a very minor one, in the ten years covered by a journal which is as a rule extremely attentive to any act of violence or popular emotion: this is the case of a peasant who protests against a *champart* (the feudal overlord's claim on the crop); a thrashing soon puts the insolent fellow back in his place—and never for a moment is there any hint of a communal movement of solidarity in his favour.

The *seigneurie* conceived as an institution has its counterpart on quite a different level, in nobility as a concept and as a source of superior social rank or status, distinguishing its possessor from the common herd. How does Gouberville, a genuine noble of an ancient line, experience his own nobility? It must be said straight away that the quasi-mystical affinities lyrically described by Noël du Fail, which appear to be the birthright of this prestigious order, have only a remote attraction for our Norman squire, who is decidedly down to earth in his attitudes. Neither the blue blood passed on to him by his father and all his ancestors, which theoretically runs in his veins, nor the red blood which he should, from time to time, if he is true to his martial calling as an aristocrat, shed from his own or other people's arteries on the field of battle, seem to bother him very much.

This double indifference, both to the exploits of the warrior and to the obsession with pedigree, is to be explained in the first place by a certain kind of psychology. Gouberville is not much of a man for the family tree, because like many of his contemporaries in rural society, "he is Nature", he lives for the moment, indifferent to historical time. Even his parents, now dead, are very far from his memory or his emotions. His mother is hardly mentioned at all in the journal. Even his father (whose living descendants he respects) is referred to only once or twice—apropos, for instance, of an old dispute over money between his father and one Gilles le Maçon. The only people who really matter to the lord of Mesnil are the living; and in the first place, for better or for worse, his brothers and sisters. As for the dead, may God rest their souls and may their memory perish here on earth. Is this so surprising? In a world where father and mother die very young and where to lose them early is the common lot, one values most of all one's contemporaries— that is the sibling confraternity.

We can go even further: this squire, barely to be distinguished from a peasant, yet graced with the title of gentleman, scarcely has a family name. The obsession with the dynastic name which we readers of Proust might be tempted to see as the authentic mark of the true aristocracy, hardly exists at all for Gouberville, and on this point he is at one with the thinking of his peers. His true identity lies not in the name but in the land, the basis of his *seigneurie*. This betokens a passionate form of attachment to the soil: the *seigneur*'s real name is in theory plain Jacques Picot, esquire. But he has been known for years as the lord of Gouberville, from the name of the village straggling along its one street, over which he is *seigneur*. Indeed another Picot, one of his cousins, actually has the effrontery to challenge the name of Gouberville as being usurped. "Picot complained, because I called myself Gouberville." Among the squire's friends, the passion for identification with the land can totally dissolve the identity of surname between brothers. True, the noble sibling group still remains one of the places where affective ties are strongest. But even this is threatened, by extravagances of nomenclature, with a permanent confusion of identities. For instance, of four brothers related to our diarist, one calls himself Monsieur de *Saint-Naser*; the next Robert du *Moncel*, *bailli* of Cherbourg Abbey; the third is Monsieur de *Vascognes*, canon; and the fourth is the lord *des Hachées* (who would one day play and lose at dice—to Gouberville—the land known as "les Hachées", but who would nevertheless keep the name he took from the place). And there are countless other brothers between whom there are nominal distinctions which in our society of fixed surnames would be quite inconceivable: "the baron de Tuboeuf and his brother Lalonde"; "my cousin de Bretteville and his brother de Briqueville"; "my cousin La Verge, brother of Jacques Picot" etc. Sometimes an entry in the journal pinpoints the elusive moment when a name changes: "Jean Merigot brought me the news of the change of name of the Lord baron of la Luthumière"; "the baron d'Auney, *now known as the lord of Neufville* is having a bridge built over the river". These petty nobles, changing their names like their shirts, have a fluctuating onomastic status, possible in our time only for women who marry more than once.

Not exactly a fanatic about his family tree then, Gouberville seems hardly to be aware, either, of the warrior values which in the old tripartite system of the *très ancien régime* were supposed to correspond to the Noble Estate. Nobles were in theory the *bellatores* (those who wage war), as opposed to the *oratores* (those who pray—the clergy), and the *aratores* of the Third Estate (those who till the land). But of course by the sixteenth century, the upper crust of the Third Estate and the higher ranks of the clergy had long since left off tilling and praying—sometimes for good. So it is hardly fair to blame Gouberville for failing to fulfil his proper function too: whenever there is an appeal for fighters, he is in any case a malingerer of the first order: any excuse (a cold, a sprained ankle) will do in order not to reply to the summons of the *ban* (call-up). In wartime, the summons would in theory oblige him to present himself for several months' service in a company of gentlemen-at-arms—whose pay incidentally was not at all lavish. But our squire, quite shamelessly and without any criticism from those around him, evades the call-up; in short he is a draft-dodger. He likes a fight of course, but only with his inferiors; they have one great advantage: they never hit back.

In the circumstances then, what does nobility mean to Gouberville? The answer is simple: basically it means belonging to a caste, privileged in various ways, of local gentlemen farmers, all more or less related to each other, with whom one exchanges courtesy calls or affectionate visits. More precisely, nobility is experienced as a special quality or degree which allows those who enjoy it not to pay royal taxes. A commoner who purchases a title is buying in the first place protection from the taxman. This is plain to see in the entries for 1555–1556, when there was a general inspection of titles of nobility in the Cotentin and Bessin, which caused a great flutter in the dovecotes or rather the manors of Normandy. "Last year those who were unable to furnish proof of their nobility were condemned to pay six years of their income ... Jacques Davy, *bailli* of Cotentin [and a pseudo-noble] was sentenced to a fine of 8000 *livres*." Upon which, Gouberville, usually so casual about his ancestry, closets himself up all day in his house and rummages through all his papers, desperately searching for the deeds of his family's title, dating back to 1400 ("it was night before I found them") and stays up copying them out until midnight; now at last, his nobility safely proved, he will be able to continue to claim tax exemption!

All things considered, Gouberville, who as *saigneur* has to assume definite leadership functions not particularly profitable to himself within the village, is thus quite generously compensated, from what is perhaps an unexpected quarter, by the fiscal exemption accorded to the nobility. This makes him in effect a fully conscious, systematic and perpetual tax-dodger. The Master certainly does not have a profit mentality in the capitalist sense of the term, but he has a caste mentality and he has a proper appreciation of the sweets and profits of privilege.

Gouberville then can tell us a good deal about the production of wealth and about the social hierarchy as seen in about 1555 in a manor of Lower Normandy. In a more intimate area of life, his *livre de raison* offers the reader information about the very substance both everyday and exceptional, of social existence: life and death, birth and marriage, food and sickness, sex and violence, as well as the more complex questions of politics and religion—in short the raw material of anthropology.

Life and death at the most elementary level means the sacred trinity of the parish registers: baptisms, marriages and deaths, each of these occasions having its own quota of specific social activity, always symbolized by the taking of food. The first of these, baptism, is not the occasion of great festivities except in the immediate family, but is a rather private occasion. Celebrated discreetly, it is followed by rejoicings only some time later, upon the *churching* of the mother, which is marked among the country people by a dinner or a drinking party with perhaps a dozen friends. This feast is held to mark not so much the arrival in the world of a new baby as the return of a young mother to fruitful and sexual life, to the cycle of nature and to the ranks of active marriage partners.

But if baptism and its subsequent celebrations only bring together a small group of people, marriage is quite different. The village weddings of 1550, according to Gouberville's account, make one think of Madame Bovary's wedding in Flaubert's novel: they are the occasion, among the local gentry or the well-to-do peasants for an orgy of feasting and conspicuous consumption. First the young bridegroom and members of his party ride on horseback to the home of the bride where her party is waiting. The bride is decked out like a Christmas tree, in jewels borrowed for the day from the manor. After Mass, both parties combine for the wedding-feast—as many as 80 guests may crowd in under the roof of a humble countryman in three sittings. The dinner is not quite as ruinous as it might appear, since gifts of food brought by the guests help to reduce some of the costs of the party: when he is invited to a noble wedding for instance, Gouberville offers a gift of game: teal, duck, rabbits and partridge, all hung until delectably high. For a peasant's wedding, he shows his goodwill a little more condescendingly, restricting his offering this time to vegetable produce: for the young couple who have invited him to their humble feast, he brings a sack of wheat, a pumpkin, two dozen pears and a jar of hippocras.

These peasant festivities, which may last for two days, are occasions for dancing or perhaps for *dictiers de Noël*, recited by a shepherd. Within the following days or weeks, there

will be a second round of ceremonies: first the "welcome
home" (a modest celebration to welcome the young bride
when she enters the home of her husband or of her parents-
in-law); then the *recroq*, another post-nuptial feast when,
under the pretext of repaying the invitation, there is a
"repeat feast" in honour of the new couple. Marriage is
undoubtedly one of the high points of social activity in a
peasant community: a whole section of a village, or of a group
of villages (a section which because of the dominant tradition
of endogamy may be identified simply with the ramifications
of a single clan) meets on such occasions, divided for the day
into "the two sides of the family".

And finally, burial is the time for social gatherings which
are of course less joyful, but hardly less important in terms of
the number of participants. The close relatives of the dead
person appear first of all at the graveside, suffering with
genuine grief, which these inarticulate people do not very
clearly distinguish from a feeling of anger or annoyance
(they will say, as Gouberville does, that they are "annoyed"
or "cross" *(ennuyés ou faschés)* at the death of a close relation.
And their affliction is so great that after the funeral service,
strange to say, it even deprives them temporarily of any
appetite. But this moment of weakness, unworthy of a
Norman heart, is quickly overcome. And they sit down to
eat: a double dinner, first a small one for the immediate
family, then another larger one for the wider family circle,
which brings together the close and the not-so-close relatives
of the deceased. After dinner, the *ayants-droit* or putative
heirs, still wiping the odd tear from their eyes, will proceed
to the division of the inheritance with that implacability
which characterizes Norman customs: these, as is well
known, totally disregard the wishes of the dead and give
each inheritor his strict due according to his rights (*c'est mon
droit et mé j'y tiens!* "It's my right and I'm sticking to it!").
So after the meal, the old oak chest is opened up; every
ducat and every crown is counted and shared out. And in
due course everything else is divided up (into equal or
unequal shares, depending on the individual standing of the
heirs): cattle, ploughs, carts, harnesses; saddles from the
horses in the stable, wool from the loft, ciders and wines

if there are any; young pigs, pewter vessels pots, pans and cauldrons; chairs, stools, tables and benches; then the year's yield of flax, sheep, linseed and hemp; and last of all the fields which for greater accuracy are divided up according to the old Viking custom, with strings: *devises* or boundary stones will then be laid along the divisions so marked.

But before dying and thus bringing joy through tears to one's heirs (if one has any property) it is normal to be ill; perhaps more than once; and possibly seriously. Sickness and the ever present threat of death, which are plainly described and philosophically accepted, are central to the journal of the lord of Mesnil-en-Val. Not that its author often has cause to mention the waves of epidemics with which historians are perhaps over-preoccupied and which, like popular rebellions in another context, are in reality the exception rather than the rule. In ten years, Gouberville mentions only one outbreak of plague, in 1562: it spares his manor, and his only action on this occasion is to offer his sister the thoughtful gift of a he-goat, whose smell will scare away the plague-bearing fleas. The illnesses which our squire most frequently has to face are the more everyday ones of the annual round: mysterious epidemics which lay low half the workers and leave the ploughs standing idle since no one has the strength to handle them. Or those tiresome and puzzling "chills" which "go from stomach to head", caught perhaps by eating shrimps on the edge of a cold sandy beach; or one day after dinner, taking a few bites from a piece of very doubtful cold beef, in a draughty kitchen. The description of symptoms in these bygone illnesses is a real headache in itself, and I shall not attempt to guess what precisely might correspond to these infectious ailments, these colds and fevers which ravaged the Cotentin from time to time and certainly caused many deaths. Eating contaminated food was probably one cause of such lethal outbreaks; another was the lack of hygiene. Gouberville for instance never shaves, buys soap once in ten years, and would not under any circumstances dream of taking a bath, even in the sea—the closest he ever comes to it is when he supervises his young haymakers' once-a-year ritual of sea-bathing in the nearby Channel. Very likely riddled with the pox, this noble person lived in something of a state of nature, a hairy and malodorous creature.

But like his neighbours, he wages a constant battle against illness. And in the first place, he seeks to cure by good food the ill-effects of the bad. To treat his famous chill caused by the cold beef, which attacks his head, kidneys, heart and all his limbs, he tries sugar plums, damsons and old wine. To settle his stomach which is also upset, he takes large amounts of calves-foot jelly. For vomiting: a shoulder of mutton, washed down with a jug of old wine will be tried, to relieve the digestive system. Needless to say, Gouberville, the local squire, considers himself "the Good Lord's physician" in the village and "treats" his vassals and neighbours free of charge. When one of his peasants is lying ill, sweating out a fever in a special bed brought close to the fire, surrounded by an anxious and noisy throng of friends and relations, the Master is sure to turn up before long. He will be there well ahead of the barber-surgeons not to mention the doctors whose faces are rarely seen in the village. But Gouberville will be there, lancing carbuncles, sagely recommending a bleeding or advising against it; devising his own remedies for anthrax out of lily bulbs; binding plasters of *tourmentine* (a medicinal plant) on his patients' broken legs. A bonesetter too in his spare time, with the aid of the curate who acts as surgeon's assistant, he sets "as best he can" (!) the dislocated knees of his tenants. Upon ladies who are seriously ill, he showers gifts of young kids and game pasties, which are supposed to cure the invalid, but which probably hasten the death of their unfortunate recipients. The sturdy squire is, as one might have already guessed, violently opposed to dieting. Accordingly, should any of his servants be ailing (and perhaps here he is on the right lines) he makes up a broth of his own concoction, based on beet, borage and spinach, enriched with verjuice, egg yolk and fresh butter, a soup which may actually have done them some good. I must not forget to mention the goat's milk he recommends for headaches; hawthorn tea for a raging colic; cabbage leaves to relieve the gathering on an injured leg; and a mysterious infusion made from watercress which has to be prepared by a priest, but whose specific virtues we do not alas know.

Of course Gouberville could not possibly handle all the illnesses in his area. In fact there was in existence in his region during the decade 1550–1560 a modest medical or para-medical network the efficacy—though not the good intentions—of which may perhaps be doubted. Relations between the squire and the different levels of this hierarchy of the health service were not always of the very warmest.

Indeed they were even cool and at times frankly hostile, at least when it came to the little group of local surgeon-barbers at the very bottom of the scale. These barbers were very humble practitioners whose consultation fee was five to eight sous (only three sous if they did not have to leave home and one came to them for treatment). They had not read the medical and surgical manuals which Gouberville by contrast knew, or claimed to know. But above all, their scientific technique, which consisted entirely of bleeding in order to remove an excess of blood or some evil humour residing in the body, was at odds with the ideas (solidly rooted in folklore and popular remedies) entertained by Gouberville. If the practice of the latter is anything to go by, illnesses did not in his opinion result from a surplus of dangerous humours (to be expelled by bleeding, or later—in Molière's time—by purging) but quite simply from lack of substance, a deficiency which one should try to remedy by the ingestion of meat, alcoholic drink, spices and simples. Once the gap was filled, health would return. These two positions, that of the barbers and that of the squire (the second being probably closer to local and peasant lore) are mutually contradictory; and it is not surprising if from time to time there should be a clash between these two schools of thought on medical care—the emptying principle and the filling principle. In such disputes, one is bound to say, *Maître* Gilles's theories always emerge triumphant simply by virtue of the principle of seigniorial authority.

Above the barbers came that other band of healers responsible for tackling the minor troubles of rural physiology, the bonesetters. These were generally priests, curates or *Missires* (another of the *Missires*' hobbies was bee-keeping and honey-collecting). The clerical bonesetter's charges were high (33 *sous* for a consultation); they could cure a sprain more or less efficiently and they too practised their own empirical medicine based on herbs and inspired by local tradition. All of which invested them with greater prestige than the lowly wielders of lancet and razor could claim.

Finally, at the top of the pyramid, distant and often inaccessible, only rarely taking the trouble to stir from the towns (where they all lived) were the licensed and patented doctors. Their fees were very high indeed (the tip for their lackeys alone cost the same as a visit to the barber-surgeon). And needless to say, the doctor in Cherbourg or Valognes was far too grand to bother to come to the bedside of some sick yokel in a remote farm in the *bocage*. So the patient had to go to the doctor; or if the patient was bed-ridden and too ill to be moved, his urine went instead: the customer's *"eaue"* or *"estat"* took the place of his medical file and a friend would carry it in a special flask to the home of the "leech". After examination of this *eaue*, the doctor would prescribe on the basis of its opacity, its colour and the particles it contained in suspension, this remedy or that: some local wine, cider from such and such a village, beer from Cherbourg Abbey etc. During epidemics, a common sight would be the procession of jugs of urine along the roads to the towns, while home in the other direction came jugs of beer.

★

The preceding remarks will perhaps have given an indication of the immense place that good rich food, both liquid and solid, has in the system of values of men in Gouberville's social category. It is the belly rather than the brain that rules his life and he has the prominent paunch of the trencherman, the florid complexion, crows-feet and swollen red nose of the incipient alcoholic. To this country gentleman, in whose eyes membership of the order of nobles renders manual work undignified, and who on the other hand as his slender library shows, attaches only minor importance to matters of the intellect, being on good terms with one's body meant in the first place being on good terms with the stomach. If it is true of the gentry, this remark is truer still of the clergy, the predatory order par excellence, at least in Lower Normandy, and great eaters and drinkers to a man (though I would not of course include the proletariat of curates, some of whom were certainly underfed). Accordingly any meeting between *Maître* Gilles and a priest of a certain rank (a prior or canon for instance) is the occasion for some impressive gastronomic performances. A few menus picked at random will convey what I mean: for supper on 18 September 1554, the menu for three (Gouberville, a prior and a *bailli*) was:

> *Two dressed chickens*
> *Two partridges*
> *One hare*
> *One venison pie.*

A "light refreshment", on 24 January 1553 (eaten by Gouberville *after* his dinner, and by three canons who had turned up, already rather the worse for drink, from Cherbourg to discuss the tithes):

> *One curlew*
> *One wood-pigeon*
> *One partridge*
> *One wild boar pie*
> *Dry white wine* ad lib.

After this post-prandial snack, the four table-companions went off to measure the tithe lands!

Dinner on 22 August 1553, for Gouberville, the vicar of Cherbourg, plus four other men and the wife of one of them was:

> *Meat worth one* livre tournois, *two* sous
> *Several chickens*
> *Eight snipe*
> *Sugar, cinnamon, cloves, pepper, saffron, ginger, in short plenty of spices to make all the meat "go down well"*
> *Four jars of wine bought at Valognes*
> *Ditto from Cherbourg*

A jar of hippocras or spiced wine (one jar = about two litres).

Were all these bouts of drinking and heavy meals of meat made up for by abstemiousness in Lent or on fast-days? Not a bit. Instead of stuffing themselves with meat, they stuffed themselves with fish. A different source of protein but the quantity remains just as excessive: the smallest fast-day meal, whether on a Friday or in Lent, if any priests or even simply friends are invited means that something like six or seven different kinds of fish will be served, with a mackerel for dessert. (And no one will, I think, object that the fish from the sea in the 1550s were any smaller than they are now!) It is easy to see that the formidable culinary traditions of the French ruling classes take their origins from the customs of these little pockets of landed gentry in the heart of the countryside, dating back to the late Middle Ages or the Renaissance. During the same period, the better-off peasants probably did their best, on feast days or at wedding banquets, to emulate these noble gastronomic feats. As for the mass of labourers or poor peasants, they probably lived close to penury or even starvation in years when the harvest failed. (In ten years of entries, Gouberville's diary mentions only one—1556—when there was a disastrous grain harvest and food shortage, a ratio for the period it would seem of one to ten, which is not unrealistic.)

In a world of comparative poverty then, the rural gentry of the Cotentin constituted, for their immediate entourage, "little islands of gluttony".[7] These "islands" were also (more than in the next century when there was a greater degree of social control) frequently haunts of debauchery and violence.

"Debauchery" of a more or less serious nature being common to all periods, we are here concerned only with concrete instances of it in the morals of the times we are studying. Let us say that in about 1555, among country gentlemen, it was hardly to be distinguished from extra-marital sexual relations, neither of them earning more than a fairly casual reproof. As such, debauchery was simultaneously widespread, considered sinful and a prerogative of the nobility. Widespread it certainly was among nobles of both sexes, where it led to an immense number of bastard children and to unconcealed concubinage (both of these it seems beating all records of the later classical age). Sinful and a matter for shame, at least if put in writing, it is mentioned in a private diary only under the disguise (rather easy to penetrate) of the Greek alphabet: Gouberville, thanks to this "Hellenic" code can set down in secret his amorous adventures, usually undertaken in the company of Simonet, his natural half-brother and companion in debauchery. His descriptions, which are brief, embarrassed, prudish and allusive, are not, need one say, Rabelaisian in tone (after all there is probably no reason to think that Rabelais was any more typical of the spirit of his time than the surrealists or the painters of Montparnasse say, were of the mentality of the average Frenchman in about 1925). And as the prerogative of the nobility, the heterosexual activity of the bachelor squire seems to have been exercised in some sort of attenuated version of an unofficial and local *droit du seigneur*, tacitly accepted by the families of the women at whose expense this right was claimed. One of Gouberville's mistresses about whom we know most is Hélène Vaultier, the sister of a tenant-farmer whose house was near the manor. This girl happened to take the fancy of *Maître* Gilles in December 1553, as he watched her going about her household tasks, stoking the fire and flailing the grain. Gilles got her with child, but continued to pay visits to her accompanied by Simonet (*"nous foutûmes Hélène"*, as he puts it). He reported the pregnancy as was the proper custom, to Hélène's brother, and apparently gave him the sum of compensation which was normal in such cases. He confessed his sin at length at the end of the year to the priest of Cherbourg, whom he had beforehand generously wined and dined. Ordered as a penance by this cleric to go on a pilgrimage, which he did, disguised as a sailor, Gilles was finally absolved of his sin, and ready as usual to begin again.

Whatever the incidence of private debauchery, violence was not necessarily associated with the nobility as a class. Gouberville for instance (apart from the domestic chastisements he hands out left and right to keep order in the manor) generally practises a policy of non-aggression. But men of comparable social standing, and in general people of high condition, were extremely prone at this period (about 1555)— quite as much as commoners—to make physical assaults on others. Of the eight killings which Gilles remarks upon in his journal over ten years, seven were committed by men of high rank—usually nobles, sometimes large landowners or "gentlemen of the robe". What we have here is a crime pattern typical of ancient times, characterized by murder, perpetrated not only by common peasants but also, to a massive extent, by members of the upper orders. It is very different from the more recent pattern of crime, which as Boutelet and Chaunu[8] have shown, takes the form of theft more often than of murder and is in any case—and this is the real difference from the Middle Ages or the sixteenth century—committed more often by the lower than by the upper classes.

Another difference from the periods nearer to our own time referred to by Boutelet and Chaunu is that the sixteenth century courts often failed to sanction or even to notice this archaic form of violence committed by the privileged men of the period. In the Cotentin during the dark days of the reign of Henri II, every one tried to dispense his own justice, like the hero of a western, by hunting down and punishing the man who had killed one of his relatives or stolen some of his furniture, money or livestock. In the less dangerous cases the affair might eventually be resolved over a dinner, offered by a third party who acted as mediator. The third party (Gouberville as it might be) would thus be setting the seal on the task of reconciliation in the course of which he would have negotiated some financial compensation to be paid by the offender to the plaintiff: in theory this transaction or settlement ended the quarrel. The Lower Normandy settlement *(appointement)* in the sixteenth century, which was entirely a matter of unwritten law, is not far removed, when all is said and done, from the legal *Wehrgeld* or financial compensation in use among the ancient Franks. True it hardly figures anywhere in the legal codes. But it did have the advantage of preventing an endless vendetta.

All this however does not mean that the judges or courts

were short of business. On the contrary; Gouberville, like all true Normans under the *ancien régime*, is obsessed with lawsuits, a futile and ruinous passion rivalled in our time only by the betting-shop. In his efforts to win his cases, he ruins himself in bribes and gifts of kids, young hares, partridges and rabbits, which he distributes to judges and lawyers. In this way he spends a small fortune—dozens of *livres tournois* or items of game in order to recover, if the judgement goes his way, a seigniorial rent of perhaps 30 *sous* a year![9] A bundle of paradoxes (to us at least) this man who is in practice unable either to sell his sacks of grain on a regular market or to connect his estate as a whole with any commercial outlets, will on the other hand spend hours haggling over a basket of apples which is to be divided between himself and the other parties to a will; loses a fortune in lawsuits and is prepared, in court or tribunal, to spend 100 *livres* to win 100 *sous*. There is obviously a considerable difference between this blind passion for acquisition (in which the important thing is to secure a rent or to seize an inheritance) and the spirit that informs a more modern economy directed towards sales and profits; innovative attitudes were not to develop in traditional France, among the Agrarians, rich and titled, until much later.

Gouberville, then, conformed neither to the spirit of capitalism nor to the Protestant ethic—despite his undeniable Huguenot sympathies. His personality seems to me to be a curious mixture of features, some very old-fashioned, others betraying here and there elements of a more modern outlook. Inherited from the past are his economic attitudes, which are directed much more towards the acquisition and conservation of property than towards profit; more forward-looking are his Huguenot inclinations and his paradoxical taste for technical innovation, in an environment of traditional autarky.

This curious mixture which blends into the seamless garment of an integrated personality is probably far from unrepresentative, since it appears again, in varying proportions, in the culture and society of the peasants of his age, as candidly observed in Gilles's daily entries in his diary.

To say that peasant culture in the anthropological sense

of the word, was during this period a combination of the archaic and the modern, is of course to state the obvious. For the historian of rural society however, the interest lies in trying to analyse more closely the ingredients of the mixture and the harmony of their proportions.

Among the more modern elements in the rural culture of the Cotentin, one has to include schooling: the peasants of Lower Normandy are already, in the sixteenth century approaching the standards of the least illiterate parts of France. In 1560–1580, their children (or at least a number of the boys) are going to school; they make up the specific age-group of "school-children" as opposed to young bachelors and married men. *Maître* Gilles, paternalist as usual, will sometimes after Mass on Sundays hear the children recite their lessons or *dictiers*, with a pinch on the cheek and a coin or two for the best scholars. Even among farm labourers in 1576, a not inconsiderable number of the men can sign their names (the women on the other hand remain steeped in ignorance). But this modest degree of education is contained within very strict limits. The Cotentin countryside is on the threshold of the "Gutenberg galaxy", true, but it is edging into the future backwards, glancing behind all the while at a past where there was no writing. Even in the manor and the presbytery, the only houses which possess printed books, the number of works on the shelves is ridiculously small: in Gouberville's house for instance, *Amadis de Gaule*, *Prince Nicolas*, *Nostradamus* and a treatise on law form the nucleus of a "library" which boasts less than ten volumes in all. Some of these books, it must be recognized, enjoy real popularity in the manor; one man in the neighbourhood is nicknamed "Nostradamus" and on rainy days, the Master himself reads *Amadis de Gaule* out loud in his Norman accent, to the assembled servants. But despite these praise-worthy efforts, inducement to read in the evenings is not very great (even in the manor itself, once night has fallen there are only candles for light; the age of oil-lamps is still to come).

All this would be useful data for a more general study of the material evidence concerning the culture, conceptual apparatus and sensibility of the local people. I will mention only one or two examples to be found in the journal: on the perception of time for instance; Gouberville owns a clock—but he is the only person who does, either in the neighbourhood or in his family. To take another topic, while the range of colours, or rather dyes, to be deduced from descriptions of women's dresses or men's clothes, is quite varied, including "white, black, red, violet, yellow, tan, dark tan and grey", one is oddly surprised by the absence in the clothing of these country people, of the colours green and blue. Can the gap be explained in the first case by a taboo (green is associated with madmen) and in the second by the high price of woad?

Whatever we may make of these very trifling yet significant details, schooling and instruction in the alphabet are still very much newcomers to village society where the greater part of cultural life depends upon ancient patterns of oral tradition and folk customs. To begin with there are the traditional winter festivities: in Gouberville's little world, people gather together for the Yule log, or the Twelfth Night cake, the costumes, mummers and drinking at Mardi Gras. In summertime, the midsummer bonfires, harvest suppers and the Mystery or Morality plays (often brought from the towns and very popular with country audiences) all continue to hold their traditional place in the year. At any season, the public executions and tortures, those exemplary displays of punishment which provided mass spectacles in the cities, offer the large number of country people who travel long distances to see them, a sight crueller than any tragedy. In the village, a variety of sports—*paume* (an ancestor of tennis) quoits, *choule* (an ancestor of rugby), bowls, skittles, *voleries* (a kind of volley-ball) are played by competing teams—especially the unmarried versus the married men. The women themselves (who in theory provide the basic principle of this demarcation line drawn within the group of males) have only a passive role to play in these games, as spectators or supporters. As for indoor games and pastimes, especially during winter, the servants play cards, noblemen play backgammon, sometimes for very high states (land, a windmill) and even priests may be found furiously playing dice on the doorstep until the small hours of the morning.

The serious mass culture of the period of course, had,

both among the popular masses and their traditional elites, a central focus: religious life, often superstitious and especially in the countryside still encumbered with pagan survivals. Gouberville and his fellows had been able to exercise their appetite for power in this area too. In the holy places they had woven their web, safeguarded their interests and placed their own men. The rural clergy, both absentees and pluralists (and connected to the noble order by privilege and sometimes by birth), were not in this respect a dangerous challenge to a squire who knew what he wanted. One priest could easily be nominally in charge of three parishes, a long way apart. In practice therefore, they had control over none of them and confined themselves to visiting one or the other once a year, on the occasion of a jubilee for instance. They might well "pray to God on behalf of their flock", but they usually did so while putting as much space as possible between themselves and their sheep. In the circumstances, real responsibility for the spiritual welfare of the countryside was left in the hands of the countless curates (not to mention the "supply" priests, *des prêtres "haut-le-pied"*, locums with no fixed living).

The power of these men to challenge the *seigneur* was extremely limited: when he shouted they jumped. How could they do otherwise? Usually penniless, the curate almost always had another job as well, usually a manual one, in order to survive. He might wind wool, mould wax, strain honey, catch swarms of bees, sow wheat, hump bundles of graft-slips, repair the sails of the windmill, act as the village postman, cart sides of beef or paving-stones—and almost anything else you can think of. The luckiest ones—but these were rare—were also physicians who thus cared for both body and soul. So Gouberville does exactly as he pleases with this impoverished band of clerics, whom he overwhelms with his hawk-eyed goodwill: the curates of Le Mesnil send a respectful invitation at dawn every Sunday, that he deign to attend one of the endless Sunday services (beginning with matins, then a Mass to Our Lady, followed by the parish service and finally a last Mass which may be a funeral or some other occasion). If the churchgoers are few, the singing out of tune or the curate drunk, the squire does not hesitate to deliver a stinging rebuke from his pew.

For Gouberville is a sincerely religious man. He believes in God with touching faith; he is even pious in the old manner and runs after indulgences. Like many other gentlemen in western France, however, he is influenced by Protestantism. His tailor is a Huguenot; and he himself goes to listen to preachers after about 1561. He sends the farm lads there too and quietly converts the most influential peasants in the village, who are his friends, to the new religion. It is possible to imagine that in areas like the Cotentin or the Bessin, an "English" type of development might have occurred, as villages influenced by their local lords and masters gradually slipped over to Protestantism, while the said lords took advantage of the change to confiscate, in the interests of piety of course, the goods of the Church. But in this case, the operation was too ambitious to succeed without opposition. To bank on a gradual, massive and peaceful movement towards heresy was to reckon without the towns, the small towns in particular, which were far more influential in France than in Britain, and which eventually tipped the balance one way or another. In urban communities like Avranches, and Valognes in particular, the population was largely composed of simple people, sometimes with a little education, but whose literary and biblical knowledge was unsophisticated. Such communities were under a constant barrage from the preaching and mendicant orders whose sermons had a very different tone from the tedious homilies of the country curate; and they were also heavily infiltrated by the craft guilds. The lower classes in the small towns therefore had several reasons to be hostile to the various sections of the cultivated elite who had Calvinist sympathies: they disliked the gentlemen of the *bocage*, the royal officers and magistrates, and the "elected" tax-farmers, who were all considered as bloodsuckers of the people and suspect of heresy to boot. Valognes and Avranches were later to become nests of *Ligueurs*; and already in 1562, these towns were employing simple-minded soldiers from the depths of ultra-papist Brittany to hunt down the *Christandins* (Huguenots). This threat of an anticipation of the Saint-Bartholomew Massacre was quite enough to make the petty lordlings isolated in the countryside see reason. Gouberville, who feared the pillaging of his manor and had already seen his most loyal farmers pilloried by the Catholics, soon "understood" as they say. We even find him at times virtually denying his Huguenot sympathies: for the sake of peace and quiet we see him sending off a kid and a hare and "a very good trout" to a prominent lady of the anti-Protestant party. In many villages in France the Reformation, which had been launched by a few enlightened but prudent individuals of the office-holding and aristocratic elite, must have finished this way: it rolled over and sank unheroically for fear of a massacre.

It is on this melancholy note that, like so many other human endeavours, the Gouberville epic ends. What remains is the enormous journal, illegible and fascinating: only fifteen years of it have been preserved and published in two massive volumes; a reproduction by facsimile or any other means is greatly to be desired. Easier to read and still fundamental is the book, which until this edition was quite unobtainable, written by the Abbé Tollemer, a nineteenth-century ethnographer from Normandy who, in about 1860–1870 discovered, took a fancy to and wrote a commentary on his "native informant" the Lord of Gouberville.[10]

9

The Chief Defects of Gregory King[1]

J.-C. Toutain's study "Le produit de l'agriculture française" (on French agricultural output since 1700) is one of the major attempts to apply quantification, on a national scale, to the *ancien régime*.[2] It is a work that should be carefully studied by any historian concerned with traditional peasantries, so that its methods can be examined, and its results put to the test.

As his original source material, Monsieur Toutain has taken the overall estimates made by contemporary observers (hence the immense interest of his book as a mine of references and a repository of information). Such estimates can however be of two kinds: intuitive guesses in the "Bergsonian" manner; or on the contrary the result of a genuine statistical enquiry. M. Toutain is prepared to give a hearing to both kinds.

Since my own speciality is agricultural history in and around the seventeenth century, I shall concentrate in what follows on the figures for the decade 1700–1710, which is the chronological starting-point of M. Toutain's study.

A convenient figure with which to begin is the example of income from cereals. The author of this study starts by taking data from Vauban's writings. The famous "square league"[3] inspired by the Marshal's experience of Normandy and the Morvan, as well as by his utopian imagination, is projected to the whole of France by M. Toutain, who then incorporates results from other sources in his study. His conclusions may be summarized in the following propositions:

1. Yield on sowing hardly increases at all between 1700 and 1790, varying in the region of 5–1.[4]

2. Yield to the hectare increases a good deal, rising from six quintals to the hectare in 1700 to 11.5 quintals per hectare (wheat) or eight (rye) in "1789".

3. The area of land under cereals (*ibid.*, p. 77–78) changes

173

little: 13,800,000 hectares in 1700, 10 million (?) in 1750, 13,600,000 in 1775; between 12,400,000 and 14,400,000 in 1789.

4. Cereal production increases considerably: it rises on initial analysis from 87 million quintals in 1701–1710 to 113 millions in 1781–1790 (*ibid.*, p. 77 ff.).

It seems in the first place that proposition 1, which has the merit of deflating the exaggerated statements, that are sometimes made,[5] is nevertheless too absolute; there is in fact a slight rise in the yield over seed, at least in some provinces, in the second half of the eighteenth century. But such a rise, it should immediately be recognized, can perhaps only partly be regarded as a genuine and unprecedented increase; in part it is also a recovery of previous levels: it brings the wheat yield, after the drop of the years 1690–1710, back to the already high and quite respectable levels that southern farmers were getting in the good old days of Colbert.

Proposition 4 (the rise in cereal production) appears to make sense, not so much perhaps in terms of the absolute figures (M. Toutain in the course of a self-critical passage later in the book, himself questions their accuracy) but certainly in relation to the general trend. Otherwise, how is one to explain the disappearance of famine in the eighteenth century? From this point of view, the convergence of certain data is remarkable: famines in France are particularly serious for example, in the decades between 1690 and 1720, during which wheat production, as we know from various sources, notably tithe-records, was indeed low, even in ordinary years. Against this background, it is easy to see why climatic abnormalities (1693–1694, 1709) should automatically assume catastrophic proportions. Such disasters cut down to the bare minimum a gross product already depressed even in years of normal harvest during these three decades.

Moreover, Monsieur Toutain's thesis, according to which gross cereal production grew between 1700 and 1790, fits in with the slight rise in bread consumption in the eighteenth century; and this rise itself accords with the elimination of famine and the drop in mortality rates. The progressive decline in the death rate in the age of the Enlightenment had been suspected by several writers. It has recently been decisively demonstrated on a nationwide scale by Louis Henry.

I am inclined to wonder however, whether the terminal figures (1780–1789) for gross cereal production calculated by M. Toutain are not excessively inflated. How is it that they are higher—by far—than those put forward by Chaptal and Montalivet for 1803–1812 (94 to 98 million quintals)?

Let us look next at proposition 2—increased yield per hectare. This seems questionable—if not in terms of the trend at any rate in the actual figures advanced. A virtual doubling of the yield to the hectare—especially when there is no increase in yield over seedcorn!—is a mysterious phenomenon. In fact proposition 3—the fixed acreage of arable land—is probably disputable too: the increase in cereal production was achieved partly thanks to higher yields, but also probably thanks to a modest increase in the area of arable land. This emphasis on acreage under grain is important—it implies that the rise in cereal production was achieved by means of an increased input of human labour. Such input must itself have been the result either of an increase in the number of people employed in agriculture; or—a theory not incompatible with the preceding one of an increase in the number of days worked in the year by the existing agricultural labour force. In other words, viewed in this light, the *annual* productivity of the agricultural worker may have increased in the eighteenth century, but not (or nothing like as much) his *hourly* productivity (which is the only one that corresponds to the modern concept of increased productivity by technological improvements.)

We might also note, concerning the possible extension of French arable land in the eighteenth century, that the concept of *recovery* is once more of fundamental importance. Eighteenth-century "growth" can perhaps be attributed partly at least to the reclaiming for cultivation of marginal fields which had been abandoned during the dark decades which punctuate the end of Louis XIV's reign.

But to return to the question of gross product, M. Toutain himself, after putting forward what appears to be a valid figure for grain *consumption* 1701–1710 (58 to 67 million quintals) admits that his original estimates of production, deduced from Vauban for 1701–1710 (87 million quintals), were therefore much too high; and he writes (p. 88): "for the decade 1701–1710, we must assume that one item in our data is wrong; and it looks as if it must be the area under cultivation, which should therefore be reduced to 10 million hectares". I would agree, if not on the exact figure, at least on the principle of reduction. And one could hardly say more clearly that Vauban's square league, with its exaggerated estimate of arable land and its unsupported assumption that triennial rotation was general, was an unreliable guide in the first place, whether for cereals (which it overestimates) or for vines (which it also overestimates) or for woodland (which it underestimates). Vauban's square league, it has to be said, is not always a faithful image of reality. It is in some ways the hobbyhorse of an old soldier: the ideal plan of a utopian garden, planted with devotion by an enlightened military man in moments of studious leisure snatched from a career in arms. The league is often used to prove an argument rather than to reflect an actual territory. Vauban himself ingenuously admits as much, apropos of his estimate of vineyards, when he writes: "I have added a few *arpents* to the estimate of the area planted with vines. . . . Which would only make people all the happier if it were the case".[6]

This brings us precisely to the subject of vines. The square league, multiplied across the entire national territory, gives M. Toutain 2,600,000 hectares of vines in France in the 1700s. This is a great deal more than under the Empire and the Restoration (2,000,000 and 2,100,000 hectares respectively), more even than during the Second Empire (2,190,909 hectares in 1858), in the days of the railway revolution which covered the south of France with vines. This is the "only plausible estimate", says M. Toutain seriously, of this figure for 1700 (p. 120). In fact these results demonstrate above all how dangerous it is to extrapolate figures from Vauban and how the reputation of the "father of statistics", despite his obvious merits as a pioneer, is sometimes exaggerated. While we are on the subject of criticisms of Vauban, need one recall that he was also the inventor of the frankly hare-brained system of the *dîme royale* which, if it had ever been applied, would have reduced

France, already extremely archaic in her fiscal arrangements, to the unenviable level of efficiency of the Ottoman fiscal system, with its squads of tax-collectors and tithe-extractors in kind?[7]

M. Toutain does in any case finally become alarmed by the fantastical accounting of his statistician. The average yield, very high for the period, of 25 hectolitres to the hectare[8] which Vauban proposes for French vineyards in 1690–1701, would, if multiplied by the number of hectares, give a wine harvest of an incredible 65 million hectolitres, that is 340 litres of wine per year for every man, woman and child in the kingdom of France. Can the average French inhabitant in the days of the Sun King, from babe-in-arms to grandfather, really have accounted for the daily "kilo of red wine" so notoriously characteristic of the Third Republic in its prime? I hardly think so. Regional exceptions apart, "this is inadmissible" as M. Toutain rightly says—and then falls back on King's estimates, of which more in a moment.

In the end then, Vauban's square league, if applied nationally, turns out to be a source of disappointment. Artificially extended in this way, as we have just seen, it gives far too many vineyards for example. Indeed Vauban himself admits as much.[9] Exactly the opposite happens with woodlands. The "league" gives only 5.1 million hectares (1.7 of mature forests, 3.4 of coppices) M. Toutain at first accepts these figures as they stand. And yet they are lower than all those for the following decades and indeed century. They are 2 or 3 million hectares or more lower than the figure suggested in the Cassini map of 1761—or the general statistical survey of France in 1830, which must be regarded as a serious source. If one blindly applies the Marshal's square league then, one has to admit that there were never so few forests standing (which might just be the case) or so few coppices in France as in 1700. But if that is so, how does one explain the enormous inroads that succeeding generations made into the total stock of woodlands? The clearances of the eighteenth and nineteenth centuries certainly took place,[10] as nobody would deny, even if one has to agree that they were not as extensive as those of the eleventh century. How could the people of the eighteenth and nineteenth centuries (let us say roughly 1730–1830) clear and reclaim land that was either abandoned under Louis XIV or had always been virgin soil, and still find themselves in 1800–1830, if we are to believe M. Toutain's original analysis, with a forest capital (both stands and coppices) *greater* than that in the time of their ancestors of 1700? Take-off does have its limits. And something seems to be wrong with the figures we are asked to believe. The square league which exaggerates the number of vineyards, tends to underestimate the area of woodlands.

M. Toutain, without being fully aware of this problem, nevertheless apparently realized that something was wrong when he came to calculate from a surface area so reduced in size, the income from forests in about 1700. He made it 25 million *livres tournois* which he admits is too small. So he decided to adopt another method of calculation He took as a new basis for his estimate (p. 194) the relation "generally admitted by writers on this period" between the value of wood and that of cereals: somewhere between four and eight per cent. And he thus arrives at a value for timber production of between 25 and 95 million *livres tournois*. But who are these "writers on this period" (p. 187 and 194)? Vauban of course yet again; and Gueuvin de Rademont, who was himself content in 1715 to extrapolate Vauban's square league[11] (Gueuvin takes as the basis for his estimates the wood and cereal acreages proposed by the *dîme royale*, and confines himself thereafter to minor corrections: he modifies the Vauban estimates regarding both the relationship between timber and firewood, and price levels.[12]) And the last writer called to give evidence by Toutain is none other than a nineteenth-century author, Moreau de Jonnès, who is also on this question inspired by the *dîme royale*.[13] So we are back with Vauban and his indestructible square league, forever bouncing up like a jack-in-the-box, with its low estimates for the area of (and income from) woodlands. This underestimate is so obvious that later eighteenth-century writers were to suggest that one should reckon on several more million hectares of forests and coppices than Vauban allows for; and the ratio of wood-values they advance is distinctly larger than the "four to eight per cent" relative to the total value of cereals produced (Toutain, pp. 128–131 and 187).

Michel Devèze's work[14] makes it possible to sum up on these questions: in 1912, the forests of France, according to the very complete records of the administration of *Eaux et Forêts* covered an area of 9,860,700 hectares. And Devèze adds: "the period at which French forests were *most reduced in size* is probably the early nineteenth century, before the widespread replanting of pines in the Landes, Sologne and Champagne. (The forested area had then fallen to barely 8 million hectares.)" If we follow M. Devèze on this, and there seems to be every reason to do so, we must concede that in the course of the centuries preceding 1800–1810, the forested area had dwindled. It must therefore have been greater than 8 million hectares in 1700. What then are we to think of the figures accepted by M. Toutain, viz: "5.1 million hectares of forests and coppices in 1700–1710"; "a large increase in the production of timber—up 72 per cent between 1701–1710 and 1781–1790"; and also (p. 121) "a large increase in the deflated income from timber ... from 116 million to 200 million between 1701–1710 and 1781–1790"? *A priori*, these hypotheses were startling enough: it is hard to believe that cereal and timber production should both have expanded at the same time, in an economy where clearing woodland is the most normal way of increasing cereal production. But they are also in contradiction with the most recent historical research: Devèze (p. 269) shows that in 28 *départements*, the forested area dropped from 16.37 per cent of the total surface area of the department in 1550 to 9 per cent in 1912. On this basis, if one applies the percentage drop nationwide (an intellectual operation whose results may not be entirely reliable, but are at least less fallible than those obtained from a generalization of the square league), France must have had 18 million hectares of forest land in 1550, as against 8 million in 1800: a difference of 10 million hectares. It was, amongst other things, the "great clearances" of the classical period eating into these 10 million hectares that made it possible first for the population to expand and then for famines to end, between 1550 and 1830. Some proportion of these 10 million hectares cleared between 1550 and 1810 was in all probability still standing in Vauban's time; so we ought really to reckon in terms of a decline or at any rate a stabilization—and not a rise—in the deflated value of timber production as the most reasonable hypothesis for the eighteenth century. It was by sacrificing woods that it was possible to grow cereals and thus for the first time without the occurrence of any major famine to fill the hungry stomachs of Louis XVI's kingdom. To explain this by forest clearances is not perhaps the whole story. But neither can this explanation be entirely ruled out.

★

M. Toutain is aware of the inadequacies of the square league, if not in relation to forests, at any rate where vineyards are concerned. So he has called upon another author: Gregory King. The reference to King is fundamental in the 1961 yearbook of the I.S.E.A. Some preliminary criticism of the basis for the English statistician's calculations would surely not have come amiss. M. Toutain's approach is generous, not to say gentlemanly: he trusts King from the start; and he accepts practically all the noncereal figures, although he does later make some minor corrections to them. But historians are doubting Thomases: they have a habit of chasing and discovering those "awkward facts" that can ruin beautiful theories.

King must first be set in period: we know that he was attempting to counter the exaggerated claims made by William Petty who, in his *Political Arithmetic* (chapter IV), asserts "That the People and Territories of the King of England are naturally near as considerable for Wealth and Strength as those of France".[15] These remarks, when they became known in France, apparently offended Louis XIV. Gregory King, who was as anxious as Petty to testify to the mighty resources upon which his country could call in times of war, nevertheless attempted to produce some rather more reasonable estimates than those of his predecessor. He admitted that the national income of France was almost double that of England. But he also thought, and tried to prove it statistically, that the war of the Augsburg League had been more harmful to France than to either England or Holland: "From the year 1688 To 1695 England has decreas'd in People 50,000 France 500,000 And Holland is Increased 40,000. That England is Decreas'd in its Income a Million, France 10 Millions, But Holland is Increased Half a Million".[16]

The hypothetical nature of these conclusions does not diminish the interest of King's work—on the contrary. His statistical analysis of the effects of war on a seventeenth-century economy remains a model of intellectual perspicacity, as M. O. Piquet-Marchal has clearly demonstrated, translating King's calculations into the present-day language of national accounting.[17] Without a doubt, King anticipates and answers the arguments of later historians who were to underestimate the influence of war in relation to the economic depressions of the seventeenth century: war, as he suggests in his figures, "restrains national saving, both public and private, slows down investment and compromises the long term expansion of the country".[18]

But it is one thing to admire the force of King's arguments, quite another to pass judgement on his figures—and in particular those for France, which are by definition the most subject to question. King was not on the spot; and we know from other sources how inadequate were the means at the disposal of statisticians likely to take an interest in France in 1696, the date of King's manuscript.

One source available to them, it is true, was provided by the various censuses under Louis XIV: partial population counts undertaken in several provinces in the 1680s; and also the national inquiry launched after the famine (1693–1694).[19] King *may* have known about this enquiry; but we have no evidence that he did. It is notable that King makes his adventurous extrapolations date from the year 1688, that is well before the national investigation referred to. If by any chance he had known about it, he would no doubt have found something in it to put in the many boxes of his statistical tables. Many of King's figures are probably founded on deductions, correctly inferred in terms of logic, but not necessarily in accordance with the facts.

The truth is that we do not know anything about the precise origin of King's figures for France, apart from what he himself tells us in his book. And his text tends to confirm, as we shall see, that he operated initially by way of brilliant and daring deductions.

D.V. Glass, the leading authority on King, whom I asked about the writer's French sources, replied (in a letter dated 3 January 1968): "I cannot give you any real indication of how King arrived at his calculations concerning France. Having read a large number of King's manuscripts, I am convinced that there must be some factual basis for his observations. Although he often went beyond this factual base, he almost always took certain data as a starting point, however plausible or implausible such data might be. Unfortunately none of the manuscripts I have seen gives any indication of the sources of his information on France." So it remains an open question. Where did King get his French figures?

On this question, Toutain hesitates between two hypotheses, which we may call for convenience hypothesis A (King worked from total figures) and hypothesis B (he worked from per capita figures).

Hypothesis A is taken from the "context" of the English work: "From King's context", writes M. Toutain, "one may deduce that per capita consumption was worked out on the basis of *total consumption*" (p. 115). Using this concept of "totality", M. Toutain divides all King's figures by 20 million, the approximate population of France in 1700. On this basis he calculates individual rations, correcting in the process the erroneous figure of 13.5 million subjects which King, as a result of an underestimate, assumed to be the population of France under Louis XIV in 1695.[20]

But did King really start with a total figure? At one point M. Toutain seems to hesitate on this question. Concerning fruit and vegetables, he writes for instance, (p. 140–141): "In the case of Davenant [Davenant was the author who later took up King's figures], we have assumed that the figure for total consumption preceded the figure for per capita consumption in his calculations. But it is possible that on the contrary King began with a presumed per capita consumption figure." M. Toutain builds up on this passing hypothesis a series of complicated calculations which he might have spared himself if he had consulted the English edition of King's book.

But in any case, apart from the one isolated instance of the fruit and vegetable figure, hypothesis B (per capita starting point) does not seem to have detained M. Toutain for long. In all other areas: grain, wine, meat, butter, eggs and cheese, M. Toutain simply keeps the Englishman's values, as they appear if one accepts that King took as his starting point total figures which one is entitled to apply as they stand to a France of 20 million inhabitants. One can see this for oneself by consulting Table 61 in M. Toutain's book (p. 199, animal produce) and especially Tables 63 (p. 202, final agricultural production) and 59 (p. 191) where there are no corrected values for meat and wine.

So which should one accept? Hypothesis A or hypothesis B? It looks in fact as if King set off from hypothesis A (total figures) and then made use, in circumstances we know nothing about, of a per capita figure (hypothesis B). Even the most rapid and superficial reading of the original English edition of King's work would have enabled M. Toutain to dispense with some of his hesitations.

I shall refer in what follows to the Baltimore edition of King, published in 1936, which conforms to the original texto.[21]

In order to estimate the income of France in 1695 King takes as his starting point the presumed "pre-war" level of 1688. He calculates this in the first place from the total area of the kingdom, estimated by him—including heath, moorland, mountains and wasteland—at 126 million acres,[22] i.e. 50 million hectares (500,000 square kilometres: roughly correct).

Then King allots, for his purposes, an average yearly rent to each surface unit (of five shillings per acre). (On what foundation? that remains a total mystery.) From this point a simple multiplication sum gives him the income from land: £32 million sterling, to which he immediately adds another £52 million (heaven knows where he got this figure) for "Trade and Business". Total: £84 million pounds sterling. And hey presto! it is on the basis of this £84 million—*and on this alone*—that is the total value of the income produced, calculated in some ten lines of quite breath-taking brevity, that King sets out to calculate the "expenses" of the kingdom of France, expenses which include food consumption and which amount in all, by a logical process of identification to ... £84 million pounds sterling.

It will be agreed, I think that the initial method by which King obtained this figure of £84 million is somewhat casual.

The flimsy foundations of these totals appear with full force in the analogous reasoning which Gregory King applies to population. King assumed that there were nine acres per head of the French population. Such an assumption is not completely unrealistic; but it has no foundation in fact. And it was suggested to the author purely and simply by a comparison which he makes with England and Holland. On this basis, Louis XIV's kingdom would have numbered 14 million inhabitants in 1688.[23]

The trouble with this reckoning is that in the area of demography we really do have some first hand information. The actual population, as is known from the counts undertaken by the *intendants*, is in the region of 19 or 20 million inhabitants. There is no reason to think that King's figure for total income is any more accurate than the figure—manifestly wrong, because purely deductive—which he devised for population.

In any case, it is certainly from this £84 million that everything else in his argument follows, including the final deductions—consequently rendered extremely doubtful—made 265 years later by M. Toutain.

In this connection, let us follow the simple and confident thread of King's argument. Starting in 1688, he wants to get to 1695: "It may well be presum'd", he writes, "That by the Interruption of Trade and the Desertion of the Refugees, the Income of France is Lessend 10 Mills p. ann."[24]

So now we have a drop from £84 million to £74 million—after all, why not?

This figure of £74 million is then broken down into various categories (*Dyet* or expenditure on food, *Apparell*, *Incident charges*, *Generall Expence*) by means of a shadowy grid or analysis—King does not tell us where he gets it. And finally, in the next paragraph, King brings us without more ado to the heading of £38 million relating to Dyet, that is expenditure on food.

This figure of £38 million is in turn broken down (according to criteria the origin of which remains equally mysterious) into figures for bread, meat, wines and spirits etc. These numbers, which constitute the ultimate point of King's speculations, are reproduced unaltered by Toutain. But as we have seen, their foundations are built on sand.

★

I think it has been established that the basic figure (the £84 million of total income) is somewhat suspect. Let us now try to probe more deeply into the "grid", the enigmatic and shadowy alchemy used by King to break down the overall figures he had conjured up with two or three strokes of the pen. Let us begin with wine.

For reasons best known to himself, King evaluates the wine consumption of the French nation at £9 million—as against £10,600,000 on bread: that is 117 and 138 million *livres tournois* respectively. At first sight, this wine/bread ratio of 9:10 for the *whole of France* and for *all French people* seems hardly acceptable. Both King and Vauban seem to have been the victim of some sort of Bacchic inflation: from their writings, especially those of the former, one might well conclude that the Frenchmen of 1700 must often have been as drunk as lords; indeed in King the ratio of the wine group to the cereal group is nearly 90 per cent (64 per cent in Vauban).

But at the beginning of the nineteenth century, when, whatever M. Toutain thinks,[25] winegrowing certainly accounted for a substantial portion of the French agricultural income, the wine/cereal ratio calculated by serious statisticians like Chaptal,[26] was only 39 per cent (30 per cent according to Montalivet). It seems indeed as though King saw the wine consumption of the French through the alcoholic haze emanating from the habitual carousing of his more prosperous compatriots. The same writer frequently goes in for these insular distortions—which would be quite forgivable, so long as one was *not* thinking of using them as a basis for a general statistical survey of France in 1695! It is probably because he is generalizing from British eating habits of the time, in which butter, eggs and cheese play an important-

and salutary—role, that King attributes to French diets in the age of Louis XIV, what is (comparatively) an improbable richness in dairy products. If we are to believe him,[27] our ancestors consumed about 106 million *livres tournois'* worth of butter, eggs, cheese, milk, poultry, as compared to 73 million *livres tournois'* worth of meat and 138 million worth of cereals. How lucky the subjects of the Sun-King were, one might think. (Lucky that is as to the *qualitative* composition of their daily fare, but not of course as to the absolute and overall quantity of rations such a menu would imply. As we shall see, this was far too low if one blindly accepts Gregory King's figures.)

Such distortions as this (relatively) unbelievably high proportion of animal proteins and alcohol should make one sceptical as to the value of King's French figures. M. Toutain himself is struck by the discrepancies; and he notes that King's dairy food figures contradict all the other known "estimates" of the eighteenth century, which give much lower figures for dairy foods than for meat.[28] His doubts do not however deter M. Toutain from considering King's figures "reasonable".[29] He even considers them to be more convincing than those of Goyon for milk, butter and cheese in 1751–1760. Apropos of the latter, who put his own apparently arbitrary value on milk, butter and cheese, of 100 million, M. Toutain declares positively: "For 1751–1760 [we have taken] Goyon's figures; *we have no information that enables us to dispute them but we shall add about 10 million, in order to account for poultry".*[30]

Why 10 million *livres tournois* for poultry (and for eggs, included in this figure apparently)? Whereas the total value of these two products had been fixed[31] by "King–Davenant" in "1700" at 50.7 million, and by other writers, no more and no less serious apparently, at at least 182 million in 1775, 135 million in 1789, and 65 million in 1803? The mystery of this temporary but staggering drop in poultry products (the figure of 10 million *livres tournois* in 1751–1760 is sandwiched between one of 50.7 million in 1700 and one of 182 million in 1775) remains unsolved. M. Toutain seems to consider that a "national catastrophe" struck French chicken farming in the mid-eighteenth century. At least that is what one may infer from his figures. But he does not acquaint us with the sources of any information which might indicate in greater detail the circumstances in which, some time during the age of Enlightenment, tragedy befell the barnyard population of France.

But to return to King, however did he arrive at these breakdowns and percentages, which are often neither reasonable nor remotely likely? I can only hazard a few conjectures. The most plausible is that while he must surely have begun with an overall model, he later turned towards a per capita analysis which provided him, or so he thought in good faith, with the "grids" he needed to break down his "general" figures.

That King was familiar with the monographs on household and individual budgets seems certain enough, at least concerning England. One of his letters indeed shows that in his *Observations upon the State and Condition of England* he evaluated all types of individual expenditure in turn, "according to the severall Degrees of Living" in British society, from the poorest to the most wealthy [32] Then, he adds, "I distributed my People into classes". On this basis, King was able to keep count of the number of inhabitants included in each sociological group; within each group, he multiplied the individual consumption figure by the total of persons; and finally produced a composite picture, which was to become famous, of national consumption in England.

As for France, it may be supposed that King proceeded, at least in part, by similar methods; once in possession of the rather doubtful figures he dreamed up to evaluate the total income of the kingdom of Louis XIV, King must have tried to find out what was the normal pattern of spending of the French family budget—so that he could then himself break down his pseudo-statistics under separate headings for different foodstuffs.

Where did King obtain such monographic "data"? From the national surveys, like those quoted by Jacques Dupâquier?[33] It does not seem very likely. Even supposing, purely for the sake of argument, that King knew of the existence of such surveys, he would not have found in them the information he needed in order to work out, for every level of society, the consumption habits of the 20 million French people.

So either (and this seems improbable) King simply invented his "grids"; or else he constructed them from data given him by some French or English correspondent living in France. (We might note incidentally that King had learned French in 1665.)[34]

But in that case, many questions remain to be answered.

Does not this mysterious correspondent seem to have underestimated some categories and overestimated others, according to his own personal whims? And how in any case would such a "correspondent" have been able to formulate figures valid for each social group and also for the whole French nation, the north, the centre, the winegrowing south and the cider-producing west? Let me repeat that much of the data reported in King's figures is suspect; the figures for animal produce (meat, butter, eggs, milk, cheese: 179 million *livres tournois*) come out much higher than those for cereal produce (138 million) which will astonish anyone who is familiar with the economy of the *ancien régime*. Conversely, when one turns away from some of these percentages (wine, animal products etc.) which are much too high in *comparative* terms, and considers the totals given in *absolute* values by King, one realizes that these are by contrast much too low![35] On the total for vegetable produce for example, they are three to five times as low as other estimates relating to the same period. And by taking King's figures into consideration, M. Toutain was led to propose a low starting-point for his calculations for the age of Louis XIV, and consequently to exaggerate wildly the rate of growth in the eighteenth century.

Moreover, if one wants to use King, whose various calculations all rest in the first place on an *overall* view of the French economy, one has to take his figures *in toto* or not at all. If one accepts 117 million *livres tournois* as the figure for the wine consumed by the French, one cannot simply jettison (and then forget all about) the figure of 138 million *livres tournois* for cereals. In fact, all the Englishman's arguments rest on the original assumption of a national "cake" evaluated at £84 million. The cake is then divided by King, by means of his category considerations (the validity of which is extremely variable and in some cases downright imaginary) into "sectors" or pieces of cake, of various sizes: £10,600,000 or 138 *livres tournois* for cereals, £9 million or 117 million *livres tournois* for wine etc. These sectors probably bear no close relation to reality, whether in absolute or relative terms. But at least they fit into a particular overall pattern, devised by King, outside which they lose what little logical significance they may originally have possessed.

But what does M. Toutain do? He takes some of the pieces of King's cake, lifts them out and sets them alongside other pieces, much more suited to a giant's appetite, and taken from a more monumental cake—Vauban's. In other words, M. Toutain uses King's figures for wine, meat, vegetables, milk, butter etc., but for bread, where King's figures are unrealistically low, he replaces them with figures more reasonable, but not necessarily more accurate and, in any case, immense by comparison, which he has taken from Vauban (sometimes revised and corrected by Vauban's commentators). Through this kind of operation, the wine/cereal ratio, which was 117 million (wine) to 138 million (cereal) according to King, becomes in Toutain 137 million (wine) (he keeps King's figure but increases it slightly by 20 million) to 785 million for cereals, or nearly six times King's figure![36]

King's wine estimate, which was in itself extraordinary enough, therefore loses any possible remaining justification, by being wrenched out of the context that gave it some *raison d'être*, however unreal, and flung into the very different surroundings derived entirely from the "Vauban complex", which is five or six times greater than the "King complex" taken altogether.

To sum up: a conceptual analysis of M. Toutain's basic data shows that his figures come from two different structures: a Vauban structure for woodland and cereals; and a King structure for most of the other products. Since these two structures are of a totally different nature, it seems illogical to try to marry them up. For such a marriage to be both happy and fruitful, King's data would have to be thoroughly transformed to make them compatible with those formulated by Vauban—assuming such a labour was worth the trouble, which is by no means certain, in view of the far-fetched character of King's data and the sometimes utopian nature of Vauban's.[37]

All in all then, it seems that M. Toutain's set of graphs describing eighteenth-century growth rests upon extremely fragile foundations. The colossus has feet of clay indeed. Looking with a critical eye at King's budget or Vauban's square league—which in any case contradict each other— has laid bare the fundamental flaws underlying the entire corpus of King–Vauban data. We know that M. Toutain reports annual increases somewhere between 0.40 per cent and 0.47 per cent for the period 1700–1790 in the production of vegetable goods (deflated value); of 1.16 per cent for animal produce and 0.60 per cent for total agricultural production (deflated value). These rates are interesting; they are not totally unrealistic; and they have helped provide material for a stimulating article.[38] But to the extent that their baseline for 1701–1710 has been proved illusory, they are literally floating in a vacuum, since they start from a point too far down on the scale, largely because of Gregory King's excessively low absolute figures.

If one compares M. Toutain's figures for France with those of Deane and Cole for England between 1700 and 1790, in terms of agricultural production, one notices that the British rates are calculated on a much more reasonable foundation. Deane and Cole mention a rise of 35 per cent in deflated British agricultural output between 1700 and 1790, as against the 60 per cent for France proposed by M. Toutain over the same period of time. The validity of this 60 per cent, comparatively a very high figure, has not been demonstrated. One cannot therefore blame the French Revolution for having interrupted a long period of agricultural growth in the eighteenth century, since such growth has probably been overestimated in the quantitative analysis referred to in this article. At least in the area of agriculture, given the present state of our knowledge, the French Revolution does not deserve the title of "national catastrophe" recently conferred upon it.

Finally then, if one is to comment on the figures given for France by Vauban and King and taken up by M. Toutain, one cannot do otherwise than agree with the cruel judgement of M.J. Marczewski: "We will not mention", he says, "among the immediate antecedents of quantitative history, the sporadic evaluations of national product and revenue for isolated years originating in both England and France at the end of the seventeenth century. They were too incomplete and broad in scope to give any indication of the economy to which they referred. In any case, their authors were more concerned in general to satisfy the immediate needs of economic policy than curiosity of a historical order."[39]

10

Tithes and Net Agricultural Output (Fifteenth to Eighteenth Century)[1]

I should like, in this article, to give some idea of recent developments in the study of tithes. It will be concerned both with research methods and with the results obtained. By "methods" I do not simply mean methodology in general; I am also thinking of the technical devices, the "tricks of the trade" which should help us to perfect the graphs we construct from tithes—if possible in standardized procedures available to all those engaged in research. As for results, I propose to set out here a provisional chronology of the development of net agricultural output as it appears so far— with more or less clarity—through the figures for tithes.

METHODOLOGY

Tithes constitute an indispensable, though often unreliable, source for the history of agricultural output. The data can be found either in the form of tithe agreements (in notaries' offices, from the fourteenth century) or in the form of tithe accounts (in the ecclesiastical archives). These two types of document can be mutually complementary, since gaps in a series of agreements can be made good with the aid of a set of accounts referring to the same tithe lands, and *vice versa*.

There is a problem: tithes were often confused, both in the documents and in reality, with various types of land rents. In many cases, in fact, tithes were farmed out: they were therefore subdivided, by definition, into the sum received by the tithe-levying body and the profit of the enterprise, which stayed in the pocket of the tithe-farmer. Our sources, in cases like this, can only tell us about the portion, the larger one of course, which went directly to the tithe-owner. In the second place, a tithe-land may be part of a larger comprehensive lease, covering not only tithes but a *seigneurie*, a large estate, a château, etc. As a general principle then, the best thing is to collect the two sets of information combined in such cases—and then to distinguish rents from tithes if this is possible. Even when a distinction between these two kinds of payment is not ultimately practicable, because in the original document they have been inextricably merged, collecting the information concerning the whole is still a worthwhile activity for the researcher. And in any case, whether one is dealing with combined or separate kinds of income, the prime object of an investigation of tithes must be to discover a number of *long-term* series, covering one or more centuries.

Such a study will first have to consider tithes in kind, paid directly to the clergy in the form of a material contribution (of grain, wine, oil etc.) Here one should record the value in figures of the offering of course, but also the metrology, the length of the agreement, and whether or not there is a signature by the lessee (as a marginal contribution to the history of illiteracy). The next stage of the research consists of drawing up a table of successive annual figures and producing the corresponding graph. This should of course be transcribed on to semi-logarithmic paper, the great advantage of which is that it makes it possible to compare any given graph with any other. In the interests of total comparability, it would also be useful if researchers could agree on the conventions for the graphic representation of chronology. I would therefore propose that the hundred years of a given century should be represented quite simply by one hundred consecutive columns in the table.

On the question of moving averages, these do not seem to me to be indispensable, at least in the preliminary stages, for the construction of tithe diagrams. Such averages either serve no purpose, as in the case of tithes in grain, where there is no need to even out the graph to make it readable; or they are misleading—when there is a series of harvests showing very pronounced biennial variations, producing a zigzag graph, as is the case for instance with olive oil. The best course is still to chart the gross payment in kind, year by year, since this really tells one everything: it reveals the short-term fluctuation as well as the long and very long-term trend. While we are on the subject, ten-yearly averages (non-moving) seem to be a bad idea: they produce a graph like a flight of stairs, with each step representing ten years, and their rigidity breaks up the living flow of real-life history.

In such a brief article, I do not want to go in detail into the problem of the representative character of tithes paid in kind. Let us simply say that they can always tell us something about the net product, and in some cases can provide graphs showing a trend roughly parallel to the general pattern of production.

Tithes payable in money can also provide a picture—more or less reliable according to circumstances—of the history of the net agricultural output. They too should be presented in the form of graphs, but should if possible be deflated[2] by means of a general price index, or if this is not available, by using some key price (such as that of grain) as a "deflater". The series of prices used for such calculations should be evened out by the use of a moving average over seven, nine, or a maximum of thirteen years. This is because tithes paid in money were usually associated with leases covering a period of several years, and it would be unrealistic to deflate them by means of prices obtained on an annual basis. Lastly, the geographical source of the prices consulted for the deflating operation should be one near the tithe lands in question. The appropriate "deflater" for tithes paid in money in the Haut Languedoc, for example, would be the market prices in Toulouse.

As a general rule, I would not recommend the practice one sees from time to time of simply juxtaposing, on the same graph, the curve showing nominal tithes in money and the nominal price curve, without deflating the former by the latter. This way of presenting the material takes it for granted that the readers of this double graph will be able to calculate for themselves, at a glance, how much the tithe should be deflated, simply by comparing it with the price curve. Such an assumption is quite unfounded. Historians are not necessarily demon calculators. It would be much better to combine the two graphs into a single one: that is, to take the trouble to work out the deflation rate and have the patience to construct a single graph showing the actual and original value of the money tithes, expressed in terms of a real commodity such as wheat.

Whenever possible, one should also work out the totals: for instance the successive totals, year by year, of all the tithes in the villages of a given diocese. It is however frequently impossible to produce such totals since many of the basic series have gaps which render any sum incomplete. In such cases, one has to be satisfied with working out averages, locally or regionally. Ideally, one might even be able to establish national averages for certain well-documented periods. With a view to the possible calculation of such averages in the future, it would be useful if data could be recorded as they are discovered. My suggestion is therefore that all figures relating to tithes should be preserved and deposited with some representative body of historians, to form a data bank.

*

After the long labour of calculation, the economic historian will remain prudent and sometimes sceptical about the value of the material on tithes that he has collected. The most impressive tithe series in the world can only give the information it has: in other words, it will always remain first and foremost, by definition, an instrument for the measurement of ecclesiastical income. It can tell us a good deal about itself; and it can be moderately helpful—or unhelpful— depending on circumstances, about anything else—agricultural production for instance. Its relationship to production will always be characterized by a variable degree of uncertainty.

This being so, it is to be hoped that historians will always do their best to obtain data about the rate[3] of tithes and the area of the tithe lands. Changes over time, in rate or in surface area, may send the income derived from any particular tithe-agreement up or down, while the basic output per unit of area may not really have altered. (But knowledge of the acreage and rate and their respective alterations should not be regarded as a *sine qua non* for collecting numerical data relating to the income from a given tithe agreement).

*

Up to this point, we have been arguing as though tithes were our only means of access to the history of agricultural production. Such a one-dimensional approach is of course misleading. Many other research techniques are open to historians. We shall mention just two of them briefly here: they are associated with the names of M M. Slicher Van Bath and Toutain.[4]

The method adopted by M M. Slicher Van Bath is based on the progress of yield over seed. This approach is one of remarkable, indeed brilliant, simplicity of principle. But the results so far published are not always convincing, at least in the case of France. The figures suggested by our Dutch colleague sometimes underestimate yields in the Middle Ages; and in particular they overestimate those of the sixteenth and seventeenth centuries. As a result they present a vision of soaring production and sustained growth of yields in France, from the thirteenth to the seventeenth century. Such an exaggerated picture is unrealistic. Actual yields were fairly stationary from about the thirteenth to fourteenth century until the seventeenth or even the eighteenth century: six or eight to one in the very good soil of the north; four or five to one in the south. The "agricultural revolution", to some extent at least, is a myth . . .

*

Whatever is thought of other approaches, investigations based on the tithe will continue to be a fundamental source. The results so far achieved by such studies help to provide the broad outlines, summarized below, of a chronology covering several centuries.

RESULTS

The following chronology calls for one or two preliminary

observations. First, periodization: it goes without saying that chopping time up into fifty-year periods is purely for the sake of convenience. Secondly, geography: the absence of western France from our records is an unfortunate gap, which should be remedied as soon as possible.

Here then is an overall summary of the question. The detailed information indispensable for a full understanding of it will be found in the section I have written at the end of the collective study, *Les Fluctuations du produit de la dîme.*

(a) *1400–1450*: there is a dramatic fall in the net output of the countryside round Paris between 1420 and 1445. A similar phenomenon can probably be expected in many other regions of France (although apart from Provence and Forez, we do not yet have any tithe-series for them). Artois and Flanders, by contrast, seem hardly to be affected by this crisis of the Hundred Years War, and are at this time going through a phase of comparatively high production.

(b) *1450–1500*: a general revival, which is perhaps wholly or in part merely a more or less successful recovery of the pre-war or pre-Black Death levels of the fourteenth century, can be seen in all regions of France, the well-documented and the not so well-documented. But in Cambrésis and Flanders on the contrary, a major regional crisis seems to take place in approximately 1480, perhaps because of the military ventures of Charles the Bold or, more particularly, those of Maximilian.

(c) *1500–1550*: this period is marked by a "national" peak—the first one to be precisely charted and measured—in the product of tithes and land rent. This peak can be observed in all areas of present-day France and Belgium. High points in the net product are reached towards 1515–1520 and 1540–1550 in the Paris region, Burgundy, Cambrésis, the Namur region, Flanders and Languedoc. A serious but temporary crisis appeared in about 1530, notably in Languedoc, where animal production was permanently affected. During the half-century 1500–1550 Alsace was apparently doing rather less well than the rest of what is now France (perhaps because of the "peasant war"?) but nevertheless achieved quite respectable levels.

In spite of the generally good results, the 1500–1550 peak

had its limits: in the Ile-de-France for instance, nominal incomes from tithes and rents in about 1520 did not even reach the corresponding figures from before the Black Death, although the currency had been devalued—those high figures of the period 1300–1340 which is sometimes half-jokingly referred to as "the crisis period". In Flanders and Cambrésis the record levels of the 1420s were not surpassed in 1550; so the notion of a multisecular ceiling on production is quite perceptible even during the economic "Renaissance".

(d) *1550–1600*: the terrible civil wars after 1560, accompanied by the refusal to pay tithes, unleashed the whirlwind and set the anemometer spinning. The sporadic withholding of tithes in this period sometimes makes it impossible for the historian to make use of tithe-payments as a measuring instrument. Certainly there can be no doubt that the product from tithes and rents fell everywhere, sometimes very low indeed, notably in Languedoc, the Camargue, Burgundy, the Paris region and in Flanders, after the sack of Antwerp. The fall in net product sometimes began very late (not until 1580 in the Paris region) and minimum rates are reached in the 1580s and more widely in the 1590s. Only Alsace, despite some negative fluctuations, seems to have been affected distinctly less than the other parts of present-day France. This is hardly surprising: still a foreign province to the kingdom, Alsace probably reflected the particular conditions prevailing in the Germanic world.

(e) *1600–1650*: at first, 1600–1620, there is a period of expansion: all of "Gaul" (i.e. present-day France and Belgium) experiences a very respectable growth of net agricultural output—until 1625–1630. It should however be noted that the maximum levels attained by tithes or cereal rents in 1625 do not, except in Alsace, go beyond the rather modest ceilings first reached in the "good" part of the sixteenth century (before 1560).

After 1630, another cyclone moves slowly across the northeast of the country: agriculture in Alsace is the first to go under, engulfed in the sound and the fury of the Thirty Years War. Then a few years later, to judge from the tithe records, Burgundy, Cambrésis and the Namur region plunge downwards in turn. The Fronde gives a rude shock to Picardy and the Île-de-France, but in the latter region tithes and rents only suffer a temporary eclipse in the years of the Fronde. The South, *a fortiori* maintains the impetus gained in the time of Sully until the beginning of the Colbert era. The healthy upward climb of the southern graphs is only interrupted, and then briefly, by a few rather violent squalls, caused by wars and outbreaks of plague, especially in about 1630 and 1650. In a general sense, it is the geography of the Thirty Years War, and of the Fronde too, which is responsible for the demarcation lines between these different economic climates. The collapse of production in mid-century in the north-east, contrasts with the steady rate (and sometimes increase) of production in the rest of the kingdom, from the Auvergne to Languedoc, in the many provinces where the expression "seventeenth-century crisis" has only a limited meaning. And if there is a "crisis", in the north-east precisely, towards 1630–1635, it is the result of the fortunes of war rather than of "monetary famine". The hypothetical ravages of the latter and its supposed negative effects on gross product ought, if one subscribes to classical theory, to reach a peak of intensity during the phase of lower prices which coincided with Colbert's ministry. But in fact the reverse is true: harvests are in general quite good and abundant during this period—and yet if we were to abide by conventional ideas, this would be the classic point of the B phase of the seventeenth century.

(f) *1660–1700*: the "early Colbert period" (the decade 1660–1670 and even the years until 1675–1680) is indeed a good one almost everywhere—outstanding indeed. Net production reaches its highest levels in Languedoc and Provence, round Bordeaux, Perigord, the Lyonnais, the Auvergne, Upper Normandy. Elsewhere there is a peak of achievement, or a postwar or post-Fronde recovery (the Ile-de-France, Picardy, the Cambrésis, the Namur region); or else a period of energetic reconstruction (Alsace and Burgundy). Expansion of the cereal output at this time rarely, except in the south, beats the records of past centuries. But it is nevertheless able, or virtually able, to ward off famine (after 1662) for the space of a generation. These years of relative plenty in cereal production, which follow the temporary famine at the time of the Accession, coincided with the most brilliant phase of the Sun King's reign. They also contributed, naturally, to send down grain prices. They made it easier, now that bread was cheap, to feed the soldiers of the large armies and the workers on the great building sites, as well as those in the newly created manufactures.

The real crisis begins after 1680: it is signposted by the fall in the tithe-product in Languedoc, Provence, Bordeaux, Périgord, Aquitaine, the Lyonnais and the Auvergne; or perhaps one should say it begins again as a kind of relapse, a more or less violent repetition of the disasters already experienced during the Thirty Years War, and warded off again for a while during the Colbert years, which were so to speak a reprieve. This renewed crisis at the end of the seventeenth century is quite perceptible, especially on the frontiers of the kingdom: in Cambrésis, Namur and Wallonia. It can be seen in the Ile-de-France too, but there more particularly after 1700. It is not possible to explain this fall in the income from tithes after 1680 by some undetected resistance on the part of the payers of tithes, since this would be unlikely in an age of Catholic reaction, symbolized by the Revocation of the Edict of Nantes.

The end of Louis XIV's reign is therefore a bad—but not catastrophic—period almost everywhere, from Cambrai to Narbonne, from Bordeaux to Lyon or Namur. An exception should be made however for Alsace and Burgundy: here the impetus of reconstruction after the Thirty Years War seems to have produced a wave of increased net production until the beginning of the eighteenth century!

(g) *The eighteenth century*: after 1720, things pick up again more or less everywhere and the prosperity that goes with recovery becomes established. Then after 1750 (except in eastern France, in Alsace and Burgundy which paradoxically fall back into stagnation after the mid-century) there is a boom. This boom reaches and sometimes appreciably overtakes the records achieved spasmodically in other periods, notably the peaks reached in the Colbert era. This final breakthrough during Louis XV's old age does not imply that there was an agricultural revolution in the technical sense. But to judge from tithes and rents, there was a certain take-off after 1750, within the general context of existing technology, probably the result of several factors combined. Among these one could safely say are a drop in the number of days unworked in the year per head of the agricultural workforce; the planting of new crops; the clearing of new land; several minor technical improvements etc.

All in all, to judge from the tithe and rent graphs on one hand, and using criteria of demographic probability on the other, the increase in real, i.e. deflated agricultural output seems to be in the region of a minimum of 25 per cent and a maximum of 40 per cent in the overall period between the decade 1700–1709 and the decade 1780–1789. Monsieur Toutain's figure of "+ 60 per cent" seems too high.

In the wider perspective, from the fourteenth century to the beginning of the eighteenth, and up until 1750, we find what might be called, to paraphrase Claude Lévi-Strauss, "a cold economy": net agricultural output is indeed subject to fluctuations—sometimes of enormous magnitude—but over the long term it is not propelled by any lasting upward movement. It oscillates, and has great difficulty in taking off. From time to time it comes up against ceilings, which, with some regional exceptions, are rigid and virtually unsurpassable (in 1520, 1550, 1625, 1670). Real growth does not seem to appear, and then only hesitantly, in most of northern France until after 1750. The great advance of the eighteenth century was that the catastrophic scale of the fluctuations now decreased. This progressive stabilization preceded the real take-off—for which it may fundamentally have prepared the way.

When viewing the history of agricultural output, the same rethinking is necessary as in the case of industrial production: what was new after 1750 was not some agricultural revolution, but a departure, without any technological upheaval, on a path of growth.

II

Mélusine down on the Farm:
Metamorphosis of a Myth[1]

The following article, on the rural and popular folklore associated with the name Mélusine in the modern period (i.e. sixteenth to eighteenth century) is intended as an extension of the study by Jacques Le Goff[2] of the mythology surrounding Mélusine in medieval times, which we know from a fourteenth-century romance. This fairy or fabled being, who would sometimes take the form of a woman, sometimes that of a siren or serpent, is said to have been seen for the first time by her future husband, Raimondin, in a forest near a fountain. After her marriage, she endowed him with an abundance both of heirs and of worldly goods. Eventually however, she disappeared, in the form of a dragon, as she had sworn to do if her husband should dare to watch her in secret on a Saturday, for on the sixth day of every week, for twenty-four hours, she would shed her woman's skin and assume the form of a siren.

IN the modern period, Mélusine disappears from literary history where the talent of the fourteenth-century narrator, Jean d'Arras, had given her a place. But she secretly lives on, or rather she now enters—or returns to—the cultural life of hamlet and village, and more generally, the broad stream of unwritten folklore.[3] Noël du Fail, in Chapter V of his *Propos rustiques*[4] which appeared in 1548, includes the serpent-woman in the repertory of tales told by a "country bumpkin" called Robin Chevet. This man was a villager from the Rennes district, a skilled ploughman and a teller of popular tales in the strictest and most professional sense of the term. He memorized the tales passed on to him by story-tellers older than he, and then related them by the fireside of an evening. "Willingly, after supper, with his back to the fire ... old Robin ... would start on a good tale of the days when the animals could speak ... how Reynard stole the

fish from the fishermen ... how he got the washerwomen
to beat off the wolf the time he was learning to fish; how the
dog and the cat went on a long journey; how Master Crow
lost the cheese by opening his beak to sing; about Mélusine;
about the were-wolf; about 'Cuir d'Asnette';[5] about the
fairy-folk, and how he often talked familiarly with them as
they passed at eventide along the country lanes." To judge
from the dates scattered here and there in Noël du Fail's
narrative, Robin Chevet was active as a story-teller in about
1490–1500, half a century or so before *Propos rustiques*
appeared. The image Du Fail presents of a popular peasant
culture, apparently going very far back in time, with its
own repertoire and forms of communal expression, seems
authentic enough to guarantee the probability that Mélusine
was an established figure in the living folklore of western
France at the end of the fifteenth century. The family fireside gathering at which Robin would tell his tales is described in very precise detail by Du Fail; it corresponds to a
pattern of traditional social activity which was typical of
Armorica and of other regions at the time. Noël du Fail had
been present at such gatherings in his youth, and the old
peasants, vine-growers and schoolmasters he met as he
went on the rounds of his estates, had told him about similar
evening gatherings that had taken place twenty years or so
before he was born. On this point, as on so many others,
Du Fail faithfully repeats the accounts of his informants.
Despite a style that is sometimes affected and flowery, and
an obvious desire to gloss over some of the more tragic aspects
of the peasant condition, which he depicts in somewhat
rosy colours, Du Fail gives us a pretty accurate picture
of country life. The details he mentions of sights still to be
seen in later centuries (houses built of daub and wattle,
the carters' drink-barrels "hooked over the lead horse's
collar") are proof of the sharpness of his observation.

All the more significant, therefore, is the long list of stories
in this ancient folklore, from the countryside around Rennes,
which are mentioned in the same breath as Mélusine. The
first two of these tales, both of which tell the story of the fox
and the fish, are not only intimately linked to a still lively

medieval culture, they also correspond to tales number 1 and 2 of Aarne and Thompson's classification of "folk tale types".[6] Hundreds and hundreds of versions of these two stories are found, right up to the twentieth century, as endlessly popular tales told throughout Europe, in every country from Gibraltar to Russia.[7] The other folktales recalled for us by Noël du Fail out of Robin Chevet's fireside repertory also form an integral part of the stock-in-trade of the oral culture of the *bocage* of western France as we know it today from documents, from literature and from the most recent anthropological research. We can therefore be certain that when he mentioned Mélusine, Du Fail was not simply echoing a literary tradition, he was reporting on the living folklore of his own times. A precursor in a theoretical tradition which, rightly or wrongly, was to be immensely popular later on, this Breton country squire did not merely provide evidence of the resilient fortune of the Mélusine myth, but also sought to explain her, along with Merlin, Oberon and "Pacolet's horse", as a folklore survival from pre-Christian tradition.[8]

A few years after the appearance of *Propos rustiques*, François Rabelais also speaks of the legend of Mélusine as being very much alive among the country folk of Poitou, in the very same place where Jean d'Arras had found her (quoted here in Urquhart's translation): "I would have you forthwith (I mean drinking first, that nothing be done rashly) visit Lusignan, Parthenay, Vouant, Mervant and Ponzauges in Poitou. There you will find a cloud of witnesses, not of your affidavit-men of the right stamp, but credible time out of mind, that will take their corporal oath on Rigomé's knuckle-bone,[9] that Melusina, their founder or foundress, which you please, was a woman from the head to the prick-purse and thence downwards was a serpentine Chitterling, or if you'll have it otherwise, a Chitterlingdized serpent. She nevertheless had a genteel and noble gait, imitated to this very day by your hopmerchants in Brittany, in their paspié and country dances."[10] And in 1532, the author of *Pantagruel*, when describing Epistemon's visit to the Under-world, depicted Mélusine there as a "kitchen drudge-wench"

("souillarde de cuisine"),[11] and her son Geoffrey-of-the-
Great-Tooth as a "tindermaker and seller of matches"
("allumetier").[12]

*

Noël du Fail's texts and the *Quart Livre* demonstrate the
persistence of the folklore associated with Mélusine, which
was evidently thoroughly rooted among the country people
of certain parts of Poitou and eastern Armorica. On the other
hand, they are much less helpful when it comes to examining
the content of these stories. A little more light is thrown
on the question, thirty years later, by the testimony of
Brantôme: the author of *Les Grands capitaines français* refers
to a visit by the Queen-mother, Catherine de Medicis, in
about 1575, to the Château de Lusignan (recently reduced to
ruins by Montpensier). Relating this episode, Brantôme
reminds the reader that Charles V, visiting Lusignan in the
winter of 1539–1540, "could not contain his raptures of
admiration and praise for the beauty and grandeur and archi-
tectural mastery of this mansion, built, what is more, by a lady
(Mélusine) about whom he heard recounted many fabulous
tales, tales which are commonly told in those parts, even by
the old women who wash their clothes at the fountain whom
the Queen-mother (Catherine de Medicis) also wished to
question and to hear". And Brantôme continues:[13] "Some
told her that they sometimes saw [Mélusine] coming to
bathe in the fountain in the form of a very beautiful woman,
dressed as a widow; others said they saw her, but only very
rarely, and this was on a Saturday at vespers (for in this state
she rarely allowed herself to be seen) bathing, half her body
that of a very beautiful lady and the other half a snake;
some said they saw her walking, fully clothed, with a bearing
of grave majesty; others that she would appear on the top
of her great tower, now as a very beautiful woman, now as a
serpent; others again that when some great disaster was
about to afflict the kingdom, or when there was to be a change
of reign, or the death or mishap of one of her kin (the greatest
of France and some of them kings), that three days before,
one would hear her cry out three times a high-pitched cry

and very dreadful: and this they held to be most true. Many were the people from those parts who had heard and swore to it, from father to son; and the same said, that at the time of the siege many soldiers and noblemen who were there swore to it; but most of all, when the order was given to destroy and ruin her castle, it was then that she uttered her loudest cries and shrieks; all this is most true by the word of honourable men. Since that time she has not been heard. A few old women, however, say that she has appeared, but only very rarely.

"For an end and for a true and final truth, she was in her time a very wise and virtuous dame, and married and widowed, and from her issued ... those brave and generous princes of Lusignan, who by their valour made themselves kings of Cyprus, and the first among them was Geoffrey-of-the-Great-Tooth who was to be seen represented on the doorway of the great tower, very great of stature."

A century later (1669), Claude Perrault gives us a dry, ironical account of the old tales he heard on the spot during a visit to Lusignan. He writes as follows on the subject of "Mélusine", of her "treasure pit", of her "château", and of "the fountain at which she was transformed": "After leaving (Poitiers) at three o'clock, at six we reached Lusignan, a little town perched on high rocks to which one climbs by a steep and narrow track. We were shown what is called Mélusine's castle, which seemed to be nothing but the walls of the town with a few towers. It was all very ancient and very ruined, built entirely of little stones, not of dressed quarry stone. A farrier's son, who heard his grandmother tell the story of Mélusine just as he told it to us, served as guide and interpreter to show us the antiquities of this celebrated place. But he could show us nothing, after promising us as we went along to show us the fountain where Mélusine used to bathe when she was transformed into Mélusine, and the pit[14] where one could hear the chink of all the gold and silver inside when one threw a stone down into it; the reason for this was that the pit had been transformed into a square hole lined with masonry, two and a half feet square and three feet deep. And the fountain had been converted into a little stretch of wall of about six feet square, at the base of which was a square hole less than six inches across, out of which, as we were supposed to believe, water had once gushed forth, but which was now completely dry. He wanted to take us to another fountain called *Cail-lerot*,[15] which cures all sorts of ailments and which is a presage of the year's fertility when it has water in abundance; but we did not dare to go for fear of making it disappear along with the other rarities, as this would have brought down a great misfortune upon the province which is not too fertile."

Claude Perrault's narrative which is as delightful as it is disappointing (for our purposes), leaves in the shadows some of the fundamental aspects of the Mélusine folklore which we know from other sources, notably from a learned memoir by Mazet (1804), to have been present in Poitevin culture in the seventeenth and eighteenth centuries:[16] "Of all the memorable items in our province of Poitou," writes Dom Mazet, "there has been scarcely anything more celebrated than the heroine of a romance, to whom was given the name of Mellusine. The multitude of great exploits attributed to her, and with which the author of the romance has adorned her history, has long served to feed the ignorant credulity of the country folk. If we are to believe them, it is thanks to Mellusine that the town of Saintes was restored from its ruins in days gone by; that the town of La Rochelle was built; and that the châteaux of Lusignan, Pons, Issoudun and several others were founded. All the remains of the monuments which used at one time to exist in Poitou, the amphitheatre of Poitiers, the aqueducts of the Romans, the ancient military roads and the walls of the city, are regarded in Poitou as the works of her hand, and are not known by the ordinary people under any other name than that of Mellusine. The author of this romance is thought to be a certain Jean d'Arras, who lived towards the end of the fourteenth century." (Dom Mazet then lists other writers, French and foreign, who have written about Melusine.) "From all the different writings of these authors, it has come about that Mellusine is heaped with praises by some, and seen as a lady full of wisdom and virtue; while by others she has been depicted as a lewd woman and as a sorceress well-versed in what used to be called the black arts . . . .

They showed her transformed into a creature of fantasy with the body of a monster, half-woman, half-serpent. This is the notion that popular tradition still has of her today. According to the chronicler's fable, it was on a Saturday that Mellusine performed her feats of magic ... [she is said to have given birth to] monstrous, misshapen offspring, such as, among others, Geoffrey-of-the-Great-Tooth, offspring who became so many heroes of the house of Lezignem (sic). This belief was founded upon the notion that their origin had bestowed upon them a nature halfway between that of the angels and of men, which was the reason why all the lords of that house were so sturdy, so brave and so mighty.

"According to the author of the romance, Mellusine took as her first husband Raimondin, Count of Poitiers. ..." (Here follows a summary by Dom Mazet of the Jean d'Arras romance, a summary influenced in greater or lesser degree by folklorist or clerical considerations, ending with the final episode telling of the disappearance of the serpent.) "Since that disappearance, according to the popular tradition, Mellusine has returned on several occasions to Lusignan and has often been heard uttering three dreadful shrieks; this has occurred chiefly when noblemen of the house of Lezignem, or one of the kings of France, were in mortal danger. It was claimed that she uttered such cries a few days before the deaths of Henry IV and Louis XIII. In order to perpetuate the memory of these occurrences, M. Robert, the President and Lieutenant-General of Basse-Marche, set down in writing the account given to him at the time by the officers of the town of Lusignan themselves and by the principal inhabitants of the place. Not content with ascribing a real existence to this chimaera and believing that Mellusine existed just as she was depicted, fathers and mothers to this day continue to perpetuate her memory and so-called reality by a host of ridiculous tales that they tell their children and anyone else who cares to listen to them."

These "ridiculous tales" are, as we know, none other than the popular versions of the myth; we only wish that some Poitevin anthropologist of a bygone age had preserved a few versions taken from the original source, that is from the lips of a story-teller. It is possible that there is one example of such a chance preservation. Biaille-Germont,[17] a *notable* of the Vendée, did, it appears, in the first half of the nineteenth century, set down one of the tales current in the countryside about the adventures of Mélusine and her son, the disagreeable Geoffrey-of-the-Great-Tooth: this dialect tale (reproduced below) may *possibly* be considered to represent one of the forms of the myth as it continued to live on among the people of the countryside—and as it was later embellished in the Classical Age by the addition of new elements including, most prominently, the introduction of new plants from America! But we must be quite clear that this particular text, if indeed it is authentic, belongs strictly speaking more to the Geoffrey-of-the-Great-Tooth cycle than to the woman-serpent cycle.

"Py-Chabot the one-eyed,[18] Big-Tooth's[19] evil spirit," (writes Fillon, who claims to be reproducing Biaille-Germont's account) "stole away the daughter of one-armed Thibault, an old man who had lost his right arm in the war, and was thus incapable of avenging such an affront. In his distress, the luckless father implored the help of the king, who was at the time engaged in thrashing the English in the neighbourhood. The king, Saint Louis (Louis IX),[20] rushed to his aid without delay, but One-eye found shelter with his victim in the castle of Fontenay. Straight away it was besieged with such vigour that the one-armed knight, at the head of a thousand stout companions, penetrated the fortress on the third day. Already shouts of victory were ringing out, already the door of the keep was yielding before the blows of the assailants, when before their astonished eyes, Mélusine rose up into the air seated astride a broomstick, carrying off with her her terrible son, and Py-Chabot, and his captive, and the 799 gallows-birds who had been defending the castle, and a huge black tom-cat, who was busy eating a sparrow that had ventured too close to his claws.

"As quick as lightning, the broomstick flew over hills, woods and ravines, before setting down its load on the Mound of Vouvent. Mélusine quickly filled her muslin apron with a pile of stones and down below, twisting and turning her hand, she built *"la grosse tour pour y caller sans bourder, tot le drigail qu'a traînait dare lé"* ("a great tower to take without delay the whole band she had in train behind her").[21] Hardly had the door closed on the last ruffian with the cat at his heels, than the king was seen riding up at full gallop. Better informed this time of the kind of foe he was to engage in battle, he signalled his army to halt. Followed by a single monk with his bowl of holy water, he advanced to within throwing distance, seized the sprinkler and with his mighty arm hurled such a quantity of holy water that it fell as a deluge of rain upon the tower which straight away crumbled, leaving at his mercy men and all, arms and baggage, including the demon tom-cat. As for the witch, for fear of being scalded by the holy water, she struck the ground with her heel; and it opened up. She vanished into the earth and came up, thirteen leagues away, at the Fumerie de Jazeneuil,[22] right under the chair of an old cross-patch called Catûche who was dozing off as she sat riddling beans under the nose of her neighbour Michâ. The old woman had such a shock that she was sent flying up over the moon before she landed back at her crony's side. And as she flew, she let slip from her hand, into a ploughed field, four beans which ever afterwards gave food to this district, where before there only grew the Saintonge vetch and Limousin chick-peas, that are eaten by half-starved hogs and the people of Bourneau.

"One-eye was hanged on the oak-tree of the Grand' Rhée as though he were Jacques Bonhommet, the miller of Pilorge; the black cat was burnt alive in front of the church of Vouvent; the 799 ruffians were served up to the crows; and Big-Tooth, protected by his rank as cousin of the king, set off dressed in a monk's habit, for Jerusalem, there to ask pardon of God for his misdeeds.

"The beautiful girl who had been the cause of so much trouble and conflict ... the following day wed Gilles Mussaprès, the handsomest young man in all Poitou.

"Since this adventure, Mélusine no longer haunts her old domains; and deprived of their fabled mistress, Mervent, Vouvent and Lusignan have fallen into decay."

There are in the end though only a handful of "contemporary" texts like this, which acquaint us, through the folklore of the *ancien régime*, with the Mélusine whom the people of Poitou, Vendée and eastern Brittany knew through their oral and popular culture.[23] Fortunately for our purpose, the rather meagre material we have so far can be illuminated, if not exactly completed, by means of some comparisons and confirmatory evidence from the province of Dauphiné.

For here, far away from Poitou, there was already well-established in the seventeenth century, a little "Mélusian" enclave, centred around the estates of the Sassenage family and the caves of the same name near Grenoble. In this connection it matters very little whether the claims of the Sassenage family to be descended from the house of Lusignan are true or not. What matters is that these claims, although scornfully dismissed on more than one occasion,[24] served as a useful pretext for the effective establishment of a Mélusine in the Northern Alps. The Poitevin name and fairy legend may have been grafted on to some obscure local serpent, hitherto anonymous.[25]

In any case, the folk-lore attaching to Mélusine in this mountainous area of south-eastern France is very similar to that described by Brantôme and Perrault in Poitou between 1570 and 1670. This similarity may well be explained by some direct link, the principal merit of which is that it conveniently underlines certain fundamental elements of the original myth. On this subject, the Dauphinois historian Chorier[26] writing in 1669, has this to say: "Very few great families when they trace back their origins do not come across some fable or other: the house of Sassenage finds Mélusine. This fable made such a great impression on the credulity of the Inhabitants of the Sassenage domains that they were persuaded that their Lord was of the blood of Mélusine and that she ended her days in that place.

"They will show you a spacious cavern in the midst of a great rock where a rushing spring of water falls and forms a stream that flows through the middle of the village. You will see two wells formed by nature close by this cavern. They say that these wells foretell the fertility or sterility of each year, according to whether they are full or less full of water on the eve of the Feast of the Kings ... They will show you the place where Mélusine was wont to take the air and to bathe, and a little further on the table where she ate, which they call Mélusine's table. The fountain of the Chasteau de Montelliez in Valentinois, which is one of the estates of that House (of Sassenage), bears the name of Mélusine: she is thought to have been seen there from time to time. There also you may see, in the thickness of the wall of the Château, adjoining the moat, a round opening piercing it from top to bottom, whose purpose no one knows. This too they call Mélusine's Hole, through which, they say, she passed her long serpent's tail whenever she wished to be seen. . . . They add that three days before the death of the head of the family (of Sassenage), or of one of his children, the lugubrious cries of Mélusine often gave warning of it; and that at such times she was seen in the form of a great lady pacing slowly to and fro."

To this day, in Sassenage, one can see in the cave of the same name, near the entrance, the two so-called Wells of Mélusine. As early as 1656, according to the local writer Salvaing de Boissieu,[27] the fairy had obligingly taken it upon herself to describe the properties to be found in her cavern for prophesying the harvest: "Here is the cave," she is said to have cried, "that I choose for my retreat," (in this Dauphinois version of her legend she was supposed to have retired to the Alps after her break with Raimondin) "and so that I may not appear ungrateful to the peoples who dwell in this country, I ordain that these wells, in which I shall bathe from this time forth, shall possess the gift of foretelling the fertility of the years, and with such certainty, that the nations shall know the truth of it. Once a year, on the same day that I first arrived in the mountains of Sassenage, these two wells will suddenly pour forth water in abundance. This well will announce the fertility of the grain harvest; and the other the wine-harvest. . . .

"It shall also come to pass one day that some of my descendants, issuing from Lusignan, will become lords of Sassenage: they will be great Warriors and they will perform many brave deeds. Finally when any one of my House is about to die, I shall announce his cruel destiny with loud cries and groans."

★

These references, fragmentary as they are, enable us to discover how certain aspects of the legend of Mélusine—

sometimes transposed or differently slanted—persisted during the modern era, in the form of tales passed on by word of mouth. From this point of view, what we shall have to say chiefly concerns the period 1570–1670, when the texts are not quite so few and far between, and where the regressive methods of later scholarship provide some help. And geographically, it concentrates on those crucial regions where the myth survived, took root and persisted, that is in the first place Poitou, and secondarily the Dauphiné.

1. The first thing to note is a very great simplification in comparison with the complicated and extremely detailed story that Jean d'Arras and Couldrette had told at the end of the Middle Ages. No doubt this simplification is partly due to the casual approach of writers such as Brantôme, Perrault and Dom Mazet, who merely recount the "popular tradition" by way of brief and sometimes scornful allusions and references. But there is no reason to doubt that the oral versions of the legend current in the modern period were in fact more simplified than were the literary versions of the legend in its heyday, in the fourteenth and fifteenth centuries.

2. Despite this inevitable lack of sophistication, we can discern, from the little we know of the oral versions, a remarkable degree of fidelity to certain fundamental themes already present in the great medieval texts. In the first place, of course, whether in Poitou or in the Dauphiné, throughout her whole career Mélusine remains a serpent, or at least a demi-serpent, and the sight of her in this shape constitutes a taboo which is hard to escape. She remains equally faithful to her constant vocation as the familiar of springs and fountains. Again, the "faery cries" prophesying catastrophes for the seigniorial or royal household she was supposed to protect, are just as piercing under Louis XIII as they were under Charles VI. In times of misfortune or crisis, Mélusine, faithful to her charge, starts up her inevitable clamour.

3. However, it is undeniable that oral tradition, or perhaps the development of this tradition, imposed certain rearrangements, certain shifts of emphasis at the very heart of the myth; though the fundamental design remained the same, as far as we can tell, throughout all its successive new forms. Let us consider the first of these changes: the theme of

demographic and dynastic fertility which is central to all the medieval versions from the twelfth to the fifteenth century, seems to have lost some of its force in the version of the legend known to the peasants of Poitou and elsewhere in the modern period. According to Jean d'Arras, Mélusine conformed to the ideal of high matrimonial fertility, already a feature of the nameless snake-women of the thirteenth century. With eight children born to her in eleven years,[28] she exceeded the fertility of the women of the region around Beauvais in the seventeenth century; she was almost the equal in fertility of the women of Brittany during the *ancien régime*.[29] At all events, she fulfilled the requirements of Goubert's standard "complete family" (ten or so children) born at brief intervals, briefer than normal in her case, since as was befitting for a rich lady, Mélusine put out her children to nurse and enjoyed the "above-average birth-rate of the upper classes".[30] This prominent medieval theme, emphasizing abundance of progeny, appears slightly attenuated in the "modern" versions of the myth. Of course, Mélusine is still a mother, the foundress of glorious lineages (the Lusignans, the Sassenages); or of extremely disagreeable individuals (Geoffrey-of-the-Great-Tooth). But her successive, closely-spaced confinements as such, no longer seem to interest her narrators as much as they used to.

On the other hand, two other attributes, not altogether unrelated to fecundity, but nevertheless distinct from its strictly maternal aspects, continue to be greatly emphasized, at times more so, in the "modern" versions of the traditional tale, than during the Middle Ages. Firstly, her role as builder, which is insisted upon by all those writers of the past who have concerned themselve with the unwritten lore relating to the Mélusine of Poitou: we find it in Rabelais (his brief allusion to the "foundress"); in Brantôme and Yver (lengthy descriptions); in Mazet; and it is also referred to by the nineteenth-century anthropologists who were regaled with many items of information on this topic by the peasants of Poitou.[31]

Secondly, the role played by Mélusine in agricultural fertility—which frequently goes unremarked in recent descriptions of her career—in fact received great emphasis in the oral culture of the seventeenth century. The Middle Ages *written* versions had touched only slightly on it, or referred only indirectly to it as an implicit corollary of the fairy's activities in clearing and cultivating the soil.[32] At any rate, in about 1400—in the literary versions of her legend—there are no references to Mélusine either as tutelary guardian of the harvests or as dispenser of new plants.

Yet the role of rural Lady Bountiful subsequently assigned to the Dame de Lusignan is clearly attested in the seventeenth century, both in Poitou and in Dauphiné, by several different authors who are not copying one another but genuinely reporting what local people told them.[33] In the cave of Sassenage, Mélusine dwelled in a fountain, and on the eve of Epiphany the level of water in the fountain clearly foretold the volume of the grain and the wine harvests. At Lusignan the fairy did not herself prophesy the harvest, but took up residence in the immediate vicinity of a spring called *Caillerot*, exactly similar in function to the fountain of Sassenage. This spring was part of the tourist itinerary for visitors in search of Mélusine. And, to take another instance, was the Poitevin fairy really believed by the people of her own province to be the original donor of the *mojette*[34] or haricot bean (which in fact, came from America in the sixteenth century and spread to western and southern France at the start of the seventeenth century)? That has yet to be established. If we can trust Fillon on this point, it looks as if the peasants of Poitou interpreted this "gift" of the haricot bean from Mélusine as a decisive factor in the improvement of their standard of living—the medieval pulses, Saintonge vetch *(gesse)* and Limousin chickpeas, were from now on eaten only by the pigs or by the inhabitants of the poorer villages. Consequently, well on into the seventeenth century, Mélusine could be regarded by the country people as having played her part in certain agricultural innovations.

On the whole, then, if we try to assess the development of the legend as it changes over time, we find that whereas the theme of the fairy as builder still prevails, her role as fertility symbol has undergone a certain readjustment—rather less emphasis is placed on the maternal aspects and rather more on the agricultural, than in the past.

Does this shift of emphasis truly reflect the evolution of the myth as it comes down from the Middle Ages to modern times? Or rather—and this seems more likely—is it simply the case that the evidence now comes from a "lower" social stratum? The prime purpose of the medieval texts had been to justify the genealogical claims of members of the nobility, who were anxious to establish totem ancestors, whereas modern versions of the Mélusine legend were gathered at grass roots level by authors whose concern was for the picturesque, and who noted down for this purpose the sayings of the washerwomen of Lusignan or the tenant-farmers of Sassenage. At this "lower" level, the informants, except in special cases,[35] seem to be quite naturally more anxious about the wine or the grain yields (and perhaps the bean harvest) than about the progenitive prowess of noble lineages.

Whatever the truth about this career in agriculture—Mélusine down on the farm, so to speak—one last point remains to be made: the progressive diabolization of the myth, in Poitou at least, especially after 1660–1670, under the influence, probably, of the Counter-Reformation, in its later stages. In Jean d'Arras's story, Mélusine was truly devout in her behaviour.[36] In between two spells of magic she did not hesitate to call upon the bishop to bless her bed. In Brantôme's time, the fairy, though religiously neutral, is spoken of as "a wise and virtuous lady", kind and charitable. But in the Classical Age, at the time when the stern preachers and priests coming from the seminaries were increasingly persecuting village superstitions, a distinct whiff of the stake is attached to the snake-woman. She is suspected of pacts with Satan and at the very least of dabbling in black magic. After all, Lusignan, where in about 1620 devils breathing fire were seen and remarked upon,[37] is not so very far from Loudun.[38] This diabolization of Mélusine is already clearly evident in Dom Mazet's text.[39]

The medieval and modern data on the subject of Mélusine —drawn mainly from Poitou but also from Dauphiné—as presented in this article, ought properly to be completed by an excursion to the east (Germany, Luxemburg, Alsace) going beyond the former frontiers of France. But the Germanic Mélusine (whose name, almost certainly borrowed,

conceals some being original to this region) raises problems
too complex for discussion within the short space of this
article. The myths concerning her tell a story in many
particulars the very opposite of the Poitou legend. The latter
was built around the general theme of a conjunction (the
meeting of Raimondin and Mélusine) followed by the
breaking of a contract or the violation of a taboo; and ending
with a disjunction (the final separation of Raimondin from
Mélusine). But in the Baden area version the story is quite
the opposite.[40] It begins with Sebald, the lover of bird
songs, breaking violently away from the embrace, now
become odious to him, of a very beautiful maiden
("Mélusine"). She had originally seduced him by her
beauty, but then, to the young man's horror, she changed,
while in his arms, first into a snake-woman, and then into a
harpy. Finally, to punish Sebald for abandoning her in
favour of another woman, Mélusine poisons the hero in the
course of a second meeting, one which this time is fatal.
The structure of this west German myth is thus quite
obviously very different from that of the Poitevin legend.
The latter has the sequence: conjunction—taboo violated—
disjunction. The former, on the contrary, has the events run
strictly in reverse: disjunction—broken contract—fatal conjunction. From the very fact of this disparity, certain crucial
episodes are constructed, in the respective versions, in radically opposite ways: in the Baden myth, at the moment of
the final conjunction, Mélusine in her serpent guise, glides
through a ceiling, drops down upon Sebald and poisons him
with her venom. In the Poitevin tale, however, Mélusine
takes her leave of Raimondin by flying away through a
window and vanishing into thin air in the form of a serpent.
The order of events and the dynamic thrust of the action thus
seem to be reversed in the two versions.[41]

*

But a study of the possible inversion of these sequences is
not the immediate object of this article. In essence, my
purpose has been to offer a diachronic analysis centred upon
the Mélusine of Poitou, together with the earlier and the

later versions of this legend in other French-speaking provinces. This legend, which Jean d'Arras told in his time, is interesting to historians because it offers the spectacle and chronology of an almost complete cycle: medieval folklore, followed by the literary elaboration of the tale on the eve of the Renaissance and finally the modern rural version (or perhaps we should say the restoration of the rural version) whose various phases we can follow through the comments of writers and scholars, the persecutions of priests and lastly the conscientious studies of nineteenth-century anthropologists. The unique nature of this story and its development diminishes neither its interest nor its influence, for the good lady of Lusignan is certainly not the only one of her kind. Mélusine was one of the more successful serpents. Like the fertile and constructive woman she was, she intelligently linked herself to the destiny of a noble line; then, when this family fell upon bad times, she was wise enough to adapt, and associate herself with other families and other mythical events. Always a generous donor of cultural goods, she devoted herself, in modest fashion, to the promotion of agriculture—and this, perhaps, was why, in the seventeenth century, she was associated with the introduction of new plants. Cultivating her public "image", negative or positive, she next served as a foil to clerical propaganda, the enemy of superstitious practices— and as a favourite subject of post-1800 anthropological studies. But for one Mélusine who thus proved capable, in a variety of ways, of making herself known, loved, appreciated or feared, how many nameless snake-women have glided undistinguished through the centuries in the company of the noble families under their protection, only to pass into extinction when the family died out? On occasion a chance document or research project brings to light one or other of these reptiles, which then gains a brief notoriety from the very fact of its extinction. One such example concerns a great peasant dynasty, the Jault clan, who lived as an extended family in the Nivernais from some indeterminate date before 1580 until their final dispersion in the 1840s. In 1847, if we are to credit tradition, precisely when the head of the family or "master of the household" had to make a decision upon the dissolution of the family community, the snake which had always watched over the family fortunes crawled out into view before the members of the assembled fraternity. Before pronouncing a final decision, the master therefore decided to wait for a sign from the little creature. This came in no uncertain fashion: it died. Its death immediately gave the signal for the dissolution of the ancient confraternity.[42] The humble snake of the Jault family certainly shared none of the fame of its illustrious counterpart of Lusignan. But in a way, and more perhaps even than Mélusine, it had carried out its serpentine calling to the very end: it had watched over the economic and demographic fortunes of the family and its own death was evidence that the line had disintegrated.

PART THREE

PRESSURE OF NUMBERS: MEDICAL EVIDENCE, CHANGING ATTITUDES AND HISTORICAL DEMOGRAPHY

12

From Waterloo to Colyton[1]

FROM Rocroi to Crulai; from Waterloo to Colyton—these four place-names could be said to sum up the course taken over the past hundred and fifty years by a certain school of history, from the resounding, action-packed historiography of the nineteenth century, *battle-history*, to the silent, mathematical resurrection of a total past represented today in *historical demography*. Crulai and Colyton, obscure little villages in Normandy and Devon, certainly have none of the echoing notoriety of the victories (or defeats) of Rocroi and Waterloo, nor have the learned works inspired by these tiny peasant communities appeared in massive editions or provided scenarios for films based on best-sellers like *The Longest Day* or *Is Paris Burning?*. And yet it is thanks to these villages and to a few others, thanks to the parish registers of Crulai, Colyton, Auneuil, Saint-Lambert-des-Levées, Sainghin-en-Mélantois, etc., and thanks also to genealogical studies in Geneva and Canada, that the decisive techniques of family reconstitution were first developed and then tested, by Louis Henry and the *Institut national d'études démographiques*, by Pierre Goubert, and by their followers. Without flourish of trumpets, these techniques have shed new light on past societies, especially on those of the seventeenth and eighteenth centuries.

Within the short space of an article, it is impossible to describe in detail the quantitative and sophisticated methods whose successful conclusion has been the complete reconstitution of hundreds and thousands of families who lived and died in the seventeenth and eighteenth centuries. For that, one should refer to the specialized works of Louis Henry *(Nouveau manuel de dépouillement de l'état civil ancien)*, and of E.A. Wrigley (Laslett, Eversley, Armstrong, Wrigley, *et al.*, *An Introduction to English Historical Demography*). What studies of this kind have effectively brought to light is the entire demographic system as it has functioned for centuries in the traditional societies of western Europe. The system, or rather, the systems have varied with the different regions, cultures and nationalities, but all have three basic components, fertility, nuptiality, mortality: in other words, births, marriages and deaths.

*

First, fertility: on this subject, the detailed statistical demonstrations of Louis Henry *(Crulai; Familles genevoises)* and of Pierre Goubert *(Beauvaisis)* seem to be beyond argument; in the age of Louis XIV (and in most regions of France) there were whole rural provinces almost completely ignorant of voluntary birth control. In these areas, the only check on fertility after a confinement was breast-feeding, a stage that might last on average a whole year, during which the young mother would be temporarily sterile. Under such conditions, most couples of child-bearing age produced a child every two years or every thirty months: biennial confinement was the regular pattern. Another fact emerges: in certain social milieux of seventeenth-century France in which babies were put out to nurse, even this form of birth control, the result of the mother breast-feeding her youngest child, did not exist; fertility went unchecked and consequently instead of having seven or eight children, couples produced ten or even fifteen.

Such are the *ancien régime* patterns of fertility and they hold good as a general rule for the country districts of France, for Canada (J. Henripin, *La Population canadienne au début du XVIIIe siècle*), and for Spain, according to B. Bennassar *(Valladolid au XVIe siècle)*. But there are some major exceptions to this general rule, and it is at this point that things become interesting for the social historian.

Geographical "exceptions" first of all. We know that in the nineteenth and twentieth centuries the south-western regions of France were among the most "Malthusian" in the world and we have long suspected that this state of affairs must have had its origins in quite early times. A recent book by Pierre Valmary *(Familles paysannes au XVIIIe siècle en Bas-Quercy)* seems to confirm this impression:

as long ago as the days of Louis XIV and Louis XV, the natives of Quercy in south-west France, although they were good Catholics, and indeed illiterate and backward, were secretly practising birth control; if we are to believe Valmary, their birth-rate was one of the lowest in the country.

Then there is another "exception", so large that it falls into a special category, different in some respects from the Spanish and the French. This is—England, no less. In Colyton, a village studied in depth by E.A. Wrigley (see *Economic History Review*, 1966), between 1650 and 1850, the villagers abandoned the lusty fertility of their Elizabethan ancestors and went in for a primitive but effective form of birth control; according to Wrigley this was the practice of *coitus interruptus* (known ever since the Bible as the crime of Onan). Thus the Colytonians of the Restoration, fathering their small families, appear quite clearly as the pioneers of contraception in Britain, an institution destined to have a great future. It remains to be seen whether, in the case of the seventeenth century, we have the right to argue from the particular example of Colyton to patterns of fertility in Britain as a whole at the time. Wrigley does not, of course, allow himself so audacious an inference. But it is reasonable to suppose, as he does, that many English villagers behaved in the same way as their Colyton contemporaries.

Let us turn from the geographical "exceptions" to the social. In France, from the time of Louis XIV onwards, the pattern of unrestricted fertility, which remained characteristic of the lower orders, was, on the contrary, abandoned by the ruling classes who deliberately chose to have smaller families of what we would call the modern type. The dukes and peers of France, the burghers of Geneva of the time of Louis XIV, and then, a little later, the Huguenot notables of Montauban, were among those who enthusiastically participated in this early propagation—secret but extensive—of contraceptive practice. On this point, Louis Henry *(Familles genevoises)*, André Armengaud and Marcel Reinhard *(Histoire générale de la population* and *Démographie et Sociétés)*, have provided convincing examples.

And then, at the end of the eighteenth century and from the first half of the nineteenth, came the spread, which soon turned into a torrent, of birth control techniques, described as the "sinful secrets" *(les funestes secrets)* and henceforth practised by peasants and artisans alike. Thanks to the published works of Hélène Bergues (Cf. *La Prévention des naissances dans la famille*), and to the studies of Ganiage *(Trois villages de l'Île de France)* and of Daniel and Henry *(Sainghin-en-Mélantois)*, we have some very sound data on this subject. In France, contraceptive practice began to spread to the general public from 1770 onwards (at the very moment when, paradoxically, the birth-rate in England was rising!) The practice became even more frequent after 1790–1800, following the upheaval of the Revolution; it was widespread and at the same time precocious, being fifty, sixty or even a hundred years ahead of the other continental European countries.

Why was France so much ahead of its time, so original in this respect? If historical demography is to attempt an answer to this question, it must broaden its normal field of enquiry and extend in particular towards cultural anthropology and the sociology of religion. That, at any rate, is what the pioneering works of Etienne Hélin and Hélène Bergues *(La Prévention des naissances ...)* suggest.

For in the Classical Age, contraception was first and foremost a matter of theology. Up to the time of the Second Vatican Council, the Catholic Church took its stand on Genesis, Chapter 38, (the crime of Onan), and by tradition was hostile to methods of contraception. Since 1600, and since Thomas Sanchez and St. François de Sales, theologians have been unanimous in condemning *coitus interruptus*. Admittedly there were divisions of opinion on the subject; the "hawks", the Jansenists, saw it as sin for both husband and wife; the "doves", the Jesuits, on the other hand, laid the whole blame on the husband and absolved the wife, who could remain in the bosom of the Church and continue to receive the sacraments. But for all that, both sides pronounced the act itself a sin.

It must not be thought that such condemnation was mere verbal prohibition. Hélène Bergues quotes several pertinent texts, as, for example, Fr. Féline's *Catéchisme des jeunes mariés* (1782), which points to serious conflicts of opinion

between the faithful and their confessors in connection with
the "act of Onan". And a rather extraordinary letter sent
by Bishop Bouvier to the Grand Penitentiary of the Vatican
describes the Catholics of the diocese of Le Mans in about
1840 "shunning the mass and the sacraments" to avoid
being admonished by their confessors who wanted to prohibit
their use of contraception. In the nineteenth century, birth
control was a continuous source of conflict between priests
and married couples, a conflict all the more bitter for being
generally kept secret.

And so we come to a first explanation of French "pre-
cocity". We know that the Revolution gave a powerful
impetus, if not to complete dechristianization at least to
religious indifference, which spread during the nineteenth
century to large sections of the French people. Quite possibly
it was this move away from the Catholic Church that was
one reason, among many others, for the particularly rapid
spread of birth control practices in post-Revolutionary
France. And, maybe, vice-versa as well. When all is said
and done, historical demography and the history of contraception will have to go beyond the sociology of religion and
seek the aid of depth psychology. As far as I know, we have
no evidence from any doctor or psychiatrist of the medical
or psychological consequences of the spread of birth control
practices in eighteenth and nineteenth century France. But,
as it happens, we do have vital evidence of this kind, about
similar phenomena in Austria. In the years 1885–1900, when
the middle classes in Vienna were beginning to adopt contraceptive practice on a wide scale, a young doctor of the town,
Sigmund Freud, observed symptoms of anxiety and even
of nervous disorder in his patients which he related explicitly
to the new conjugal practices (cf. *Letters to Wilhelm Fliess*).
The young Freud's writings on these problems are open to
discussion as regards their scientific interpretation of the
facts observed. But for the historian of sociology and psychology at all events, they contain extremely valuable medical
evidence. Here is an instance when that longed-for collaboration in the social sciences, between history and psycho-
analysis, could become a reality.

Historical demography then has the merit of providing

us with guide-lines that can take us very far along the road of social history. We can see this clearly in connection with fertility. The same is true of another of the basic themes in population studies—marriage rates.

The central role of marriage in traditional societies has been given much prominence by anthropologists. But demographic historians, too, have proposed a *philosophy of marriage*, though from a somewhat different point of view. Here I shall confine myself to two questions, connected as it happens: first, the age of marriage, and second, the significance of marriage in the life of the individual (in the seventeenth and eighteenth centuries).

The age of marriage: demographic historians have put paid to the myth of early marriage (at 15 or 16 years of age), a myth put out incidentally by excellent scholars working on the seventeenth and eighteenth centuries, but drawing on individual cases and on a few literary and non-statistical sources. In fact, our seventeenth-century ancestors, at least among the ordinary people, often married rather late: the girls at 24 or 25, the men at 26 or 28. On this point one need only mention, apart from the authors already referred to (Henry, Goubert, etc.), the statistical proofs of Peter Laslett (*The World We Have Lost*), of Gouhier (*Port-en-Bessin*), of Godechot and Moncassin (*Démographie et subsistances en Languedoc*).

Now to the second point: the significance of marriage in the life of the individual. This raises the whole question—of little relevance at first sight—of pre-marital conception; (and also of "extra-marital" conception, in other words, illegitimate births).

Pre-marital conception is of course assumed to have taken place when a couple have their first child before they have been married for eight months. An occurrence of this nature, common enough in present-day society, where it is looked on with indulgence, takes on an unexpected importance for the demographic historian. Set out in the form of statistics, pre-marital conceptions provide us with a quantitative history of social mores, and all the authors previously quoted, Goubert, Gautier and Henry, Ganiage, Wrigley and Laslett, allow them an important place in their statistical tables. From these deviations we can learn how far young people and engaged couples respected the commandments of the Church and the sexual taboos that went with them.

In France, in the majority of *rural* areas (except for the Ile-de-France and certain villages in the north, and also suburban villages like Sotteville, close to the freer morals of the big towns[2]), these phenomena are statistically insignificant; taken together, pre-marital conceptions and illegitimate births account for only a small percentage of all known births. From this we must therefore conclude as does Henry in *Crulai*, basing his conjecture on an impeccable set of arguments, that the French peasantry of the seventeenth and eighteenth centuries were abstemious in their private lives and held the moral teaching of the Catholic Church and the commandments of their priests in the highest respect. In seventeenth-century England, however, according to Wrigley and the village monographs quoted by Peter Laslett, rural morals, though still rather strict, were much more free than in France. Bold fiancés, or gallants such as Pepys and Boswell, took many a liberty with the virtue of young girls. Illegitimate and pre-maritally conceived children make up quite a high percentage of births in the parish registers kept by the priests of the Anglican Church. (But would the result be the same if one were to analyse the records of the nonconformist sects whose ways were more austere?)

Be that as it may, the customs of the two countries, England and France, seem to be somewhat different from the picture that is sometimes painted of them. It is tempting to think of seventeenth-century France as flirtatious and frivolous, libertine even, and of England in the same period as austere and puritanical. But the true picture, as far as the rural masses were concerned, was the exact opposite of this popular image; strictly speaking, it was France that was austere and England that was libertine.

The sometimes unexpected conclusions of this kind to be found in historical demography add fresh importance to the old sociological problem posed by Max Weber at the start of the century and present it in a completely new light— the problem of austerity, of asceticism in traditional society.

Max Weber gave us a masterly description of the ascetic type such as was to be found in seventeenth- and eighteenth-century society among the Puritans and the Methodists, the Huguenots, the Pietists, and also, if we take into account a few minor differences, among the Jansenists of the *grand siècle* and the Enlightenment. But Max Weber went beyond mere description. It was his considered opinion that the ascetic personality was the direct antecedent of the rise of capitalism. Recently, Herbert Luthy's little book *Le Passé présent* has brilliantly argued against Weber's theory; he proposes a more convincing sociology of triumphant Protestantism and nascent capitalism.

But historical demography makes things clearer still. In the perspectives opened up by this discipline, the ascetic personality within a traditional society no longer appears as the guarantee of a capitalist *future*, but simply as the response to the exigencies of a social *present*. For these austere young people who married late and remained chaste until marriage, regardless of the exigencies of nature, derived their attitude from a coherent system of cultural values and justifications.

To take socio-demographic justifications first, by marrying late and remaining chaste they limited the number of their children and they were practising that elementary form of birth control based on virtue which, according to Cantillon and Malthus, forms the basic condition of social happiness. To take an example, in a society in which contraception was not practised and biennial confinement was the norm, a young woman who married as a virgin at the age of twenty-five would have, on average, in the whole of her maternal career, two or three children fewer than if she had been married seven years earlier at the age of eighteen.

As regards ethical and religious justifications, these derived quite naturally from the ideologies of austerity, from Calvinism or Jansenism which flourished in western Europe from the sixteenth to the eighteenth century. Pierre Goubert has demonstrated this clearly: the countryside around Beauvais, where there were no illegitimate children and none conceived before marriage, a region of austerity then in the age of Louis XIV and more particularly in that of Louis XV, was a predominantly Jansenist area.

In the Huguenot Cevennes, towards the end of the seventeenth century, the correlations seem to have been even closer (I have tried to show this in my book *The Peasants of Languedoc*). These correlations combine, within a coordinated whole, demographic structures (based particularly on long and strict pre-marital chastity), basic personality traits (formed from early childhood by the austerity of both family and religious community life), and finally the psychology of deeply-rooted emotions (characterized by extremely marked hysterical tendencies). In this instance of Huguenot Languedoc in past centuries (where research is favoured by the wealth of documents) knowledge of the demography of the region has made it possible to move towards total history.

After fertility and marital (or extra-marital) patterns, comes the third panel in the triptych, mortality. Historical demography is among other things a meditation upon death.

The Malthusian approach was the one originally adopted, whether explicitly or not, by historians of death. In this perspective, demographic history is thought of (when applied to a society of the old type based on scarcity) as describing a dramatic confrontation between a population tending to increase and a static food supply.

In such conditions, every twenty or thirty years, population and production have their reckoning: the *subsistence crisis*, the rationale of which has been demonstrated by Ernest Labrousse (*La crise de l'économie française*) and Jean Meuvret (in *Population*, 1946). Its pattern, repeatedly confirmed, goes as follows: after a poor cereal harvest the price of grain rises sharply; immediately poor people begin to die, of hunger or of deficiency diseases; the annual number of burials doubles or trebles; the survivors, afflicted by famine or unemployment, put off their marriages until later, or if already married they avoid or desist from having children. There are more graves and fewer cradles. This is what happened in France in 1661, 1694, 1709, etc.

In this whole process, the scarcity and high cost of grain plays the principal role: the incidence of death depends upon the price of corn, "*La population est fille de la mercuriale*" (Goubert)[3].

This theory of the *subsistence crisis*, which is both logical and soundly constructed, has rendered great service to historians. It constitutes a serviceable conceptual tool, and a diagnostic pattern of social change (E. Labrousse). It was, in fact, the disappearance of crises of this kind, in about 1750, that marked in France the start of the economic *take-off*, the beginnings of modernization, the first steps in the decline of traditional, "feudal" society.

But man does not die from lack of bread alone. Demographic historians are becoming increasingly interested in the crises of high mortality resulting solely from epidemics, in which the cost of bread plays no part at all. In connection with these various diseases of former times, of which we know so little, Joseph Ruwet has recently drawn attention to the high death-rate in Aix-la-Chapelle in 1668–1669 (dysentery) and 1689–1690 (dysentery and syphilis), at a time when the price of corn was not moving much at all. In these two instances, temporary shortage of grain was quite certainly not to blame! It was the deplorable standards of hygiene and also chronic under-nourishment—those two other negative features of earlier societies—that were responsible for such catastrophes.

*

But above all, historical demography is seeking to move beyond the brief and often localized disasters caused by food crises and fatal epidemics, in order to discover something more about the much wider contexts, both diachronically and synchronically.

Diachronically, the new discipline is studying the shifting balance, century by century, between life and death; it is seeking to establish a chronology over the long term which will also be based on the population/production relationship. Such a perspective has direct relevance to economic history, which proceeds on the basis of the *secular trend*.

Synchronically, the most recent development in historical demography envisages taking the broad spatial view—making a systematic geographical study of death, for example. Straightforward geographical analysis of this kind is based on one or two major contrasts; the subsistence crises already referred to were fraught with danger in the France of Louis

XIV where they struck repeatedly. In seventeenth- and eighteenth-century England, on the other hand, they seem to have been less severe, to such a degree that in a recent publication, Peter Laslett could ask: "Did the English peasants really starve?" Similarly, infant mortality (an interesting index of the standard of living) was devastating in seventeenth-century France. Out of 1000 French babies born at that time, 250 died in their first year. In England however, a land on which the gods apparently smiled, the corresponding rates were much lower, generally less than 200 per thousand.

In pre-industrial society, there were already striking contrasts then between the demographic patterns of England and France with respect to both mortality and morality. In England, the population was fairly small, the death-rate relatively low, contraception already widespead, morality laxer, marriage later. In France, there was over-population and a high death-rate, fertility was unchecked, contraception unknown, rural morality austere, marriage earlier. Geographically, the demographic patterns of former times were more liberal north of the Channel, sadder and stricter south of it. And each of the systems, the English and the French, had its own logic and its own form of articulation, each deserving the most thorough investigation. This is a field in which the concept of *structure*, so dear to the linguists and anthropologists might well render useful service to the historians of vanished population patterns.

At all events, in barely two decades, demographic history, the sector of historical research concerned with population studies, has attained the enviable position of having matured into a science. The reasons for this success are obvious; the demographic historians were wise enough to borrow quite early the tried and tested techniques of the advanced social sciences. In addition, they have given a new direction to these techniques by applying them to the study of population in past societies. We have long had a history of population. From now on, we have historical demography. And so, to use the language of Michel Foucault and François Furet, we have moved on from the descriptive *picture* to the logical *system*.

These transfers of methods, together with technological

importations from the human sciences into history will, no doubt, have a part to play in other fields—in the historiography of society, for example. Social history already has an honourable place in the canon. Will there one day be such a thing as historical sociology? Such a development is much to be desired and is not beyond the realms of possibility. Two recent books, *La Sociabilité méridionale*, by Maurice Agulhon, and *The Vendée*, by Charles Tilly, indicate a promising move in this direction, in which the still-vigorous approach inherited from the Marxist tradition blends paradoxically with the subtle newly-imported methods of contemporary sociology, in order to study past societies.

13

From Brantôme to Paul VI[1]

ONAN, the son of Judah and Shua, refused to have a child by
his wife, Thamar, and "when he went in unto his wife ...
he spilled his seed on the ground. ... And the things which
he did displeased the Lord, wherefore he slew him." Sustained by this old story, taken from Chapter 38 of Genesis, the
Church has long refused to sanction the use of any contraceptive practices, even those less crude and more efficacious
than the method mentioned in the Bible. One practice only
has found grace in Rome, the "Ogino" (rhythm) method;
not that it is particularly effective; but its great merit is that
it has nothing in common with the "act of Onan".

Will this traditional attitude change? It is quite possible. A
Vatican working party on birth control met this month [April,
1965] in Rome. Among its members were doctors and sociologists. The proceedings of this tribunal are so far secret; but
thanks to Hélène Bergues's excellent book,[2] we can all become
acquainted with the historico-theological background of the
affair, a very important one, since it concerns four centuries
of controversies and dogmatic assertions, alternating with
the anguished appeals of the faithful and their spiritual
counsellors.

*

It was at the very beginning of the Classical period that
the essential texts and condemnations first appeared. In
1607, the Spanish Jesuit Thomas Sanchez, in his *Disputation
on marriage* labelled *coitus interruptus* or sexual withdrawal as
"*a mortal sin against nature*"; and in the following year,
St. François de Sales, in his *Introduction à la vie dévote*,
after praising "nuptial intercourse which is so just, so
remarkable, so useful to the public good", declared that
it was essential to detest before God "the infamous and
execrable practice of Onan in his marriage". Here we have

in the writings of both de Sales and Sanchez, the two chief condemnations: the sexual act, when uncompleted, is both a sin against God and a crime against nature.

As it happens, Catholic theoreticians of the Counter-Reformation had very little difficulty in gaining acceptance for their strict point of view. At the start of the seventeenth century, contraceptive practices were experimented with only in "avant-garde" circles: either by lovers and adulterous couples in high society (on this point Hélène Bergues quotes Brantôme's admiring comment on the noble Chevalier de Sanzey who "ground very well in his lady's mill without spilling any water"); or, by prostitutes, in whose chambers that great connoisseur and explorer of secrets, Mathurin Régnier, found the whole range of contraceptive devices available at the time.

But in the vast majority of cases, married couples did not yet, in the *Grand Siècle*, practise any form of "family planning". A fertile wife, as Pierre Goubert has shown, regularly bore a child every two years, making an average of eight children for every complete family. This high birth-rate was only too tragically balanced by savage infant mortality.

From 1650–1700 onwards, the situation—very slowly—changed among the upper classes. The French higher nobility and even more so the austere burghers of Geneva began to restrict births by whatever means were available, which still generally meant the method of Onan. Madame de Sévigné, a loving mother and a nagging mother-in-law, scolded her son-in-law, sermonized her daughter and without any hesitation informed her of certain methods of birth control ("*restringents*"),[3] imploring her to avoid pregnancy as she would the small-pox: "You are obeying me by not becoming pregnant, take the same care to please me by avoiding small-pox."

During the reign of Louis XV, from 1760 onwards, the new customs prevailed both at court and in the town; occasionally they even spread among the peasantry. Confessors and statisticians took fright; in 1778 Moheau uttered a cry of alarm: "Already the sinful secrets have reached the countryside; nature is being deceived even in the villages." A Norman priest, Father Féline, attempted to analyse the situation in his *Catéchisme des gens mariés* (1782). "The crime of the infamous Onan", he writes, "has become very common among married couples." The reason? Husbands have now become too ready to please their wives, too "sensitive" to their complaints; they therefore indulge the excessive "delicacy" of their wives by sparing them multiple pregnancies, "but they do not on that account renounce *the right they think they have to satisfy their desires*".

The unwillingness of women to bear many children, their husbands' indulgence, masculine sensibility—such, in brief, according to Féline, was the psychological context in which the modern practice of contraception was taking place. But despite what might be thought laudable sentiments, the Norman priest persisted in maintaining the terrifying prohibitions of the Church.

The Revolution, by "dechristianizing" society, widened the breach between the Church's doctrine and the behaviour of married couples; for the prohibitions ceased to have any effect and couples became more knowledgeable. Fertility rates in France fell drastically after 1790–1800 (half a century in advance of other western countries). At the same time, the different Churches adopted different attitudes: the Protestants on the whole, despite their faithful adherence to biblical teaching, allowed and tolerated contraception; the Catholic Church, however, took up a position of rigid intransigence which left only the slightest margin for compromise. In this respect the affair of Bouvier of Le Mans was typical.

In 1840, J.-B. Bouvier, the Bishop of Le Mans, became alarmed at the state of morals in his diocese. He affirmed that young married couples, *"while continuing to practice the conjugal act"*, contrived to avoid having large families. When they were interrogated and subsequently condemned by their confessors, these young couples grew tired of their crises of conscience and in the end abandoned the sacraments and gave up religious observance. Indifference and contraception went hand in hand. A great schism developed between the Church, which refused to budge, and conjugal life which was undergoing a process of change.

"Overwhelmed with anxiety" by such a state of affairs,

which was unanimously reported by all his confessors, J.-B. Bouvier turned to Rome for guidance and help. And the reply that was given on 8th June 1842, by the Grand Penitentiary of the Vatican, is a model of strictness qualified by masterly subtlety. "Yes", said the Penitentiary, "*the husband sins when he withdraws from the place of consummation and spills outside the receptacle, but the wife, on the other hand, if she is constrained to it by her husband, may submit passively to these practices, without thereby committing any sin.*" This became a text of the first importance, which was to be taught in the seminaries and reproduced in Bouvier's theological manuals, in edition after edition. By its prohibitions, it continues the ancient condemnations; but by its tolerance, its subtle distinction between husband and wife, it has contributed—among many other factors—to the establishment of one of the basic elements of religious practice in our country, which has continued up to very recent times, with its characteristic sexual dichotomy: the husband, the sinner, is effectively excluded from religious observance; whereas, the wife, resigned, innocent, "passive", continues to attend church, to take part in the mass and the sacraments.

This official position of the Catholic Church scarcely varied throughout the following hundred years. It is only now that the whole question is under review. And we wonder, with some curiosity, what will come of these debates in the Vatican Commission: a new set of "subtleties"? Or perhaps a clear choice, without either hypocrisy or ambiguity?

14

Demography and the "Sinful Secrets": The Case of Languedoc in the Late Eighteenth and Early Nineteenth Centuries.[1]

FROM the point of view of sources and documents,[2] four periods can be distinguished in the demographic history of Languedoc.

The first period is before about 1570. We know little about the population of Languedoc in this period, except indirectly from fiscal sources, of which there is however an ample supply (tax registers, *taille* records).

The second period runs roughly from 1570 to 1770. For this period, we have parish registers of baptisms, marriages and burials, and also census returns of varying validity.

In the third period, from 1770 onwards, by order of the *Contrôle général*, parish priests and local officers *(sub-délégués)* were required to make annual returns to the *Intendance* of baptisms, marriages and deaths. Totals were cast, and therefore we have annual records for this large province, relating to something like 70,000 births and a slightly smaller number of deaths. Furthermore, details are available for a precise computation of the diocesan populations in 1788 (in Languedoc, the civil dioceses and the *subdélégations* coincided and at the end of the *ancien régime* formed the basic administrative unit).

The fourth period is that of the systematic census, characteristic of the nineteenth century. In Languedoc (especially in the Hérault) this last period, the most favourable one for the demographic historian, begins in the Year IV, with an accurate census giving the details of each household.

The account which follows refers to the third and fourth periods, i.e. the late eighteenth and the early part of the nineteenth century. The particular questions considered here relate to overall population numbers; to the death-rate (was

239

there a "revolution in the mortality rate among ordinary
people"?) and to the birth-rate (when were the "sinful
secrets" of contraception propagated?)

*

To start with the overall population, let us look first at the
figures for 1788. The *Intendance* asked for details of this
count from its local officers *(subdélégués)*. They, in their
turn, consulted the village priests who were well-informed
about the number of their parishioners. The basic figures
transmitted by the clergy were then totalled for each diocese.
Ballainvilliers used these lists—which he occasionally muddl-
ed or improperly altered—in his *Mémoires* on the province
of Languedoc. Léon Duthil in his huge thesis of 1911, also
published these statistics, but in round figures. These two
sets of alterations, first by Ballainvilliers, then by Duthil do
not appear to be have been particularly necessary. It would
be preferable to consult the original figures which are preserved, in the case of a fairly large number of dioceses, in
dossier C39 in the Departmental Archives of the Hérault.
These original figures do not have the value of a contemporary census. Nevertheless, they are far superior to the
usual "counts" of the last years of the *ancien régime*: the
latter, we know, often resulted from a simple multiplication
of the number of births by a more or less arbitrary birth-rate
coefficient (for example, a coefficient of 25, suggesting a
hypothetical rate of 40 per 1000.) Such a procedure—
which, incidentally, was recommended to the administration
by Necker—is not entirely unjustifiable; but by the very
nature of its initial assumptions it rules out any subsequent
calculation of the actual birth rate.
The Languedoc count of 1788 has nothing in common
with these purely deductive operations. It was the result of
an estimate, an approximation made on the spot by thousands
of *curés* in thousands of parishes, an approximation in which,
as usual, "accuracy is in inverse ratio to precision". But
nevertheless, it is an approximation of some value: for
statistical over- or underestimates made by each priest
within the limited sphere of his own parish balance out in

the diocesan totals. The statistical target is always somewhere within the *curés'* sights, even if they do not in all cases score a bulls-eye by hitting the exact figure.

If, for example, in the case of the diocese of Lodève, we compare the data of the 1788 count with data from the Year IV census, we find both in the figures for individual villages and in the overall figures, a remarkable similarity of statistical results. The "concordance tests" work out satisfactorily.

From this point on, it is possible to make a general comparison between the known total population of 1788 in twelve Languedoc dioceses and the number of births in these same years (1787–1788); we can be quite certain of these numbers thanks to the returns of the parish priests and the totals submitted by the local administrative officers (preserved in the Departmental Archives of the Hérault).

Let us take the example of the diocese of Narbonne. There were 60,850 inhabitants in 1788; 2,435 births in 1787; 2,396 births in 1788. The birth-rate in the Narbonne region for 1787–1788, reckoned at 2,415 births per annum (i.e., an arithmetical average for the two years) is therefore established at 39.7 per 1000.

Extending the same method, we can obtain the birth-rate for 1787–1788 for the twelve dioceses of which the census returns are preserved in dossier C 39.

In these various dioceses, except for Castres and Uzès, (where Protestant births are in any case counted in with the others), the proportion of Huguenots is negligible, unlikely to disturb the demographic historian's calculations. The birth-rates obtained all lie, in round figures, between 35 and 40 per 1000, tending to cluster around an average of 38 per 1000. The "population/births" graph, in which the points representing the birth-rates tend to group very closely along a straight line, testifies significantly to this *de facto* convergence; it is likely that this average figure of 38 per 1000 corresponds to the demographic reality.

Let us make some inter-regional comparisons. In Catalonia between 1785 and 1790, a rate of 36.5 per 1000 is considered to be a minimum: "in the countryside, birth-rates above 40 per 1000 are common".[3] In Provence, in a score of towns and villages, the average birth-rate is 40.75 per 1000 in 1716,

39.7 in 1765.[4] All round the Gulf of Lions in the last thirty years of the eighteenth century then, one birth per annum per 25 or 26 inhabitants seems to have been a constant norm.

These figures are significant, no doubt, only within certain limits, for birth-rates, as we know, are neither very precise nor subtle tools of measurement since they take no account of age-group structures. (Fertility rates are better scientific criteria.) But despite this drawback, the Languedoc birth-rate, as reckoned on the eve of the Revolution, when it seems to be established at 38 per 1000, enables us to make certain comparisons.

Thirty-eight per 1000 was approximately the birth-rate in India up to 1915; it was also the birth-rate in Puerto Rico, before the spread of contraceptive practices brought the rate down to 32 per 1000 in 1959.[5] Yet, although it may seem high, this figure of 38 per 1000 is by no means a maximum, representing some "natural" or uninhibited birth-rate, without limitations of any kind. To take just one example, the countries of Latin America, which are at present among the most prolific in the world, in general exceed 38 per 1000 and even 40 per 1000 when we relate the rate of their births to their population. In Venezuela, the most authoritative study so far indicates a figure of 43 per 1000 for recent years.[6]

The Languedoc rate of 38 per 1000 in the 1780s is not therefore incompatible with the (restricted) spread of certain "Malthusian" practices. Around Toulouse and Montpellier in the reign of Louis XVI, contraception existed probably only as an exceptional and individual practice, or among social groups very much in a minority.

A letter from the *Intendant* of Languedoc to the *Contrôle Général* dated 29 May 1778, might well serve as testimony on this point. "Here is a summary of the figures", the provincial administrator writes, "to inform you of the difference between the years 1776 and 1777. You will see ... that in 1777 there was an increase of 2,200 in the number of births; it may be attributed to greater prosperity in trade."[7] The lower birth-rate of 1776 is thus by implication stated in this text to be the result of a deliberate intention on the part of potential parents: young people either hesitated to get married because of economic difficulties, or else couples already married temporarily limited births by some crude form of contraception.

Another problem: is the Languedoc rate of 38 per 1000 on the eve of the Revolution comparable to the rates observed at the same time in the rest of the kingdom?

At first sight, the answer appears to be yes. Forty per 1000 is the figure generally quoted as representative of the French birth-rate in the second half of the eighteenth century.[8] Necker himself, in a letter to the local administrator in Carcassonne in 1789, recommends taking 4 per cent or 40 per 1000 as the basis for population estimates inferred from the number of births. And, far away from Languedoc, in the prolific *généralité* of Valenciennes, the birth-rates between 1774 and 1787 seem to have been between 37 per 1000 and 43 per 1000![9]

However, we must not generalize. As a matter of fact, as early as 1785 to 1789, a certain number of regions of France (unlike Languedoc) did not reach even these rates of 38 per 1000 or 40 per 1000. At Crulai in Normandy,[10] a village studied in depth by means of the reconstitution of families, the birth-rate between 1675 and 1760 was only 36 per 1000. It fell even below this figure on the eve of the Revolution. And for the nation as a whole during the same period, the scholarly reconstructions carried out by Bourgeois-Pichat suggest a birth-rate of 36.4 per 1000,[11] that is to say distinctly lower than the rates found at that time in Valenciennes and in the majority of the dioceses of Languedoc.

At the end of the *ancien régime*, Languedoc therefore appears (completely unlike its contemporary self, which is very "Malthusian") as one of the most prolific of the French provinces, positively swarming with children. A map showing the surplus of births over deaths on the eve of the Assembly of Notables[12] would display a pattern the exact opposite of the twentieth-century situation: Languedoc and the Dauphiné were national leaders in terms of demographical increase, whereas the north-western regions, without exception, trailed behind. The "sinful secrets" of contraception, already known in some small measure in certain regions of the kingdom, were practised to a very much lesser degree in the southern province. And it was at Caen, not at Montpellier, that Father Féline published in 1782 the celebrated *Catéchisme des gens mariés*, denouncing "the crime of the infamous Onan, most reprehensible and very common amongst married couples".[13]

*

It might be objected that my basic figures relate only to twelve out of the twenty-two dioceses of Languedoc. In ten dioceses, the priests' population counts have not been preserved. Would these ten dioceses, on the eve of the Revolution, have had birth-rates similar to those of the other twelve?

It seems that they would. Let us take for example the area corresponding to the present *département* of Hérault; this territory consists, almost entirely (we shall take into account this very slight difference) of the five civil dioceses of the *ancien régime*: Montpellier, Béziers, Saint-Pons, Lodève, Agde. For these five dioceses, I have not been able to find the exhaustive population counts supplied by the priest and totalled by the *subdélégués* in 1788. But the Hérault census of a little later, in the Year IV, is reliable. It was conducted on a house-to-house basis; it is confirmed, by comparative tests, and for that year (Year IV) it gives a figure of 275, 628 inhabitants in Hérault. These 275, 628 inhabitants of the Year IV correspond to the population of the five *ci-devant* dioceses mentioned above, plus that of the nine *communes* and one *canton* (Capestang) added to the five dioceses at the time of the subdivision into *départements* effected by the Constituent Assembly. These additional nine *communes* and *canton* had, in the Year IV, a population of 9,022 inhabitants. In other words, the population of the five *ci-devant* dioceses, at the time of the Revolutionary census, was 275,628 minus 9.022, i.e. 266,606 inhabitants.

Such a figure is certainly very little different from that of 1789 (were immigration and natural increase between 1789 and the Year IV partly balanced by the first departures into the army?) In fact, in 1790, the estimate made by the National Assembly, quoted by Young, gave a figure of 264,000 inhabitants for the Hérault, i.e. approximately 255,000 inhabitants for the five dioceses. The *Intendant* Ballainvilliers had, in

1788, put down a figure of 273,000 inhabitants for the five dioceses.[14] But his figure is too high because of an overestimate by 10,000 of the population of the diocese of Lodève. Ballain-villiers' corrected total comes to 263,000 inhabitants, which is not far off that for 1790 (255,000) and for the Year IV (266,000). We can therefore take as a maximum figure, reasonably approximate, and in any case unlikely to be better-ed, 265,000 inhabitants in the five dioceses in 1788–1789 (the real figure is probably a few thousands less). Now the annual average number of births, still in the five dioceses in 1787–1789, is 9,783 including 200 babies born to Protestant families. Hence a birth-rate of 37 per 1000 *at an absolute minimum*, hardly less than in the twelve dioceses previously mentioned, where the average was 38 per 1000.

The presumption of a birth-rate in pre-Revolutionary Languedoc of 37–38 per 1000 is therefore based on figures for a wide geographical area: twelve dioceses out of twenty-two plus the territory of a present-day *département*, that is, a total of sixteen dioceses out of twenty-two.[15]

Another objection or question might be raised: are these rates of 37 per 1000 or 38 per 1000 established for two or three years (1787–1788 or 1787–1789) purely fortuitous, tran-sitory and accidental? Or do they correspond, on a local level, to old, long-established and persistent demographic structures?

It seems that they do: calculated over six years (1784–1789), and taking into account, year by year, the natural increase in the population (excess of births over deaths), the birth-rates in Hérault (five dioceses) and in Languedoc (twelve dioceses) regularly work out at about 37 per 1000 and 38 per 1000 respectively. This is quite satisfactory as confirmation.

But one cannot legitimately use this procedure to go very much further back chronologically. To reconstitute the population of a Languedoc diocese in 1770, for example, is a hazardous operation. True, I know what the population(P) of this diocese was in 1789; I also know the annual figure of its natural increase (excess of births over deaths) C, C', C'' C''' ... , C^n in 1789, 1788, 1787, 1786, and so on, going back to 1770, and thus I can in theory, reconstitute the population in 1770, P', by the formula:

$$P' = P - (C + C' + C'' + C''' + \ldots + C^n)$$

But the figure thus obtained for P' would not have allowed for immigration, which was so important in old Languedoc, and especially in the *ci-devant* dioceses of present-day Hérault. Since the figure obtained for P' does not distinguish the influx resulting from immigration in the intervening years 1770–1789, it will therefore be necessarily too high; and conversely, the birth-rate, calculated from the number of diocesan births in 1770 and from P', will, on account of this over-estimate of the overall population, be much too low. This approach must therefore, unfortunately, be rejected.

In spite of this, however, we can, with the aid of certain documentary data, go back further in time. In the first place, we have a large though partial sample for 1773; in the Languedoc administrative subdivision of Tournon, otherwise known as the Vivarais, a very thorough count,[16] including "boys and girls, fathers, mothers, grandmothers, grandfathers, servants male and female," also "including attorneys'-clerks and shop-assistants," gives a total for 1773 of 90,118 inhabitants. Now, in this same Vivarais administrative area and at the same period in time, the average number of births (an average calculated over three years: 1770–71–72) works out at 3,517 births per annum: i.e., a birth-rate of 39 per 1000, a rate hardly any higher than it was fifteen years later in the other parts of Languedoc.

Before these dates we have only a scattering of birth-rates, calculated on the small number of inhabitants of a few parishes. It appears that Blagnac for instance, had a birth-rate of 38.6 per 1000 in the period 1630–1700; Lévignac, 40 per 1000 in 1700–1735; Lussan, 53 per 1000 in 1741; Pépieux, 50 per 1000 circa 1708; Villemoustaussou, 36 per 1000 in 1740; Rabat, 37 per 1000 in 1701–09.[17] Taken as a whole, these birth-rate figures for Languedoc before 1750 settle around a median of 39.3 per 1000 and an average of 42.4 per 1000.

A table grouping the various figures for the Midi (Languedoc and Provence) referred to in this article is set out on page 247.

Judging by this table, which it would obviously be desirable to complete and fill out as new discoveries are made, it would

Date	Sample	Birth-rate per thousand (%$_0$)
1716	15 Provençal localities	40.7 (average)
17th century to 1740	6 Languedoc villages	42.4 (average) 39.3 (median)
1765	19 Provençal localities	39.7 (average)
1770–1772	Administrative district of Tournon (90,118 inhabitants)	39.0 (average)
1787–1788	12 Languedoc dioceses (out of 22)	38.1 (average)
1787–1789	Area corresponding to present-day Hérault (265,000 inhabitants)	37.0 (average)

appear that the birth-rate in the Midi in the last third of the eighteenth century underwent a slow and imperceptible decline, probably attributable to the very limited communication—in whispers, so to speak—of some of the "sinful secrets". Nevertheless, despite this very slight decline, which in any case debatable, the birth-rate in the South remained fixed at a very high level for 1787–1789, (even) higher on the whole than the national average.

These persistently high birth-rate figures in the South, and the slight delay in the adoption of the earliest Malthusian practices (which had, however, begun), correspond to some very clearly defined sociological factors. First and foremost, to the low status accorded by the men of Languedoc to their women-folk: it is well known that the South of France is generally less literate than the North; but female illiteracy in the Midi during the eighteenth century, reached frightening proportions. Unlettered and harshly treated,[18] and without any very great objection on their part, the women of Languedoc had one "vocation": having babies.

This was a prolific society, then, and if further proof is required, one has only to look at the towns of Languedoc.

At first sight, one might well believe that these towns were already practising contraception: in the decade 1770–1780 the B/M ratio (number of baptisms in relation to the number of marriages) is 3.9 or 4.0, roughly four births per marriage; at the same time in the surrounding country districts, this ratio was higher, about 4.5 or 5.0 per marriage. The towns, Montpellier, Nîmes, Toulouse etc., if we are to believe these figures, were therefore in Turgot's time "Malthusian islands", surrounded by a countryside still backward and tradition bound—islands of "vice" to use the expression by which Malthus censoriously characterized the very contraceptive practices with which, ironically, his name was later to be associated.

But this crude B/M ratio, so enlightening at first sight, carries a risk of error. If one takes the trouble to look beyond the B/M ratio and calculate the birth-rates for the towns in question, one finds that these wholly urban rates are in fact equal to, or scarcely any lower than the average rates for the predominantly rural Languedoc dioceses. In 1787–1789, the birth-rate in Montpellier works out at 39 per 1000, in Nîmes at 37 per 1000, in Toulouse (this one may be questionable) at 39.9 per 1000. Despite appearances then, the towns also remained extremely prolific; they too were swarming with children, and there were as many born in the town as in the country districts. True, the B/M ratio is lower there; but this was not so much because town dwellers produced fewer children as because there were more marriages in the towns. This propensity to marry in the towns is easily explained: the town population was, on average, younger as a result of the immigration of young men and women from the surrounding countryside; perhaps too remarriage was easier there and more frequent than in the villages. If the B/M ratio was low in the towns, it was not so much that B (the dividend) was dropping; essentially it was a case of the divisor M being very high.

*

When the birth-rate is high and the death-rate comparatively low, the result is naturally a surplus of births. From a "population-growth" point of view, the situation in the dioceses of Upper Languedoc was very "satisfactory". The death-rate in 1787–1788 was 26.6 per 1000 in the diocese of Alet; 28.6 per 1000 in the diocese of Limoux; 24.7 per 1000 in the diocese of Comminges; 28.0 per 1000 in the diocese of Rieux; 29.1 per 1000 in the diocese of Bas-Montauban; 25.7 per 1000 in the diocese of Lavaur; 28.3 per 1000 in the diocese of Albi; 26.2 per 1000 in the diocese of Castres; the annual surplus of births over deaths consequently reached and exceeded 10 per 1000; at such a rate the population of Upper Languedoc would have doubled in two generations. (But this rate was not maintained in the nineteenth century.)

In Lower Languedoc, at least in the few dioceses where I have been able to calculate the rates, the situation appears to have been less satisfactory. In the diocese of Lodève, the death-rate stood at 32.1 per 1000; in the diocese of Uzès at 34.1 per 1000; in the diocese of Carcassonne at 32.4 per 1000; in the diocese of Narbonne at 35.0 per 1000. In the five dioceses which make up the present *département* of Hérault, the death-rate was 32 per 1000 during the 1780s; and as high as 33.4 per 1000 in the three years 1787–1789. To what are we to attribute these differences in the mortality rates between the east and the west of the province? Inequalities in the standard of living perhaps? More probably it resulted from the unhealthy nature of the east: the Languedoc coast is bordered with swamps and marshes, the haunt of mosquitoes and the source of malarial fevers and viruses.

Despite these local difficulties, the overall picture was excellent. Calculated from the figures for all twelve dioceses, east and west, the average death-rate in 1787–1789 was 29.2 per 1000 as against a birth-rate of 38.1 per 1000. The annual surplus of births was 9.1 per 1000. As in Catalonia at the same time, the surplus of births was considerable.

Do these mortality-rates reflect a situation of very long standing? Apparently not. The earliest mortality-rate we know, that of Blagnac (1630–1700) was 38 per 1000, exactly the same as the birth-rate.[19] At some point, a "social revolution in mortality rates" must have occurred.[20] Graphs plotted from the Languedoc parish records enable us to date this episode precisely: it varies from region to region, taking place a little earlier in one place than another. In about 1740, 1750 or 1760–1770 depending on the area, the local burial curves become regularly lower than the corresponding baptism curves.[21] According to a recent study,[22] this fall in the Languedoc mortality rate seems to have affected adult mortality most. The combination of the beginnings of economic growth, the slow improvement in the standard of living, the elimination of famine and the modest increase in real wages is sufficient to explain this improvement, here as in Catalonia, from about the middle of the eighteenth century. Adults in Languedoc lived in conditions a little less bad than in the past, and consequently they lived longer.

And so, in this region, towards 1785–1789, we find a demographic situation which was to recur fairly often, in several different countries, in the nineteenth and twentieth centuries. On one hand, mortality-rates fall off, under the stimulus of an initial upturn in the economy; on the other hand, the birth-rate stays at its traditional healthy level. As a result, the human race expands.

After 1789 these basic figures changed. First, let us look at the mortality rate: it is certainly difficult to discover exactly what it was during the Revolution and the First Empire. Many Languedoc soldiers died outside the *départements* of the former province, or outside France even. And it is only with the return of peace in the first years of the Restoration that a valid comparison of the rate with what it had been in the *ancien régime* becomes possible. In Hérault this rate fell from 33.4 per 1000 in 1787–1789 to 27.4 per 1000 which was the average rate during the five-year period 1816–1820. This was the normal, standard fall, a continuation of what had already been registered in the eighteenth century under Louis XIV and Louis XV.

Easier to recognize and more significant also, is the fall in the birth-rate after 1789. In the eighteenth century this rate held firm, fell very little, seemed to have the consistency of a natural law, and regularly reached a very high level: in this respect, the population was still displaying a quite outmoded demographic pattern in contrast with the "modernism" of the falling death-rate. But in the following era, during the Revolution, and above all under the Consulate and Empire, the pressure within this situation began to be relieved: the "sinful secrets" of contraception hitherto shared only by a minority of initiates, spread widely throughout the Languedoc area.

In 1813–1820, in fact, the systematic returns of the prefectorial administration indicate birth-rates very much lower than those of pre-Revolutionary days: 1813, 32.1 per 1000; 1814, 33.8 per 1000; 1815, 32.9 per 1000; 1819, 33.4 per 1000; 1820, 32.3 per 1000.

There was a similar fall in the *départements* of Upper Languedoc: in 1787–1789 the birth-rate at 38 per 1000 was still quite close to the barely higher figures for the time of Louis XIV. But forty to fifty years later (1830–1840), the birth-rate was working out somewhere between 21 per 1000 minimum) and 27 per 1000 (maximum),[23] i.e., lower than the national average (29 per 1000).

In this case, the position is therefore completely reversed since pre-Revolutionary Languedoc had a birth-rate *higher* than the national average. And in these circumstances there can be no talk of a continuity with the pre-Revolutionary period, for the tendency towards restriction of births had scarcely begun before 1789. During the Revolution, the Empire and the Restoration monarchies, the birth-rate fell dramatically, like some geological fault. In little more than a single generation (from 1789 to 1830), a radical change in the behaviour-patterns of a great number of married couples had taken place; a break on what was already a massive scale with the traditional concepts of conjugal morality; and the statistically significant introduction of contraception, or, to use once more Malthus's term, "vice".[24]

For it is hard to see any other factor which would explain this early evidence of a limitation in the number of births. Could it have been the result of the departures of men into the Revolutionary and Imperial armies? In fact, these departures and mobilizations led rather to an increase in the number of marriages, for marriage was a young man's hope of escaping conscription. And in any case, the fall in the birth-rate persisted well beyond 1815, well beyond the Empire wars.

We should probably therefore abide by the simplest

explanation: contraception. In Hérault, where there are good chronological and statistical records, contraception made rapid progress between 1789 (the *terminus a quo*) and 1813 (the *terminus ad quem*); i.e. during the crucial years of the Revolution and the Empire. Was this an isolated case? Probably not; elsewhere too, in Normandy,[25] in the Ile-de-France,[26] the decade of the Revolution seems to have marked the decisive turning-point after which the "loss of innocence" of the population, scarcely apparent under the *ancien régime*, progressively accelerated. More generally, on a national level, Biraben's graph[27] showing the decline of fertility in France, confirms and refines this chronology: the decline began as early as 1789; it continued during and after the Revolution.

*

From the data quoted in this article, it is now possible to construct an approximate chronology of contraception, and of its progress in Languedoc, a province where it was to have above-average success. What is now required is a more precise formulation of the "problematic" approach to be adopted towards the phenomenon.

First, there is the question of the "sinful secrets". Was there, as in other regions of France and as in nineteenth-century Austria[28] a preference, as compared with other methods, for *coitus interruptus* with its not inconsiderable consequences, psychological and sometimes psychopathological?[29]

Then there are the problems relating to the social, cultural and religious context in which the propagation of contraceptive methods took place. It was closely connected, apparently, in the particular case of France, which was ahead of most other countries in this respect, with an essentially masculine disaffection from the Catholic church.[30] Was this disaffection, in certain cases at least, prompted by Revolutionary dechristianization, which coincided in time with an obvious wave of birth control? This is one working hypothesis among several others. The French Revolution, a total phenomenon, may have acted at many levels (legal, religious, cultural) on family structures.

In any case, this double disaffection, mutually and reciprocally conditioned, both from the Church, and from traditional child-bearing patterns, was to become definitive by the end of the nineteenth century when the new identity of the Midi was to take shape: republican, anti-clerical, and resolutely "Malthusian".

BIBLIOGRAPHY

ARMENGAUD, A., "De quelques idées fausses concernant les pays de la Garonne vers 1840", in *Revue d'histoire moderne et contemporaine,* 1960.

BAEHREL, R., *Une croissance, la Basse-Provence rurale,* 1961.

BEN SAMOUN, Y., *La Démographie de Blagnac (Haute-Garonne),* unpublished thesis (Université de Toulouse), quoted by BLAQUIÈRE, *Annales de l'Institut d'Études occitanes,* 1960.

BERGUES, H., ARIÈS, P., HÉLIN, E., HENRY, L., RIQUET, M., SAUVY, A., SUTTER, J., *La Prévention des naissances dans la famille,* Paris, 1960.

BOURGEOIS-PICHAT, J., "Évolution de la population française ... ", in *Population,* 1951, p. 635, and 1952, p. 319.

DUTHIL, L., *L'État économique du Languedoc,* Paris, 1911.

ESMONIN, E., "La Population en France de 1770 à 1789", in *Bulletin de la Société de démographie historique,* 1964, n° 1.

FÉLINE, Le P., *Catéchisme des gens mariés,* Rouen, edition 1880.

FLEURY, M. and VALMARY, P., "Les progrès de l'instruction élémentaire en France de Louis XIV à Napoléon III", in *Population,* 1957.

FREUD, S., "Lettres à Wilhelm Fliess, 1887 1902", in *La Naissance de la psychanalyse,* Paris, trans. A. Berman, 1956.

GANIAGE, J., *Trois villages de l'Ile-de-France,* Paris, 1964.

GODECHOT, J. et MONCASSIN, S., "Démographie et subsistances en Languedoc du XVIIIe au début du XIXe siècle", in *Bulletin d'histoire économique et sociale de la Révolution française,* 1964.

GOUBERT, P., *Beauvais et le Beauvaisis au XVIIe siècle,* Paris, 1960.

HENRY, L., cf. BERGUES, 1960.

HILAIRE, M., "Communication", in *Cahiers d'histoire,* t. IX, 1964, n° 1, p. 109.

LABROUSSE, E., in MOUSNIER, R. and LABROUSSE, E., *Le XVIIIe siècle,* Paris, 1953.

LE ROY LADURIE, E., *Les Paysans de Languedoc,* Paris, 1966.

MANDROU, R., in DUBY, G. and MANDROU, R., *Histoire de la civilisation française,* Paris, 1958.

MOHEAU, *Recherches et considérations sur la population de la France,* Paris, 1778.

REINHARD, M. and ARMENGAUD, A., *Histoire générale de la population mondiale*, Paris, 1961.

VILAR, P., *La Catalogne dans l'Espagne moderne*, Paris, 1962.

VILBACK, R. de, *Voyage dans les départements de Languedoc*, Paris, 1825.

ZOLA, E., *La Terre*.

15

Amenorrhoea in Time of Famine (Seventeenth to Twentieth Century)[1]

IN 1946, in the course of his research into famines in the age of Louis XIV, Jean Meuvret[2] noticed that such famines were accompanied not only by high death-rates, which one might expect, but also by a very pronounced drop in the number of births. He was the first to suggest a sophisticated diagnosis which went some way towards a causal explanation, without however claiming to have provided a definite solution. Checking through the parish registers and in particular the figures for baptisms, he decided that the appropriate basis of reasoning lay not in births, but in conceptions. Accordingly, working backwards nine months from the baptismal dates, he succeeded in following the month-by-month change in the number of conceptions. At once something that had hitherto merely been suspected became abundantly clear: at precisely the time when the price of grain was reaching its peak and deaths from hunger and epidemic diseases were increasing, the number of conceptions fell dramatically. The graphs illustrated this very strikingly. The link between famine and sterility that, rightly or wrongly, gynaecologists had discerned during two world wars, was now plainly visible during a seventeenth-century subsistence crisis, thanks to Meuvret's ingenious calculations. What remained to be explained was the physiological process: why should normally fertile married women suddenly become barren during the worst weeks and months of a famine?

Eight years later, Pierre Goubert was asking the same kind of question.[3] From documents in the Beauvais archives, he was making a study of the catastrophic famine of 1693–1694 whose murderous character he had already noted. He drew attention to the fall in the number of births (down by 62 per cent in six parishes) just as prices and deaths reached their

255

peak. Quoting a text from Genesis, his first suggestion was that this mysterious "strike of the womb" could be explained by some kind of birth control in times of catastrophe.

Different explanations, however, were being offered by other researchers. Joseph Ruwet, who was also studying the 1693–1694 famine—in Liège in this case—recorded that there too, there had been an alarming drop in the number of conceptions.[4] Without discounting the hypothesis of some elementary form of voluntary birth control, he also suggested a number of other possible factors to explain temporary falls in the birth-rate in times of crisis: sexual abstinence through a sort of provident asceticism or lack of appetite, a temporary fall in the number of marriages, and, lastly, a probable increase in the number of early or spontaneous abortions resulting from the poor state of health of the pregnant women, caused by hunger, disease or epidemic disorders. Incidentally, Ruwet also remarked that the events of 1694 may have taken a similar course to those recorded in the Low Countries at the time of the famine of 1944–1945: in these two years, half of the women of child-bearing age in Holland's larger towns became victims of temporary amenorrhoea (cessation of menstruation accompanied by sterility). Was it not possible, asked Ruwet, that what was true of 1944 was also true, *mutatis mutandis*, of 1693 and 1661?

This thesis, together with his own research and recent progress in demographic history finally led Goubert, in 1960, to revise his original assumptions. The work of Louis Henry, in particular had shown that birth control was much less widespread among the poorer classes during the seventeenth and eighteenth centuries than historians had previously thought.[5] In 1960 therefore, Goubert discarded the theory he had once held that voluntary contraceptive practices were the cause of the fall in the number of conceptions in times of famine. Dismissing this explanation and possibly exaggerating a little his real thoughts on the matter, he wrote: "The more one knows of the Beauvais and other peasants of the seventeenth century, the less one is inclined to believe them capable of resorting with any frequency to the most elementary forms of birth control, even in times of crisis."[6] Logically, having reached this conclusion, the author of *Beauvais et le Beauvaisis* suggested that amenorrhoea in times of famine might be a significant (though not necessarily the only) cause of temporary sterility. In this connection, he recalled that Moheau, writing in 1778, had taken for granted "a failure to reproduce the species, since sick and exhausted people are incapable of doing so".[7]

Finally, Goubert prudently raised the question of documentary evidence: "We continue to hope", he wrote, "that the writings of some doctor of a past age will provide us with evidence of ... the phenomena of amenorrhoea in times of famine."[8]

*

The problems put forward for historians' consideration almost ten years ago have not yet received any very new or consistent answers or solutions. Without wishing to venture into the terrain of medical history, with all its technicalities[9]— certainly not my field—in my capacity as a social historian who has occasion to work backwards from present-day evidence, and also so that I may make some indirect contribution to our knowledge of the subsistence crises of former times, I should simply like to re-open the file on amenorrhoea in times of famine. It is a much larger file than one might gather simply from the now familiar references to the effects, already mentioned, of the famine in Holland.

In conclusion, I shall attempt to broaden the scope of the debate; I shall also try, if possible, to answer Goubert's specific question about potential evidence from the writings of doctors of a former age.

*

The first rigorously kept records on the subject of famine or wartime amenorrhoea (*Kriegsamenorrhoe*)[10] are the work of a Polish doctor. In August 1916, J. von Jaworski, gynaecologist at the Saint-Roch Hospital in Warsaw, discovered among the poorer of his women patients coming for consultation, an unusually large number of cases of amenorrhoea (failure to menstruate) accompanied, with few exceptions, by temporary sterility.[11] He thought the possible cause was the shortage of food which was becoming increasingly more serious in the Central European Empires, because of the war. The working-class population of Warsaw in 1916 was so undernourished that many women and girls who were on the point of starvation were at the same time suffering from abnormal failure to menstruate. Hence the expression "starvation amenorrhoea" sometimes employed to describe this condition.

Well in advance of anyone else, Jaworski published a report in the *Wiener Klinische Wochenschrift* of the first hundred cases he had diagnosed. Very soon, similar phenomena were being reported from almost everywhere. German doctors were being consulted by numerous young women, anxious or overjoyed, believing themselves to be pregnant.[12] After examination, they were told to their amazement that they were not pregnant, simply suffering from amenorrhoea. In Vienna, the "epidemic", diagnosed in the course of social security examinations, started in October 1916. In Hamburg, the first cases were reported on October 2; in Freiburg in November of the same year. All the great cities of Imperial Germany were affected, Berlin, Cologne, Kiel, etc. Only the area around Tübingen appears to have been spared. The "epidemic" reached its climax in the spring of 1917, around March-April.[13] In most cases the amenorrhoea condition cleared up fairly quickly—in two or three months, or in some cases six months. Among certain exceptionally weak women (as for instance patients in a Berlin clinic for epileptics who were on a restricted diet) menstruation failures lasted very much longer, up to two years on average. Various symptoms, including of course sterility, accompanied these attacks of amenorrhoea.

From the very beginning, with Jaworski leading the field, gynaecologists blamed the poor diet. In Hamburg, Spaeth maintained that the great wave of menstruation troubles followed the introduction of meat rationing and the rising price of foodstuffs: "Eggs are not to be had ... instead of potatoes we have beet." Women were badly affected by this deprivation. "No doctor with eyes to see will deny it." Elsewhere it was the lack of bread, flour, fat, or meat that was blamed. Moreover, very frequently, when the cause was removed by giving whenever possible a more nourishing diet to the women who suffered from this strange disorder, a cure resulted. "Fortunately for the future of the Fatherland, everything goes back to normal when the food improves", wrote Giesecke. Hoping for a restoration of the birth-rate, he prescribed milk, eggs and fresh vegetables for his patients. In Schleswig-Holstein in 1917, bacon, eggs, bread, flour and oatmeal were in very short supply and these shortages were considered to be the reason for the high incidence of amenorrhoea. In Berlin however we do, at last, have some statistics to go on: in the Berlin clinic already mentioned we are able to compare precise data relating to amenorrhoea and the food ration. Between 1914 and 1918, out of 142 women inmates, aged between 16 and 44, 129 (i.e. 90.8 per cent—an enormous proportion) were affected by amenorrhoea, in the majority of cases from 1916 onwards. These disorders followed drastic reductions in the daily ration of food. Meat rationing in Berlin did, in fact, begin at Easter in 1916; in October, milk was rationed; simultaneously Jerusalem artichokes and swedes replaced potatoes and were also used to make bread and conserves *("Murmelade")*. Following these restrictions, amenorrhoea beat all previous records in this clinic, in the last quarter of 1916 and the first quarter of 1917. As it happens these shortages can be expressed accurately in figures:[14] non-working patients who were fed at the clinic were consuming, on average, according to the institution's accounts, 2,955 calories per day in August 1914, but only 1,961 calories by December 1916. Their intake of fats in the same interval fell by 69.2 per cent.

The dietary causes of amenorrhoea were, in the opinion of the German doctors of that period, corroborated by sociological data. In the Viennese practice of Dr. Czerwenka (1917) for example, two groups can be distinguished:[15] on the one hand, women suffering from amenorrhea, who were of working-class origin, and registered on the social security panel; and on the other hand, the better-nourished women in his private practice, who escaped the disorder. In Koenigsberg, in the same year, Dr. Hilferding[16] remarked upon similar occurrences: in his hospital surgery, visited each

year by thousands of social security patients, the number
suffering from amenorrhea rose from 0.55 per cent in 1912
to 14 per cent in 1917 (reckoned in percentages of the
total number of his women patients). Among the better-off
patients attending Hilferding's clinic, on the contrary, only
5 per cent of the women (10 out of 100) were affected. And
finally, in Hamburg [17] still in 1917, we find the same contrast
between paying patients, totally exempt from amenorrhoea,
and the under-nourished young women registered in the
Krankenkasse, working girls, servant girls, shopgirls, large
numbers of whom no longer menstruated.

The most detailed research was that carried out at Kiel
by G. Teebken:[18] it concerns 375 cases of amenorrhoea for
the period 1916–1919. Of the women affected, 33 per cent
were working girls and house-servants, 7.5 per cent were
"white-collar workers" (post-office employees, shop assist-
ants, laundry supervisors etc.) and the remainder mainly
housewives whose husbands were workmen or artisans.
Whereas 65 per cent of the clientele of the polyclinic studied
by Teebken was composed of town dwellers, the proportion
of women suffering from amenorrhoea was 84 per cent urban
and only 16 per cent rural: evidently the poor standard of
living in the town during the food shortages was to blame.
Chronologically, amenorrhoea began to appear in August
1916, after the start of the lowering of the bread ration and the
introduction of meat rationing: cases multiplied in the
autumn of 1916, when individual rations fell to 1558 calories
(48gms. protein, 27gms. fats, 274gms. carbohydrates).
They reached their peak in the winter of 1916–17 when
swedes completely replaced potatoes and *"Marmelade"*.
From the autumn of 1917 rations improved; large supplies
of potatoes were distributed, and the incidence of amenorrhoea declined. What happened in Kiel during the harvest-
season of 1916–17 amounted to a moderate subsistence
crisis, comparable to one of the relatively less severe famines
of the *ancien régime*—one whose effects could be measured
much more accurately, thanks to the observations of doctors,
than ever they were in the seventeenth century.

In Lille,[19] in territory invaded by Germany, but also an
area famous for studies in demographic history, the situation

in 1914–1918 seems to have been much more serious: out of 200 Lille women hospital patients interrogated by Dr. Boucher, 79 who had been in normal health before the war, were affected by amenorrhoea; in 57 cases this lasted for more than six months. Half of these cases occurred during the last year of the war, "the year of the harshest restrictions.[20] Without denying the influence of psychological factors, Boucher chiefly blames "severe under-nourishment";[21] he refers to the drastic reduction in food supplies—worse than in Germany; and he points out that out of twenty or so women who kept records of their weight during the war, twelve of them supplied him with "precise figures of loss of weight of 10 or more kgs."[22]

In Germany, meanwhile, from the last year of the war (1918), things began to improve: the incidence of amenorrhoea declined. Did the German food supply become more substantial again after the severe shortages of the winter of 1916–17, known ever since as the "rutabaga [swede] winter"?[23] It is quite possible, but it is doubtful whether the 1917 harvest restored full rations. Are we to believe with Selye[24] and others, that after the first savage shock of the shortages of 1916, the human organism gradually managed to adapt to scarcity? We do not really know and we must be wary of offering an explanation: *ne sutor ultra crepidam*. But, for the historian, simply from a bibliographical point of view, certain facts stand out: after that year (1918), talk of amenorrhoea, once the subject of lively discussion in the German medical press, died down.[25] In 1920, the food supply was restored almost to normal and German women "statistically" no longer had any problems of that nature. It was in Russia now, during the critical years (1917–1921), that observations relevant to this topic took place: in 1916, in Petrograd, where there were catastrophic shortages of bread and fats, Leo Von Lingen encountered his first clinical cases of abnormal amenorrhoea which occurred here as elsewhere.[26] Within the space of a few years he recorded 320 cases, the majority occurring in the winter of 1918–19, when the young women in the working-class districts of Petrograd suffered and worked in extreme conditions of unbelievable cold and hunger. Subsequently Leo Von Lingen left the country and his observations were interrupted. But a Soviet surgeon, W. Stefko, was in practice there during the famine years (1920–1921). Following a number of operations performed for a variety of reasons which enabled him to carry out a histological study of the ovary, he diagnosed, in the case of 120 women affected by food shortage and amenorrhoea during those years, the virtual cessation or interruption of the physiological processes involved in ovulation.[27]

The second world war is, alas, a rich source of similar data; and the dossier on amenorrhoea once again becomes very substantial during the tragic decade between 1936 (the war in Spain) and 1946 (the last year of food shortages).

This time our information comes from further afield than the Austro-Germanic world, from the whole of Europe in fact, including France, where the food restrictions of 1940–1944 were more severe than during the 1914–1918 war. During the earlier conflict, doctors in the allied countries[28] had known about wartime amenorrhoea only from hearsay and from reading obscure articles in the gynaecological journals of Germany and Austria. The exhaustive search made by Teebken[29] in 1928 located only one single article devoted to the subject in the medical press of England, France or America for the war and post-war period. This had been published in *The Lancet* in 1918,[30] and proves, on reading, to be only a brief, anonymous and not very well-informed piece.

Twenty or twenty-five years later, the situation in the major countries of the west had altered.[31] In Spain there were many cases of amenorrhoea in Madrid and Barcelona in 1936–1938 and it was not until after the Civil War that the numbers declined.[32] In France, from 1940 and especially from 1942 the doctors were on the alert: in June 1942, during the "difficult summer gap" (stocks of food commandeered by the occupying forces, harvest not yet in), obstetricians in Paris were alarmed by the increasing incidence of amenorrhoea. Signs of puberty (first menstruation) appeared later than usual in Parisian schoolgirls, at thirteen and a half or fourteen years of age, instead of at twelve and a half, as had been the case in 1937, among girls of school age in the working-class suburbs. Many women who were overworked, subject to nervous disorders and above all suffering from lack of food, ceased to menstruate. All things considered, it seems clear that the year 1942 marks the climax of the incidence of amenorrhoea in France during the second World War (just as 1917 had in Germany during the first). After 1942, French food stocks still remained low; nevertheless, as a result possibly of physical adaptation[33] or for some quite different reason, the number of amenorrhoea cases levelled out or even began to decrease. To return to 1942, such was the extent of the phenomenon that a young doctor from Finistère, Laurent Quéméré, made it the subject of a thesis which he presented in Paris in November of that year.[34] Unfortunately, Quéméré confined himself to a synthesis of certain observations made by the German writers and by Boucher in 1914–1918. His amenorrhoea cases were one war late! We have to wait until the following year to obtain a few figures which are reasonably satisfactory but rather approximate and too general (even in the opinion of the authors) to be wholly reliable. According to Guy-Laroche, Bompard and Trémolières, four to seven per cent of French women of child-bearing age, were affected by "wartime amenorrhoea" during these last years of the occupation. In one large factory, the figure reached 12.6 per cent of the female personnel. The first figure (four to seven per cent) comes close to the scientifically attested figure of 5.11 per cent proposed by Teebken for Kiel,[35] in 1917.

Whatever might be the exact percentages, their geographical distribution is worth noting: the under-nourished Midi[36] appears to have been particularly affected, especially around Toulouse, Bordeaux and Montpellier. If we wish to find a particularly clearly defined and tragic "regional" example, we must leave France and go to the north-west of Holland, which in 1944–45 experienced distress comparable with the worst medieval and Classical Age famines— and this in the middle of the twentieth century.

On 17 September 1944, at the request of the Dutch government in London, a general transport strike began in Amsterdam, Rotterdam and the Hague.[37] Liberation seemed to be around the corner . . . in fact it did not come until May 1945. But the strikes persisted, the railways remained paralysed. In reprisal, the Germans blockaded the roads and canals. The towns received little or no food. A starvation winter followed. In the Hague, every week from January to May 1945, more than one hundred people died of hunger; in Rotterdam more still. The official rations for pregnant women (who were relatively privileged) fell to 1,144 calories a day at the start of 1945. Proteins, fats, carbohydrates, all were drastically reduced at the same time. As a result, amenorrhoea leaped to enormous, quite historic proportions, far beyond the figures for Germany in 1917 and France in 1942, where malnutrition had tragic consequences in only a minority of cases among the very poor. In the cities of Holland during this last winter of the Nazi occupation, practically all the women went hungry. The result was that only 30 per cent menstruated normally. The number of conceptions, deduced from the births nine months later, fell to one-third of the normal figure. Amenorrhoea (and the sterility associated with it) was evidently one of the causes —though not the only one—of this temporary fall in the birth-rate. In Utrecht, another researcher independently published similar findings: with every other factor accounted for, the winter of hunger in this city was responsible for amenorrhoea in 33 per cent of the women of child-bearing age.[38]

These horrifying percentages, never before seen in medical literature, pale into insignificance by comparison with the figures revealed, in the immediate post-war period, of the plight of women deportees: in the camp at Theresienstadt, 54 per cent of the 10,000 internees ceased normal menstruation after one, two or three months inside. After eighteen or twenty months in the camp, the great majority of the survivors among this 54 per cent were menstruating regularly again. This was not because the living conditions in Theresienstadt had improved but because the phenomenon of adaptation had taken place: the organisms of these women had become involuntarily "accustomed" to the intolerable.[39] Many similar occurrences were noted, especially in Auschwitz.[40] Hungarian doctors, also,[41] in 1944–45 reported some horrendous percentages, some of which may have been exaggerated:

	Percentage of women suffering from amenorrhoea
Women living in Budapest during the siege 1944–45	50 to 60%
Women deported by the Germans	99%

In the two works he has devoted to the subject, A. Netter makes the following comment: "All states of malnutrition, and especially protein deficiency, can cause amenorrhoea. This was frequently observed during the last war, particularly in the case of deportees ... when the deportees returned home and the consequences of famine had been remedied, the one single factor remaining to cause amenorrhoea was the remembrance of the terrible psychological conditions associated with deportation."[42]

Together with the severe lack of food which was so obvious a feature of the death camps, psychic and psychosomatic factors have, it appears then, played an important part in the onset or prolongation of amenorrhoea. Famine, after all, is a total phenomenon, not only producing malnutrition but also causing debilitating anxiety. These psychosomatic factors[43] are indeed referred to in the published writings of American doctors imprisoned during the Second World War in Japanese camps, where there were also many women from the United States. In Manilla, in the Santo Thomas camp normal menstruation had ceased in the case of 14.8 per cent of the women detainees. But this condition pre-dated the food shortages; in the majority of cases it had begun with the bombing of the city and during the first days of internment: the cause, quite simply, was anguish and shock.[44] Similarly, in Hong Kong, in Camp Stanley (1942) 60.6 per cent of the women detainees were afflicted with amenorrhoea. Very often it occurred during the first days of food restrictions and simply as a result of the psychological shock of internment. The diet at Camp Stanley was very inadequate it is true, but it was no different from what Chinese women had subsisted upon, long before the war, without any signs of amenorrhoea. But as Dr. Annie Sydenham, who observed and published these data remarked, it was not so much the meagreness in absolute terms of the daily ration that counted, as its sudden deterioration "in quality as well as in quantity".[45]

Even in the United States, where food restrictions in 1941–1945 were insignificant or non-existent, there was a rise in the number of cases of amenorrhoea during the Second World War: in the hospitals of Dallas (Texas) menstrual disorders of this kind affected only 82 patients out of 9,141 between the ages of nineteen and thirty-nine in the "pre-war" year 1940. But in 1945, at the conclusion of four years of accumulated tensions resulting from the war, these disorders were experienced by 368 patients out of 2,398.[46] The difference between 1940 and 1945 looks as if it is statistically significant.[47] These American women under stress at the end of the war were not under-nourished. But they were the wives, daughters or fiancées of combatants, and were therefore in a state of anxiety, which would have greatly contributed, among other possible causes, to explain their condition.

In any case, if we are to believe the specialists, "war-time amenorrhoea" seems to be the result of a multiple assault upon the female organism: anguish and restrictions, food shortages and mental distress combine in an inextricable complex of causes.[48] Such a complex is not however, necessarily associated with the traumatizing background of a world war. Peace may equally be a time of famine and disruptive anguish. This fact, which is of the utmost importance for the interpretation of the famines of former times, has been demonstrated on a number of occasions. In 1948, for example, Theodore Heynemann, summarizing many observations noted in Hamburg during the preceding years in the University hospitals,[49] could speak of *Nachkriegsamenorrhoe* (post-war-amenorrhoea). The term would seem rather strange . . . if the problem were not a real one. In a word, Germany under Hitler, fairly well fortified against food scarcities, thanks to forced levies on conquered peoples, escaped the worst shortages, and the amenorrhoea which these entailed, until the beginning of 1945. Paradoxically, it was in 1945 and 1946, and so mainly *after* the war, that serious food restrictions, in calories and proteins, had their greatest effect on German women; to which, of course, must be added the psychological factors resulting from total defeat. Whatever the reasons, the number of cases of amenorrhoea in Heynemann's clinic rose from 16 (0.8 per cent of his women patients) in 1938, to 396 (8.7 per cent) in 1946. The percentages of similar cases had fluctuated between 2.1 per cent and 3.5 per cent from 1939 to 1944. They rose to 7.6 per cent from May to December 1945, to reach a maximum later, as we have seen, in the following year, and eventually decreased from 1947 onwards, with the return to more normal conditions.

★

It was in this year 1947, in fact, as the world emerged from the tragedy of war, that two American researchers, Strecker and Emlen, decided to conduct experiments on mammals having certain similarities to man, in order to examine this difficult problem of the link between famine and sterility. Their method consisted of creating a subsistence-crisis, with scarcity or famine, in a colony of mice. The student of social history not necessarily confined to mankind[50] is unfortunately obliged to consider the possibility of comparative experiments on animals, although they may seem cruel. This is because subsistence crises are tragic episodes in the demography of early Western societies. A rise in the death-rate, a fall in the number of marriages, a disproportionate collapse in the number of births, or rather, of conceptions, all interact with machine-like regularity. And so it is important to know what happens in similar circumstances in the case of animals, whether at liberty or in the laboratory.

Strecker and Emlen carried out their crucial experiment using mice caught in the city of Madison.[51] They confined the little creatures in carefully stopped-up empty rooms in a disused barracks in Wisconsin. They fed them on wheat, maize, meat, salt and cod-liver oil. They checked their numbers and weighed them at fixed intervals.

The subsistence crisis was created quite simply by a policy of *laissez faire*. While the mouse population in the barrack-rooms continued to grow, the total amount of food supplied to the whole community remained fixed at a constant daily level. At first, the individual ration was more than sufficient. As the population increased, at a certain point it became inadequate and scarcity began.

The first consequence was the effect upon infant mortality. Young mice born before the famine managed all right. They did not die. But out of thirteen mice (from three litters) born immediately after the famine began, twelve died within five weeks of birth. Stecker and Emlen were unable to determine the exact cause of these deaths. Were the under-nourished mothers short of milk and lacking in care for their new-born babies? It is possible, but not certain. For all these infant deaths occurred after weaning. They might have occurred simply as a result of competition for food, the over-weak baby mice being pushed away from the feeding-troughs by the more vigorous adults. If this was so, the young ones were condemned to death by starvation: a form of infanticide.

But another effect—and a very important one—was the decline in the fertility of the mice in times of scarcity. The sexual appetite of the subjects of the experiment diminished as a result of their enforced fast, while their appetite for food, constantly frustrated, became more acute. This reduction in sexual activity is quantifiable. The two researchers studied *in vivo* or by autopsy a large number of mice: in the starving mice they found few, if any, of the usual signs of genital activity: pregnancy, perforated vagina, etc. Concerning the latter, the percentage of female mice exhibiting such a characteristic fell from 70 per cent among the well-nourished to 17 per cent among those who were short of food. In the males too, the researchers observed various symptoms of a diminution of the sexual function after the onset of food scarcity: decrease in the size of the testicles, etc. According to a whole series of signs, observed by comparative dissection of fasting and non-fasting mice, it appears that the percentage of sexually active males fell from 100 per cent to 80 per cent from the start of food shortages. This fall was therefore less serious than the corresponding fall in the case of the females: from 70 per cent to 17 per cent as we saw.

This experiment is conclusive. It destroys the commonly

accepted view according to which animals, since they do not
know how to limit their numerical increase, are inevitably
doomed to physiological decline and death as soon as a
serious subsistence crisis develops. In this particular experiment at any rate, this was not what happened: death was
restricted to the very young. And an involuntary but very
effective "policy" of a fall in the number of conceptions
began to apply. Through the operation of certain physiological mechanisms, this prevented the normal multiplication
of the mice, the consequences of which would, in times of
scarcity, have been catastrophic. The adults became sexually
abstemious—no doubt of that—but they did not die. Better
still—they did not even lose weight. By severely limiting
their numbers they succeeded, more or less, in maintaining
their food ration. To put it one way, using a somewhat
simplified, inexact and determinist metaphor, one might
say that these mice were born Malthusians whose organisms,
when constrained to it by necessity, preferred "virtue" to
"deprivation". In more scientific language we might well
repeat what A. Netter[52] wrote in this connection, on the
subject of secondary amenorrhoea caused by malnutrition
or by some other condition seriously affecting the constitution: "It would be an error to treat amenorrhoea in such
circumstances; for it is undoubtedly a defence mechanism:
it is as if the organism were suppressing the *luxury function*
i.e., the function of reproduction, in order to preserve the
vital function—the function of survival."

*

As we reach the end of what is really a survey of the literature on this subject one conclusion seems obvious: scientific
studies of animals akin to man, and above all, the bitter and
often repeated experiences of the world wars, scientifically
recorded, demonstrate clearly that there is a link between
acute famine and temporary sterility. This article is not the
place to comment on the physiological nature of this relationship, but there is no denying its existence. Amenorrhoea
resulting from famine is clearly one factor accounting for
the drastic fall in the number of conceptions[53] at the worst

times of subsistence crises, such as those studied by the historians of the seventeenth century.

In conclusion, the question posed by P. Goubert is still waiting for an answer: "We continue to hope that the writings of some doctor of the past will provide us with evidence ... of the phenomena of amenorrhoea in times of famine."[54] My so far incomplete and *ad hoc* research into this subject in works of the seventeenth and eighteenth centuries, has borne little fruit. *Emmenology* (the science of menstruation) by the English doctor J. Freind (who died in 1728) has nothing to tell us: Freind sympathizes with the unfortunate condition of women and he reports that in his day girls reached puberty at the age of fourteen, but he has nothing further to say on the phenomena in which we are interested. On the other hand, the materialist-philosopher and doctor La Mettrie, in his commentary on the work of Boerhave, is more explicit, without however having anything particularly pertinent to say on our subject. He does not establish a direct link between famine and amenorrhoea; but he does note that *atrophy*, which he defines by the symptoms of under-nourishment—"emaciation", consumption, extreme loss of weight—is accompanied by cessation of menstruation: "victims of *atrophy*," he writes, "commonly menstruate either very little or rarely."[55] Is it exaggerating, if we pursue to its conclusion the reasoning implicit in La Mettrie's argument, to say that in times of famine, the number of "atrophic"—and therefore amenorrhoeic—women increased considerably?

Whatever one might think of this analysis, the conclusions set out in a comprehensive study by V.C. Wynne-Edwards[56] are fully substantiated: it is quite correct that man (like the animals) possesses mechanisms capable of controlling births on a massive scale in times of distress and serious scarcity. Voluntary contraception is not the absolute *sine qua non* for the attainment of this objective. In women, as in rats and mice, virtually automatic processes are ready to function at any moment, ready if necessary to suppress the "luxury" function of reproduction; they constitute an unconscious control so to speak, that humanity exercises over itself. Such processes revealed themselves in Europe during the famines of the Classical Age, as they did two and a half centuries later, during the world wars of our own time: the latter have enabled us to take the measure of the former. In both cases, amenorrhoea resulting from malnutrition is indeed *the cry of silent suffering*[57] of millions of under-nourished and deeply traumatized women.[58]

Since the publication of this article in *Annales*, in 1969, I have at last discovered the text that Pierre Goubert was appealing for: "The causes of retention and suspension (of menstruation) are several, as, for instance, acute or long illness, grief, fear, *hunger*, and heavy toil ... or pregnancy" (Ambroise Paré, *Oeuvres complètes*, Paris, 1840, Book XVIII, chap. 61).

16

Chaunu, Lebrun, Vovelle: The New History of Death[1]

THE historical theme of changing attitudes towards death, and, indirectly at least, towards life, has recently been the subject of various works by historians. I am thinking in particular of the writings of Pierre Chaunu, François Lebrun and Michel Vovelle. In this paper, I should simply like to present a résumé of the results obtained concerning the last few centuries, and in particular the seventeenth. These relate, as it happens, to Christian countries, especially France, about which more is known, thanks to its wealth of notarial archives. Such documents enable us to explore the attitudes towards death, not so much of the great writers and thinkers—of, say, Pascal, Montaigne or Bossuet—but rather those of the anonymous individuals who made up the élites, the bourgeoisie and the provincial nobility; and if we dig even deeper, those of the ordinary people of town and country.

Pierre Chaunu, who recently published a brilliant article on this theme,[2] considers that the seventeenth century and the early years of the eighteenth were marked by what amounts to the *socialization of death*. Death itself was a spectacle for the near and the not-so-near relatives; burial was an occasion for a grand festival in which the whole town took part, and of which the French expression *"les pompes funèbres"* (still to be seen outside undertakers' parlours) and Churchill's funeral in England (of which there has been no equivalent this side of the Channel) even today still convey a faint but authentic echo. In the seventeenth and eighteenth centuries, public expression of grief by members of the family of the deceased and, when called upon, by professional mourners, sanctioned a salutary outburst of emotion and a release of suffering. Paroxysms of weeping, whether sincere or merely histrionic, allowed the mourning to take its proper course in a world where, by definition, there were no such things as psychiatrists or tranquillizers.

273

The average man, having an immediate or long-term hope of salvation, probably faced death with more serenity than does his counterpart today. True panic was concentrated not so much upon the last moments of life as upon the dread moment of appearance before the Sovereign Judge. The truly devout, echoing Saint Teresa of Avila, even went so far as to pray for the moment of death. "I die because I cannot die", said the saint. Not that one can always be absolutely certain of the significance of this longing for prompt death: near-certainty, perhaps, of celestial salvation—or a death wish, in the case of the less pure of the saint's followers?

From 1740–1750 onwards, says Chaunu, the "desocialization" of death, to which reference has already been made, took place. The excessive display of funeral parades with their processions of the poor, of penitents, of bearers of torches and palls emblazoned with coats of arms, inevitably evoked from those of Jansenist consciences, what one may agree with Michel Vovelle in calling a protest against pomp. People asked for simpler funerals. Death was thus gradually withdrawing from urban or surrounding society and retreating into the private world of the family (as is illustrated by certain paintings by Greuze dating from the beginning of the neo-classical, or *style Louis XVI* period). Nevertheless, republican ceremonies in the nineteenth century, such as were seen at the funeral of Victor Hugo, occasionally indicate the existence of what was now no more than a residual folk-memory of funeral processions. In Corsica, the cult of the dead flared up probably for the last time on the occasion of the burials of the famous Pigalle family, in their gigantic tombs on their native Isle of Beauty, between 1920 and 1930.

However even this "desocialization" of death and its confinement within the privacy of the family was only one step. At the next stage, already reached in American civilization, normal everyday death can become totally individual, to be experienced simply as a personal tragedy. The segregation of the older generation in the luxuriously-appointed ghettoes of Florida enables the young and middle-aged to accord only the bare minimum of importance to the death and burial of faraway, cosmeticized grandmothers. Death, as Chaunu has written, has virtually replaced sex as a taboo subject in what was once the Victorian category of the obscene. "Each for himself, and God for nobody" (Chaunu). Or as the famous slogan of the funeral home has it: "You die, we do the rest."

The civilization of the Baroque, at the height of its career, had been capable of integrating both skeleton and coffin into the mazy arabesques of its tortuous decorative style, so beloved of the Bavarian rococo. Industrial, or post-industrial society, on the other hand, in its most characteristic form of mass self-expression—advertising—banishes death, old age and ugliness, in order to celebrate the values it most admires. The divinities thus honoured, with a sometimes suspect sincerity, are, of course, youth, vitality and physical beauty, particularly as represented by a desirable woman.

In this deodorized world, however, death, like some irrepressible demon, makes a regular weekly appearance at the hour of reckoning of the weekend road toll. The tragic significance of car accidents lies in the fact that it is often, indeed principally, the young who are killed, making a mockery of the statistics of increased life expectancy. *Thanatos* also regularly appears in television programmes, showing the events of the Third World, far or not so far from home (Vietnam or Sinaï). The planet has indeed become a "global village", where for the first time, news of death, often on a massive scale, circulates from one end to the other of the inhabited world; but these items have now become too numerous and too varied to make possible any deep show of grief. We might also note the rise of the mythical cult of death in the cinema of ultra-violence.

Should this mythical "socializing" of death cause us to regret the passing of an age—not really a very pleasant one—when "socializing" fulfilled a genuine function? François Lebrun's book, *La Mort en Anjou au XVIIIe siècle*, goes some way to help us to an answer. This work has the considerable merit of combining the most scrupulous and quantitative of demographic research with the study of cultural data and collective mental attitudes in a large province of France. Beginning with a forthright statement of the absence of any demographical increase in the eighteenth century in Anjou, Lebrun is able to reveal, thanks to the help of the parish registers, the formidable hold of death, and the short expectancy of life among the people of this province in the period in question. Infant mortality of 300 or even 350 per 1000 in the first year of life; the indifference with which adults, both peasant and middle-class, accepted the death of very young children (who would be assumed in any case, to go straight to Paradise) are among the phenomena carefully recorded by Lebrun. They lead him to support the theory that the feelings aroused by the death of a young child, and especially of a baby, were not as intense in the seventeenth and eighteenth centuries as would be the case today: an Angevin lawyer of 1660, Pierre Andouys, records with neither comment nor surprise, the death of four of his children at an early age, all within the space of less than two years. It is only on the death of his fifth child (then aged five and a half) that Andouys deigns to insert a comment in his diary. And this comment testifies more to the egocentricity of the author than to his sensitivity: "May this child", he writes, "do me the grace of praying God for me." On this point, however, perhaps it would be as well to reserve judgement on François Lebrun's opinion—which is still perfectly valid, of course, but only as a first impression. The family diary of a modest lawyer or cattle-merchant of the seventeenth century is not always the most appropriate place in which to look for cries from the heart.

In other respects, Lebrun's work already gives a hint of several of the discoveries which were to be fully brought to light by Vovelle: in Anjou the change in the wording of wills, eliminating religious references, took place between 1760 and 1775: from this time on, when making their wills, adults, whether in good health or in bad, either ceased or neglected to commend their souls to all the saints in heaven; or at any rate, they left out some of them, the saints of popular folk-lore or the saints of the Counter-Reformation. They also left off their former practice of burial inside churches, even before the royal decree of 1776 banning this practice. And finally, the cemetery, which for ages past, had been an open public place, used not only for burials but also for fairs, folk dances, village fêtes and even for the nocturnal trysts of young lovers, had, by the middle of the eighteenth century, become an enclosed space, the dark interior of which was henceforth hidden away from the rest of the world by surrounding walls; which meant that the dead, too were securely shut away. If we are to believe François Lebrun, these various developments constituted a double separation: the living became separated from the dead and also from the hosts of the saints. It was as if the Christian, or formerly Christian community, were shaking off the ties binding it to the Church Triumphant, in other words to the community of saints; as if, moreover, this community were also freeing itself, to some extent, from its links with the Suffering Church, in other words, from the community of souls in Purgatory. The "desocialization" of death, of which Pierre Chaunu speaks, can be said then to amount to a divorce, dissociating the village of the living from the village of the dead.

In a thesis as yet unpublished,* Michel Vovelle fully develops this analysis.[3] Wishing to view the subject of human attitudes towards death in a perspective both broad and historical, he has made a study of wills and testaments, documents which can be listed in series and thus lend themselves to quantification. From sources of this type, one would not of course expect to find insights comparable to those on the same subject in, say, Pascal's *Pensées*. Vovelle however, armed with information from his thousands of wills, goes further, in a certain sense, than the historians of literature or the students of Pascal. For he has made contact with the average man, *homo historicus*, so to speak. As he card-indexes the last wishes of the people of Provence, is Vovelle's technique so very different from the methods of the French Institute of Public Opinion, or Gallup, when they take their opinion polls? Purists, perhaps, will turn up their noses at this method, but those who believe in the value of social history will read Vovelle, when he is published.

Here to begin with, is his first conclusion: in about 1720, baroque extravagance still surrounded death and burial in Provence—the region which, for reasons of circumstance and principle was to provide the initial field for research into the

*It has now been published. See footnote 3.

historiography of wills and testaments. The burial of any notable person, or even of a local tradesman, would mean a *tour de ville*, a funeral procession round the streets; in the procession there would be a band of marching musicians and either thirteen or twenty-six children (thirteen boys and thirteen girls) representing the twelve apostles and Judas. During the burials, bells would be tolling their loudest from a hundred belfries in one of the southern towns so typical of the French provinces, an opportune reminder that before the towns became the notorious centres of ungodliness they are in our time, they had originally been the scene of the maximum displays of Christian observance. Such observance, during the period famous for the Revocation of the Edict of Nantes, was enacted within a rural environment which, although Christian, remained faithful to a more informal spirit world, still heavily redolent of folklore and pagan survivals.

From 1750 onwards, among the upper classes and especially the aristocracy, requests for simplicity in funeral ceremony became increasingly more frequent, though they may not always have been sincere. In the Nice region, still very Italian and very baroque in the eighteenth century, one gentleman asked in his will that his burial should take place "in all simplicity" ... only to stipulate immediately afterwards that all he wished was that he should be accompanied to his last resting-place by twenty-six poor children and three rows of penitents, that the bells should be tolled so many times, and much else besides: the strictest incognito as it were, remarks Vovelle wryly. So the demand for simplicity was not necessarily always genuine. But all the same, there was unquestionably a trend towards the decline of baroque ceremonial.

Furthermore, in Provence as in Anjou, fewer people insisted on choosing their place of burial. Those who did so, usually chose in their wills to be buried in a convent, or perhaps under the flag-stones of the parish church, near the altar of a saint. To renounce sleeping one's last sleep close to a saint was to forfeit the benefits of a flood of indulgences and chances of grace. According to what was, it must be admitted, a primitive and superstitious theology, such benefits flowed more or less freely as one lay nearer to or further from the altar in question. Such a renunciation meant one of two things: either a Jansenist attitude (which defied superstition, saw the problem of grace in an entirely different light, and sought an authentic relationship between the individual soul and God), or something else altogether: indifference, to some extent at least, which made light of supernatural aids during and after death.

Another aspect of the quantitative historiography, "à la Vovelle", of attitudes towards death, relates to the study of requests for masses for the repose of the soul of the departed, and of the offerings of candles for the same purpose. An English critic has recently exercised his irony at the expense of the quantitative school—justifiably perhaps in this instance – on the use, as a criterion, of the average weight of votive candles, which did, in fact, radically diminish after 1770. But the tally of the number of masses requested does seem to be much more convincing. At the end of the seventeenth century, testators endowed foundations for masses in perpetuity which, in theory, should still be being said today, provided that the celebrants had remained sufficiently conscientious. But over a very long period of time, inflation nibbles away at the fees for such masses "in perpetuity". That was why, after 1700, testators, who had remained very pious and faithful to the extravagant devotions of the Age of Baroque, no longer requested masses in perpetuity, but rather by the thousand, provided they were rich enough and eminent enough to indulge themselves in such luxuries. Then, after 1760, this practice also declined. After this date, fewer and fewer testators, a minority even, asked for masses to be said after their deaths. And the number of masses of those who still requested them fell away sharply, to such a point that certain stereotyped images which are commonly (and quite justifiably) employed of the nineteenth and twentieth centuries, were already beginning to apply as early as the second half of the eighteenth century. For instance in Provence during the Enlightenment, women were more constant and more faithful in their requests for masses at death and after death than men; and yet, at the start of the eighteenth century there had been as many devout men as devout women; but after 1720–1730, the new attitudes, either Jansenist or indifferent, *vis à vis* Christian rites of death became more widespread in the male half of the population than in the female.

In connection with this study of masses said for the dead, Vovelle has also calculated the chronology of the varying factors, based either on Jansenism or indifference, which may legitimately be held responsible for the decline in the celebrating of masses. A strictly baroque and ultra-devout period was followed, from 1730 onwards, by a Jansenist interlude; this in turn gave way to an immense surge of indifference (much less acute of course than nowadays) during the second half of the eighteenth century. Between these two episodes—the Jansenist and the indifferent—there were several short revivals of baroque piety around 1750, but they were far from widespread in the Provençal region.

For the moment let us concentrate on the latest problem in time, the rise of indifference: not that one can go so far as to talk of "dechristianization" exactly, but one can recognize that several indications point in that direction: the research done by François Furet, based on the statistics of printed texts, and even that by Daniel Mornet, on the intellectual origins of the French Revolution, are supported by Vovelle's analyses; if I may, for once, use the outmoded language of causality, I would say that, with respect to the religious indifference and the "dechristianization" of the upper classes and even of the mass of the population, the French Revolution was as much effect as it was cause.

Another very striking index of attitudes detected by Vovelle concerns invocations to the Virgin: in the early years of the eighteenth century, 80 to 85 per cent of wills in Provence commended the souls of the faithful to the Virgin Mary; if they felt it necessary, the commendation was accompanied by a legacy to a Lady chapel in some church or convent. By the end of the eighteenth century, these figures have fallen to 25 or 30 per cent. It is true that we are speaking of Provence where, in spite of invocations (of relatively late date) to Nôtre-Dame-de-la-Garde and to the Holy Mother, the cult of the mother of Christ never reached the intensity one finds for instance in neighbouring Italy. But despite this incontestable difference in voltage, so to speak, it is nevertheless quite clear that the popularity of the Virgin Mary was in decline among the people of Provence during the eighteenth century. The same might be said for the good (or the guardian) Angel, and for the patron saint; and also more generally for all the heavenly saints: a certain number of them were mentioned in the usual fashion in the last wishes of Provençal citizens at the start of the eighteenth century; but they were almost entirely absent from wills, after having been more or less gradually neglected, by the last decades before the Revolution. This inglorious rout of the saints was accompanied by an erosion of respect for convents and monasteries; during the Century of Enlightenment, these establishments gradually lost their prestige, to such an extent even that monks were no longer asked out to dinner. There was also a decline in legacies willed by testators to relatives— cousins, uncles, nephews—who happened to be members of the clergy: the reason quite simply, was a certain decline in the number of vocations in these days of the *philosophes*, and consequently, on the whole, testators were left with fewer and fewer ecclesiastics in their families. Associated with such changes of attitude towards death, attitudes towards the poor also changed: no longer were they seen as the image of Christ on earth, nor as having the capacity in the hereafter of making corresponding payments into the accounts of those who had offered them "alms" on earth. The poor became the object of the anonymous charity of the government or the town: politicians, councillors, bureaucrats, could therefore proceed with the clearest of consciences to shut them up in poor-houses. All at once, the poor became invisible, either because they had been shut away, or because they had become as it were transparent, insubstantial. So no one gave them anything any more. As for the companies of hooded penitents who invested the pious energy of their members in duties and prayers at the funerals of the poor or of their fellow-members, after 1750 they were no longer in demand by polite society and by the nobility. At the end of eighteenth century, their companies tended to become simple clubs devoted to gastronomy, folklore and licentiousness, even free-masonry (cf. the works of Maurice Agulhon).

*

At this point, at the end of an account in which I have tried to present the conclusions of recent research, I should like to offer a few general reflections. In the first place, as Michel Vovelle remarks, it seems that we must categorically reject the hypercritical position which casts doubt upon the value of series of wills as documents reflecting mental attitudes towards death. It goes without saying that each one of the items of evidence put forward by Vovelle could be attributed to the personal idiosyncrasies of the notaries who drew up the wills; or else could be explained by an increased demand, expressed by testators, for a purer, more direct and less materialistic religion and consequently for smaller and less costly attendance at their funerals and for a decrease in the weight of wax-candles to be burned in the church service. But taken as a whole, the "Vovelle index" points too consistently in the same direction to indicate anything other than a progressive sense of detachment with regard to the supernatural, and a move towards a greater decline of Church influence and a "desocialization" of death. What we must recognize, after 1750, is indeed (in spite of, or because of the intermediary Jansenist phase about 1730–1750) an undoubted move towards religious indifference which led to a desanctifying, to a demystification, as it were, of death; and even to the inclusion in one's will of certain preoccupations with life, quite unheard of in the Baroque Age—think, for example, of the panic terror of being buried alive that was so characteristic of so many testators in the eighteenth and nineteenth centuries.

Vovelle and especially Chaunu, confront us, moreover, with a strictly historiographical problem: according to the author of *L'Europe classique*, the appearance of the subject of death on the contemporary historian's agenda, is, in fact, inseparable from a crisis of civilization characterized, as we are all aware, on a very much broader plane, by the widespread challenging of values, by the remote but frequently discussed question of an ecological Day of Judgment etc. This, to paraphrase Chaunu, would explain why "the kind of history written by Labrousse, Meuvret or Goubert, which centred on questions of growth or non-growth, is now being superseded (in part) by the kind of history associated with Vovelle and Lebrun, who are concerned with the serially-documented images of death in human society". Without denying the relevance of such an analysis, let me say, however, that it seems to me to be particularly French. In the United States, as we well know, the crisis of civilization is just as evident and even more pronounced if anything than in France. Yet when I look at the current trends in American historiography, I see in them nothing remotely resembling the fascination that death has for the French historians. Transatlantic historians, or at least the most *avant-garde* among them, are currently interested—whether because it is fashionable or particularly relevant at the moment—in the past history of the Blacks and other ethnic minorities in the North American continent; in the history of women, associated with the recent resurgence of interest in feminism; in the history of cities, rising out of the modern urban crisis; and lastly, in detailed studies of econometric and statistical history, or quite simply, in the history of other countries and other continents. To my knowledge there is no Vovelle, no Lebrun in Yale or in Harvard, and if Philippe Ariès has followers in the United States, it is because of his social studies of childhood, not because of his recent researches on death under the *ancien régime*. The present interest in the history of death, as I have described it, seems to me to be specifically French, or perhaps Italo-French or Dutch (I am thinking of the work of Tenenti and also of the still relevant studies of Huizinga) rather than truly international. American lack of interest in this subject is however easily explained: in spite of, or because of, the present crisis, United States' historians are influenced by the dominant trends in their national culture, and they remain profoundly and incorrigibly optimistic. Perhaps one has to be a European, a fellow-countryman of Pascal, to think that history is a meditation on death as well as a reflection on life.

Even on this point, however, in so far as Vovelle's work is

concerned, it would be wrong to end on too one-sided an impression. The second volume of his book is much less concerned with the subject of death as such. Vovelle's interest here, expressed consistently throughout, is quite simply research into the religious sociology of the Provence of the past. There is, it seems, a "hereafter" to death, if not perhaps in "another world", then at least, in the works of good historians. Thanks to Vovelle, religious sociology—the sociology of death and of earthly existence—has, in the history of the *ancien régime*, gone beyond the stage of counting heads—whether of those who take the sacraments or of those who attend mass. It is leading to a truly serial, mass-scale history of religious attitudes.

PART FOUR

HISTORY WITHOUT PEOPLE: THE CLIMATE AS A NEW PROVINCE OF RESEARCH

17

Writing the History of the Climate

IN the year 1601 a group of panic-stricken villagers addressed a very curious petition to the Chamber of Accounts of Savoy. They were from a poor and almost unknown parish in the Haut-Faucigny, called Chamonix. Until this date, no one had paid any attention to these mountain settlers, except for a few cheese-merchants and chamois hunters, and, occasionally, the priests who made their way up into the mountains to levy tithes (only to be received quite often with sticks and stones). But now, unexpectedly, in the year 1601 the natives of Chamonix brought themselves to the attention of the authorities. "We are terrified of the glaciers," they wrote in their local patois, "particularly the Argentière and the Bois [the latter better known today as the Mer de Glace] which are moving forward all the time and have just buried two of our villages and destroyed a third . . ."

The petition of the Chamonix villagers aroused no alarm, no interest even in the government of Savoy. It was simply filed away in the archives, at the back of a cupboard where, in 1920, three and a half centuries after the events it described and just when scholars were beginning to take an interest in historical glaciology, it was discovered by the archivist Letonnelier.

The phenomena described in the 1601 text were not the only ones of their kind. Throughout the Alps at the very end of the sixteenth century and the beginning of the seventeenth, the glaciers were making frontal assaults and the record of these events probably provides the best possible introduction for anyone who is interested in the climatic and glaciological history of the seventeenth century. At Grindelwald, in the Bernese Oberland, the glaciers began their advance in about 1600–1601 and took over the site of the disused chapel of Sainte-Pétronille and several hitherto well-stocked barns. At Vernagt (in the Tyrol) as at Ruitor (Aosta), between 1596 and 1603, fast-moving rivers of ice formed barrier-lakes,

287

the overflow from which spread across the meadows and destroyed whole parishes. Everywhere, at this time, glacier tongues settled in very advanced positions which they were not completely to abandon until 250 years later, i.e. from 1855–60, when the great thaw of the Western ice-fields began—a thaw still in progress today. Climatologists, have been so struck by these two and a half centuries of glacial dominance (1600–1850) that they have named this period, mistakenly perhaps but picturesquely, the "little ice age".

The "little ice age" is not the only episode of its type on record in recent history ("recent" history of the glaciers means the last three or four thousand years as opposed to their "geological" history, which is reckoned in tens of thousands or even millions of years). Over the last few years, the Austrian glaciologist Franz Mayr has embarked on the promising project of studying the glacier of Fernau (Tyrol), the tip of which extends directly into a peat-bog. In the stratified layers of peat and moraine gravels which form the subsoil of this swamp, Mayr has discovered the traces of five multi-secular advances by the Fernau glacier (separated from each other by long intervals of retreat). These advances occurred in the fifteenth and fourteenth centuries B.C.; during the first millennium B.C. (two instances); in the fifth to eighth centuries A.D.; in the thirteenth century; and lastly, of course, from 1600 to 1850.

Since the middle of the nineteenth century, there have been, so far at any rate, no further instances of such phenomena. The Mer de Glace which from 1600 to 1850 curved round, in Hugo's phrase, "like the bend of an arm" ("comme un bras qui se recourbe") above the Chamonix valley, has since then entirely disappeared from this part of the landscape, and is no longer visible from the little winding plain which stretches from Chamonix to Les Praz and Les Bois. The Rhône glacier, which in all the old engravings formed a gigantic "pecten" or comb-like mass of ice blocking the bed of the Gletsch valley, has now retreated very much higher— a kilometre—into the rocky defile below the Belvedere Hotel: the "pecten" of ice has been melted away by the rise in the temperature.

One could cite many other examples: it is common knowledge that all the glaciers in the Alps have retreated spectacularly in the last hundred years. Some of the smallest have even disappeared altogether. The principal factor in this retreat is, *in the main* (a *detailed* account of the causes would require a completely different article[1]), the rise in the temperature, as it has been recorded in meteorological stations over the last century. The rise has been modest, but it has had "multiplicator" effects. Since 1860, annual average increases of a few tenths of a degree centigrade, or of barely one degree, at the most, have been enough to thaw gigantic glacier tongues in the mountain ranges of Western Europe.

*

So it is a story of fluctuations over whole centuries (set against the background of a climate which is stable only in the very long term), that the great glaciers of the Alps and the meteorologists' observations have to tell. A story of fluctuations, that is, and not one of "changes in the climate", an inappropriate expression one sometimes hears. Such fluctuations have been long and slow, and of variable duration. It would be pointless to try to find in them "cycles" or regular periodicities of eleven years, thirty-five years etc. These exist only in the imaginations of those earnest researchers who followed the example of Jevons and Moore (1923) and allowed themselves to become obsessed by the eleven-year sun-spot cycle, thinking that they had rediscovered it in the fluctuations of our terrestrial climate.

The last word in this story of climate fluctuation, we may suspect, has not yet been spoken. The detailed research of meteorologists such as Mitchell, Lamb, Von Rudloff, Callendar and Willett shows that the century-long rise in the temperature has now come to a halt, after reaching a peak between 1940 and 1950. Even the retreat of the glaciers has now apparently stopped as a result. In the course of the last twenty years, a new cooling phase has set in. Does this phase really herald, as it is sometimes claimed, a return to the slightly colder conditions of the previous phase? Or is it perhaps just a passing episode, temporary and insignificant? Only time will tell.

*

The important point is that, during the last generation, thanks to an intellectual endeavour little known to the general public, a scientific history of the "recent" climate, with its own methodology and results, has finally been established. In this respect, the situation has radically changed. Twenty or thirty years ago, the history of the climate was still a sort of happy hunting ground for hasty historians with a penchant for simplistic theories of causality. Those were the days when, if one needed a quickly-cobbled explanation for some great phenomenon of the past, apparently insoluble by any other causal analysis, the answer given by anyone with the slightest taste for the sensational, was that it could all be explained by a so-called "change in the climate". Huntington "explained" the decline of the Roman Empire by a variation of the cyclone paths which led to a progressive and disastrous drying up of the Mediterranean Basin. Olagüe attributed the decline of Spain to a similar kind of drought, but he placed this episode in less remote times than Huntington. Brooks sought to explain the migrations of the Mongols in the Middle Ages by the vagaries of rainfall: from time to time, drought reduced the pasture lands of Central Asia to scrawny scrub, and this, he claimed, drove the Mongols, a race of shepherds, to migrate towards rainier skies. It would be easy to list other speculations of the same type, as naïve as they are sterile.

We are no longer at that stage. The history of the climate has moved from the age of metaphysics into the age of science. From now on, glaciology combining with meteorology will be able to chart real fluctuations which have not been invented merely to prove a theory. In adjacent fields, other disciplines, which substantiate these first conclusions, are coming to the fore. In the U.S.A., *dendroclimatologists* are at work examining very old trees and producing rainfall-graphs covering periods of more than a thousand years, thanks to the annual growth-rings of sequoias and other conifers. They are able to do so because in the arid south-west of the United States, drought years produce very thin growth-rings, whereas a succession of thick rings of rich growth is the sign of comparatively wet years, favourable to forest growth. In France we have no thousand-year-old sequoias. But *phenology*[2] can tell us the dates of the ripening of flowers and fruits. The earlier the ripening, the warmer the growing season and vice-versa. Using this providential correlation between temperature and ripeness, phenologists are working on the records of the annual wine-harvest dates which can be found in the archives in Burgundy, Switzerland and the Midi, going back to the beginning of the sixteenth century. Converted into graphs, the wine-harvest dates can, as the meteorologist M. Garnier demonstrated in 1955, justify some definite conclusions as to the nature of the summer climate, hot or cool, year by year over the last four centuries, that is to say well before the start of accurate temperature readings. In Germany and Holland, experts in *palynology*, the science of pollens, have been exploring peat-bogs: they hope to find, trapped between the layers of peat, the "recurrence surfaces" in which the intermittent growth of sphagnum moss and other moisture-loving plants provides evidence of decades of humidity in the Middle Ages. And medieval historians and archaeologists have not been idle: in recent years, John Titow and Gabrielle Démians d'Archimbaud have made some important contributions to our knowledge of thirteenth-century meteorology. Finally, on the highest level so to speak, the science of *dynamic climatology* has recently been given fresh impetus in the USSR by the work of Dzerdeevsky. This discipline classifies and describes the changes affecting the general circulation of the atmosphere. Its aim is to explain climatic fluctuations established empirically by meteorologists and historians.

These findings all converge. Focusing on the climate, they have pioneered a specific historiography of natural conditions, a "geographical history" or *geohistory*. And this is how, in the pursuit of a fascinating subject, a dream has quietly come true—the famous dream of interdisciplinary research, long hoped for by specialist scientists who, as they worked in their separate fields, continued to be nostalgic for the lost world of the unity of knowledge.

18

The History of Rain and Fine Weather[1]

IN recent years, methods in climatic history have undergone some significant and highly interesting developments. Before saying something about them however, I should like to begin by recalling some of the best known of the various techniques employed in historical writings on climate, as applied to the last thousand years.

1. Concerning the latter part of this period—the last two centuries—the climate historian's task is, quite simply, to collate, verify, tabulate and publish basic series of meteorological observations. From the eighteenth century and the early years of the nineteenth onward, such records are in fact quite plentiful. As a model in this respect one may refer to the series of temperature readings for England and Holland for the last three centuries given by Gordon Manley and the Dutch researchers in this field.[2] The advantage of having thermometric series from neighbouring regions is that they can be checked for their mutual correlation: consequently, whenever any new records are discovered, they can be tested for correlations and their reliability can be established. Then, once one has an indication of the overall picture, the series enable the historian to detect on a regional, national, or even European scale, any intermittent fluctuations of temperature, tending towards warmer or colder weather which may have lasted chronologically a decade, a number of decades or even a century. And bearing in mind future research, we should not forget that in addition to such temperature records, there also exist early series of rainfall and barometric pressure records for the nineteenth century, and some even for the eighteenth century. Although often less reliable than the records of temperature, they are nevertheless extremely valuable for defining the weather patterns and atmospheric

293

conditions of the past. Huge numbers of valuable dossiers of this kind still lie buried away, even today, in the archives of observatories, medical and provincial academies, and learned societies.

2. For periods earlier than the eighteenth century, *dendrochronology* (the study of the growth-rings of trees) produces knowledge of the first importance on the subject of drought in arid or sub-tropical countries; on rainfall in temperate zones; and on cold conditions in northern lands. In the present article, we shall be concerned principally with the fluctuations of these three phenomena.

3. *Phenology*, the study of the annual dates of the flowering and fruiting of plants, has so far related exclusively to a series of documents almost unique of its kind: the wine-harvest dates *(vendanges)* registered in the archives. From these we may learn whether the March–September period in any given year was, on average, "warm" or "cool". Whenever we have a series of such dates for an area or group of areas, they shed light on the temperature fluctuations from one year to the next, or one decade to the next—though not as yet from one century to the next.[3]

4. The *"événementiel"* (recorded events) method relies on the painstaking accumulation of empirical and qualitative observations of climatic conditions recorded at the time by contemporary witnesses in private correspondence, family diaries, parish registers, etc. John Titow gave us a model of the method in 1960, in his impressive article on the climate of England in the fourteenth century *(Economic History Review)* and we also have the 1949 publication by D.J. Schove[4] of a comprehensive study of the climatic fluctuations of sixteenth-century Europe and of the progressive cooling of the winters from 1540–1560 to 1600.

5. The *glaciological* method was recently demonstrated by J. Grove à propos of Norway in the seventeenth and eighteenth centuries (see his article in *Arctic and Alpine Research*, 1972). This method involves a combination of

different types of research: analysis of documents (the Chamonix archives; the records of the sub-glacial farms of Norway; the Icelandic sagas); investigations calling on *geomorphology* (the study of moraines); *palynology* (the study of marshes and peat-bogs situated downstream of glaciers) and *nuclear biology* (the carbon 14 dating of the débris of trees left behind in moraines or found rooted in rocky beds lately uncovered by retreating glaciers). These studies have made it possible to track the secular, sometimes multi-secular ebb and flow of the glaciers and thanks to them we know the movements that have taken place in the ice-fields of Europe throughout the whole of the last thousand years; they offer an invaluable, if distorting, guide to weather pattern changes and in particular to changes of temperature.[5]

At this point however it seems to me essential to say a few words about the methodology, the fundamental aims even, that are associated with such techniques.

The *aim* of climatic history is not to explain human history, nor to offer simplistic accounts of this or that remarkable episode, (e.g., the crises of the fourteenth and the seventeenth centuries or the dramatic upturn of the eighteenth) not even when such episodes prompt us, with good reason, to reflect upon the great disasters of history. In the initial stages, its "aim" is quite different. Essentially it is to produce a clear picture of the changing meteorological patterns of past ages, in the spirit of what Paul Veyne calls "a cosmological history of nature". True, this "chronological cosmology", modestly limited to a study of regional climates, may serve as a discipline for future reference for a quite different and more ambitious project with human history as its object. The "spin-off" of the history of the climate does indeed have a bearing on the chronology of famines and also, perhaps, of epidemics, but these are merely consequences derived from it. However important and even exciting they may be, they remain marginal. The historian of the climate should ignore the tactics of the moment. It seems to me that his strategy should be, first and foremost, to place himself in the front line, shoulder to shoulder in interdisciplinary collaboration with the natural scientists. And if, at the outset, they treat him as an intruder, a deserter from his own discipline with nothing of any value to impart, so much the worse for them. The historian should simply swallow the insult and carry on doing his best to get them to accept the specific contribution that he alone is able to make. Several years ago, Pierre Chaunu said that the first duty of the economic historian was in all modesty to supply the professional economist with his basic material. Similarly the climate historian's first duty is to supply the natural scientists—meteorologists, glaciologists, climatologists, geophysicists, etc., with archival material. The reasons for such a division of labour are obvious and unsensational: by his training (in palaeography, knowledge of Latin and above all mastery of the "historian's craft") the professional historian alone has the key to certain types of data hidden away centuries ago in bundles of illegible old documents. Meteorologists have long ceased to be Latin scholars, let alone—and who can blame them!—palaeographers or "historiometricians".

My second comment concerns the necessarily climatological background to all research conducted along these lines. Unless he is to confine himself to a bare recital of the variations of the climate of the past, the historian of rain and fine weather has a duty to work at his assignment primed with a complete understanding of the basic data relating to movements of air masses and atmospheric circulation. The general theories and syntheses relating to such data are well-known and are constantly under review. The latest and most up-to-date account is by H.H. Lamb; (in 1970 I published a summary of this major work, but this should not be thought a substitute for consulting the original).[6]

These then are the essential presuppositions upon which, for the past fifteen years, my own investigations and those of several other researchers in the field of the recent history of the climate have been based. With these in mind I shall confine myself to pointing out the most recent developments, some of which are continuing along lines already referred to, others of which, on the contrary, are breaking entirely new ground. I shall also, in passing, note some of the most glaring gaps in our knowledge in the hope that one day new labourers in the field will come along and fill them.

1. With reference to the first method mentioned above—
collecting, tabulating, constructing, putting into graphs and
whenever necessary completing by informed extensions,
some of the very early meteorological series—I have to say
that recent results have not always reached the standard set
by Gordon Manley in the 1950s with his series of British
temperature readings for 1690 to 1955.[7] Since Manley the
most impressive achievement remains that of von Rudloff
(1967). In an important work almost unknown in France,
the German meteorologist has, with the aid of dozens of
previously published series, constructed a picture of the
changing pattern of the climate of Europe from 1700 or
1750 up to the present day. The pattern has of course its
characteristic phases: first, the little ice age; next, fluctuating,
irregular rises of temperature after 1850 or 1900 of the order
of one degree centigrade at the very most; lastly, the recent
cooling down period since 1953–1955.[8] The merit of von
Rudloff's book lies less, on the whole, in his definition of
these broad phases, for that had been done before, than in
his precise and subtly differentiated descriptions of them,
with the seasonal changes clearly marked.

But we do not always see evidence, even when it is staring
us in the face; even in this case when perspectives have been
opened up for us elsewhere by Manley or Rudloff. As far as
France is concerned, I shall therefore merely express a
regret which at the same time shall be my own apology—
mea culpa. Here in France, we are still waiting for someone
to establish a reliable, annually numbered series of monthly
temperatures running without interruption from the early
eighteenth century up to the present day, an enterprise
eminently possible thanks to the excellent archives of daily
records preserved in the Paris Observatory and elsewhere.
It would chiefly concern the northern half of the country,
more precisely the Paris region and the north, where these
series of old readings are the most plentiful. But our professional meteorologists are wholly engaged in the crushing
task of providing a daily forecast of tomorrow's weather!
They therefore have neither the opportunity nor the leisure
to provide us with the information we need. Even M.
Dettwiller[9] in his splendid book about the climate of Paris

did not consider it appropriate to pursue his investigations further back than the nineteenth century. We can only hope therefore that one day a professional historian, or perhaps a team of experts drawn from various fields, will undertake this truly long-range serial project.

While we wait for someone to produce these immensely long series of graphs, work has already begun on some vast documentary seams of meteorological data and is yielding interesting, if as yet incomplete, results. For instance, preserved in the Paris archives of the Academy of Medecine, are the findings of a weather survey—very topical and random as to method—which was the work of a team of observers, led by Vicq d'Azyr, covering the years from 1775 to 1790. It contains more than 150 series of daily meteorological observations drawn from the "whole world" (of that time) but mostly from France.[10]

During the past few years, the use of the computer has made it possible to sift this enormous jumble of old papers and records, to separate the wheat from the chaff, the good series from the bad. All those which are sufficiently long—covering more than four years—have been mutually correlated. Next, by means of a statistical test which is now normal practice in history and sociology, we were able to select, from the random heap, particular sets of series which produced a high correlation coefficient when matched regionally with their counterparts (above 0.80 and preferably above 0.90) over a great range of monthly data. The research team of the 6th Section of the *École pratique des Hautes Études*, which has embarked on this investigation, has thus been able to eliminate or leave out of selection the series drawn from southern France: these are inadequate, poor in mutual correlation and appear to be the work of observers lacking in zeal, conscience or scruple. On the other hand, a certain number of local series emanating from the Paris region, from western France and especially from the extreme north of the country (Arras, Montdidier etc.) emerged triumphantly from the computer-statistical tests that we applied, with mutual correlation coefficients above 0.90. They were therefore retained for the "follow-up studies" and thanks to them we have been able to lay the foundation for a thorough study of the climate of the last two decades of the *ancien régime*. By way of spin-off (cf. *supra*) this research has even produced a contribution which promises to add to our knowledge of the crises arising from crop surpluses that left their mark on the pre-revolutionary "intercycle" previously described in the works of Ernest Labrousse. Our team has been able to show that, as far as their climatic aspect is concerned at least, the phenomena of over-production of wine and the correspondingly low prices revealed by Labrousse, were largely the result of a succession of warm years, and especially of hot springs and summers, around and after 1780. Similarly, study of the graphs makes abundantly clear the meteorological conditions which led up to the bad harvest of 1788, itself the cause of the *"Grande Peur"* and the social disorders of the spring and the critical summer of 1789. Notable among these conditions, of course, was the hail-storm of July 1788, which has long been common knowledge. But also—and this is a piece of information discovered by our team—the scorching of the grain just as it was on the point of ripening before the harvest of 1788; and earlier, in the autumn of 1787, rainstorms in the sowing season. All these items of evidence demonstrate the ineluctable element of chance which must be taken into account in any attempt to analyse the causes of the French Revolution.

2. Turning to the second discipline mentioned earlier—*dendrochronology*—it appears to me that the methodological advances that have quite recently become available to the historian, have taken two different directions. Firstly, the old formula or prescription of dendrologists of the past—as well-tried as it was unilateral—has now been superseded. It consisted, it will be remembered, of relating a dendrological series (taken for example from a particular variety of pine-tree from some particular region of Arizona) to a climatic parameter, rainfall perhaps, or in certain circumstances aridity (the latter being associated both with precipitation —or rather the lack of it, and with evaporation caused by high temperature). Instead of this type of approach, which is both limited and subjective, present-day American dendrochronologists, Harold Fritts, for instance, prefer

more universal and comprehensive methods. Currently and on into the future, their aim is to chart the annual or decennial growth of the conifers throughout an enormous continental area, such as the entire south-west of the United States. At the conclusion of this operation, they will have a chronological series of geographical charts—a film almost—each one of which will depict against a background of the territorial map, a network of isochronic forest-growth lines, strong or weak according to the region. By looking at this succession of maps one will be able to see, not only an "episodic" but also a "spatialized" image of the successive changes of the climate and even of the ten-yearly movement of the air masses throughout the whole of the continental area under scrutiny. Harold Fritts has produced series of charts for vast regions, stretching from the present-day territory of San Francisco down to Los Angeles, that are extremely instructive in this respect. They reveal the succession of massive long-term waves of heat-drought or coolness-humidity which have by turns swept over the Pacific coast and the interior of the country, since the sixteenth century.

Secondly, Fritts no longer restricts his study to one single parameter (aridity in desert zones or perhaps summer temperature in Arctic forests); he is interested in the totality of weather patterns in any given year (with all their varied components of rainfall, temperature and seasonal changes); for this total annual pattern is, in fact, statistically associated with "an annual average tree-ring concomitant" thin, medium or thick. When it becomes possible to establish such a link between this or that "weather pattern type" and this or that "tree-ring type", the historian studies his graphs and can then compose a total history of the climate for any given region with all its complex fluctuations and temporal variations.[11]

This innovatory dendrochronological methodology pioneered by the work of Harold Fritts, is specifically American. In Europe, we have not progressed so far—more is the pity, particularly when one thinks of the range of questions that might be raised, and solved, by research of this kind, questions that would be of interest not only in the abstract realms of diachronic cosmology, but also in matters of human history.

In the course of the last ten years or so however, European

dendrochronology has turned up some new results which, in both subject matter and methodology, are not without interest. The most important studies in this field are those of Huber for the district of Hesse, and of Hollstein for the western areas of West Germany (the annual oak series, 820/1964 A.D.). Exemplary in its techniques of proof, the recent, final section of Hollstein's series is based on the study of some fifteen living trees, some a hundred years old, some older still. For his graphs of the earlier centuries ("modern", medieval or "early-medieval") Hollstein has used dozens of timber samples taken from ancient beams, mainly from old buildings or historic monuments, some even from archaeological digs. After careful dating,[12] these samples have made it possible to extend far back chronologically into the past the German tree-ring series derived from living trees. Huber's researches, which were started more than thirty-five years ago, and subsequently Hollstein's, have drawn on hundreds of thousands of annual growth-rings and consequently, between them, the two authors have been able to reveal or to discover certain important episodes in the climatic history of western Europe. They have suc-ceeded in brilliant style in confirming the existence of the *Sägesignatur* ("saw-tooth signature" or zigzag pattern) which had already been modestly hinted at in an earlier publication. During the eleven years from 1530 to 1541 in West Germany, in the Alps and in the Franco-Swiss Jura mountains, hot summer succeeded cool summer, and dry summer wet, in unvarying biennial sequence. This shows up both in the zigzag pattern of the graphs of old tree-rings and in the vintage dates in these parts of France and Switzer-land, where the grape harvests between 1530 and 1541 alternated regularly between early and late. The biennial alternation that took place during these eleven very distinctive years also constitutes, when viewed over the long term, one of the very rare periods of, let us say, recurrence—one dare not call it rotation—which western meteorology has from time to time recorded, with approximate accuracy. But it is very seldom indeed that this "biennial alternation" attains the clockwork regularity one finds on both sides of the Rhine throughout the 1530s.[13]

The 1530–1541 *Sägesignatur* thus provides a readily recognizable "fingerprint" so to speak, making it possible (as a kind of bonus) to identify any timbers displaying it, whose age was previously unknown, as originating in the sixteenth century. Huber's and Hollstein's series have also made a great contribution in method and content to the historical study of both climate and agriculture. They have for example confirmed the very wet period in the years 1310–1320. During every season of most of the years in this decade, bad weather cast its shadow, with a number of incredibly heavy rainstorms. The excess of water rotted newly-sown seeds and ruined harvests; hence the great famines of 1315–1316. It also produced tree-rings that were unusually thick and luxuriant; (for of course trees indigenous to western Europe generally thrive on wet weather, differing in this respect from grain-crops, which are imports from the arid East and have never really become acclimatized to the leaden skies of the temperate continent). On all the German dendrochrono-logical graphs the 1310 decade is therefore marked by a dome-shaped curve indicating thick rain-gorged tree-rings, thus providing a perfect example of the way in which wood and corn (or lack of corn) give proof of their complementary yet opposite histories.

Following the example of Huber and Hollstein, certain researchers on the other side of the Rhine are attempting to establish annual dendrological series in other regions of Germany to cover the last thousand years. (See for example the work in course of preparation by Mme. Siebenlist.) We must hope that on the model of the project initiated in Nancy by M. de Martin, the same will be done for France and in particular for our eastern provinces. Here it is always possible to make comparisons with the long German series which have the singular merit of existing and of being geographically extremely close; one might therefore expect some rapid progress and even the cutting of a few corners.

Finally, still on the subject of tree-rings, I must mention one last method, which it is important for the historian to know about, even if he cannot employ it himself. It can provide him with a sensitive and precise image of the "intra-annual" climate of years and periods very remote in time. This latest method involves examination by microscope and X-rays of each growth-ring of a particular piece of wood with reference to a particular year. The growth and the dimensions of the cells which compose the tree-ring alter appreciably with the progress of the vegetative season, and also with the fluctuations, towards more wet, dry, hot or cold weather of the successive months and weeks of the year in question. It is therefore theoretically possible, thanks to the microscopic examination of the cells ranged in concentric "beds", to obtain first-hand information on the climatic influences prevailing successively throughout the spring, summer and autumn of, say, the year 1284 or 1558, as it might be in Lorraine or in Würtemberg! It is only fair to say that studies along these lines (Fletcher's research in Oxford and Polge's in Nancy) have often reached the laboratory stage, but have seldom reached publication.[14]

One last word on dendrochronological methods. The compilation along the lines proposed by Huber and Hollstein of very long millennial or intermillennial series for Germany, France and Great Britain will render great service to the historians of the climate. But such series will be even more useful to archaeologists working on the medieval or early modern periods, who are interested in dating the timbers of old buildings, whether intact or in ruins. They will be able to date with absolute certainty oak beams forming part of any building they are examining. To do so, they will simply have to compare the growth curves drawn from these beams with the outline of the master-diagram for the thousand-year history of all oak trees in the area under scrutiny, or in a neighbouring region. (Cf. on this point the study of houses in Lorraine which P. de Martin has proved, using this method, to date from the period of reconstruction following the Thirty Years War.)[15] The dendrochronological method thus appears to have a fundamental importance for chronological dating. On the other hand it is more marginal to the major preoccupations of historians of the climate.

3. However, the history of the wine-harvest dates remains central for our purpose. The perfecting of methods in this field, and the discovery by Madame Micheline Baulant of *ad hoc* archives in the Paris region have enabled us to extend

further back in time the phenological series hitherto available to us. They could formerly be regarded as reliable from 1600 onwards. We now have reliable series dating from 1490–1500 onwards, throughout the sixteenth century. From a methodological point of view, it may be interesting to note how this "reliability" was originally established. Mme. Baulant had discovered some fragmentary series of phenological documents, with many gaps and missing entries. These documents related to several series of wine-harvest dates from vineyards round Paris. Fortunately, as it happened, each of these series had its own specific gaps which could be filled in or estimated, thanks to data furnished by the other series in the Paris region. Companion series were also available for the sixteenth century in Burgundy, Franche-Comté and French Switzerland. They generally contained fewer gaps than the series mentioned above from the Ile-de-France. In the first phase of dealing with this "hotch-potch", the most complete, or rather the least incomplete of the Paris region series (the records for Chartres, as it happens) was used as a standard of reference. The other Paris series were matched with it by making corrections where appropriate.[16] And now, from these various graphs, rectified or not, it became possible to construct an "average" Parisian graph, more or less complete and without major gaps, a synthesis of all the basic series drawn from vineyards scattered around the capital. The next step was to compare this Paris graph with those for Burgundy, Franche-Comté and Switzerland, to see whether the curves matched. The result proved satisfactory—mutual compatibility of vintage date fluctuations: from year to year, within decades or over decades. On the basis of this satisfactory correlation it was considered legitimate to strike a balanced average of all the series mentioned above, from Lausanne to the Ile-de-France, with the result that we now have a unique comprehensive graph for the whole of the northern vineyards of France and Switzerland. Close study of the graph thus constructed proves that it has not been artificially distorted by any intra-secular tendency, towards either the advancing or the retarding of the wine harvest. Had any such tendency shown up, it would have been human in origin (we happen to know

that in the seventeenth and eighteenth centuries, the Burgundy wine-growers—to give one example—put back their
harvests, later and later, from one decade to the next and
from one century to the next, in order to have grapes bursting
with ripeness and yielding juice of very high sugar content
which would convert in due course into a more alcoholic
wine. This retarding of the grape harvest to produce the
"noble rot" was practised increasingly from one century to
another, so there can be no question of attaching any particular *climatic* significance to the lateness of the harvests
as between centuries that appears on the Burgundy graphs
from 1650 to 1780).

The new sixteenth-century graph, however, displays none
of these "human, all too human" symptoms. Interpreting
the climate from it therefore becomes all the more exciting.
Indeed it soon becomes apparent that it has much to tell us
about the changes in the spring and summer temperatures
throughout the whole of the sixteenth century, and not only
about their short-term fluctuations; and, thank heaven,
nothing at all about the personal idiosyncrasies of the wine-
growers which in the circumstances, would be irrelevant to
our purpose—the history of the climate. From this point of
view, the most interesting conclusion to be drawn from this
comprehensive document concerns the cooler nature of
the spring-summer season during the second half of the
century, especially from 1560 to 1600—a cooling process
perfectly in accord with the substantial advance of the
Alpine glaciers which were helped on their way by the
absence of summer melting during this same period. Study
of the vintage dates exhumed from the archives brings us to
the same conclusion then as the documentary evidence from
the Alps, long since gathered by the glaciologists—a genuine
example to support the ideal of "interdisciplinary research"
so often praised in the abstract, so seldom realized in practice.

Meanwhile, back to our wines, in barrel and bottle.
Bacchus, our patron deity in this respect, has an inexhaustible
store of knowledge for us about the climate. Not only the
wine-harvest dates, which historians from now on will have
at their fingertips,[17] but also the quality of the wine, furnishes
first-class documentary evidence of the weather patterns of

past ages. Angot's statistical study of the subject suggests that
in the case of our northern vineyards and also those of
Germany, where the ration of sunshine is often insufficient
for the grape the following maxim applies: good wine = hot
summer, hot summer = good wine. The excellent post-war
vintages (1947 for example) bear this out and meteorological
series set against the wine connoisseurs' tables demonstrate
it with remarkable accuracy. Conversely, in cold, cool or wet
summers, for lack of sunshine the grapes wither or become
watery before they have had time to ripen satisfactorily and
to produce a sufficient quantity of sugar to yield a good
degree of alcohol in due course; hence the very poor wines
produced, for example, after the 1675 and 1968 grape
harvests. Angot was a pioneer in this field, and drew attention
to the remarkable possibilities that would be opened up by
the systematic annual study of the quality of wines in recent
centuries for the historiography of the summer climate. In
1895 he published an excellent annual series, covering
several hundreds of years and relating to the changing
qualities of Burgundy wines as far back as the seventeenth
century. Unfortunately, after Angot, French historians
missed a good opportunity. With their access to archives,
they would have been well placed to take advantage of this
method, but they have failed to pay any attention to the
records of vintage qualities, good, bad or indifferent. In
Germany, however, and in Luxemburg, Müller and Lahr
respectively have established some remarkable series relating
to the quality of the wine year by year, based on a number of
vineyards situated near the Rhine, the Neckar, the Black
Forest, etc. Von Rudloff has made use of these series to
substantiate his history of the climate in the West from 1670
to the present. A few words on this topic might therefore
not come amiss.

The various adjectives or epithets applied to the quality of
German wines in this or that year ("acid", "detestable", or
"delicious", "extra-good", etc.) are more subjective and
less precise, needless to say, than a wine-harvest date, which
falls plumb on to a given point in a chronological table. It is
nonetheless true that the Lahr–Müller method, however
qualitative it might be, lends itself to the serial processing,

dear to the *Annales* school of historians. Used in this way, it provides remarkable indications of climatic trends. Turning once again to the case of the sixteenth century (ever instructive and already several times referred to) I find that the *quality* of the wine can also, in its own fashion, tell us much about the secular trend. The years 1453–1552 taken *en bloc*, or decade by decade, were, on average, years of good German wines (which does not of course mean that certain individual years during this heaven-blessed century did not produce sour or tart wines). On the other hand (and here we have to make the opposite reservation) the five decades in Germany from 1553–1562 to 1593–1602 were, on average, characterized by bad vintages when the wine was sour.[18] The evidence of a century and more of series from the other side of the Rhine is all the more relevant in this connection since the German vineyards in question are typically marginal and northerly, and therefore extra sensitive, in positive terms, to sunshine, which is rarely excessive and often deficient in this region. And it must be remembered that in those days there was no adding of sugar, or chemicals, to doctor failed wines or fake an acid wine into a *grand cru*. It appears quite clear then—and here we have corroboration from three different sources—that the evidence from the glaciers of the temporary cooling of the climate between 1500 and 1600 is borne out by the two available viticultural series— the wine-harvest dates and the quality of the wines (bad, in this case). The summers (and the springs) of the years 1553–1602 were decidedly less warm than those of the years 1452–1553. As a result the wine-harvests were late, the wine was bad and the glaciers increased in size, becoming danger- ous even, so much so that in 1595–1605 they buried several villages in Chamonix and Grindelwald. Proof *a contrario* might be found for example in the frequently delicious wines of the 1860s and 1870s, and 1940–1953 in Germany and France, years when summer temperatures were at their high- est for the nineteenth and twentieth centuries respectively.

We must hope, therefore, that the Müller–Lahr method will be tried out in France too, for France, according to a truism, useful to our purpose, has been the home of good wine ever since the Middle Ages. Our connoisseurs have kept faithful records, in note-books of every kind, of the good years and the bad, the delicious wines and the detestable. We must order these records into series better than Angot did almost a hundred years ago and then we must construct reliable, up-to-date graphs of the annual quality of the wines of Burgundy, Champagne and the Île-de-France since the sixteenth century. This will put into our hands a powerful research tool well able, in conjunction with other methods, to resolve many questions concerning the climate of the modern period.

4. I referred at the start of this article to the "*événementiel*" (recorded events) method of historical study and its possibilities for regions such as ours where archives are plentiful. Recently, François Lebrun has greatly enlarged its scope in his book *La Mort et les hommes en Anjou aux XVIIe et XVIIIe siècles*. He has listed, for the province of Anjou, month by month and year by year, all the spells of hot and cold weather, wet and dry, with approximate indications of their intensity. His sources are parish registers, family diaries and other such documents. The final graphs and diagrams in the book, which present in visual form the results of Lebrun's research, consist of several strips of histograms in the lines of which one may read the illustrated history as it were of the climate of Anjou over a span of two centuries. Constructed as they are, these diagrams have made possible the formulation of a northern typology of events: famines in the seventeenth century and grain-crop deficiencies in the eighteenth, in which both of these phenomena—especially the first—are seen as expressions of the adverse meteorological conditions of the little ice age. Thanks to Lebrun, the climatic combinations most conducive to the onset of great famines are now known, and according to our author they are of two types:

a) *either*, the association (for one or several consecutive years) of *very cold winters and cool and wet springs and summers* (in other words, the most typical combination of the little ice age: cold winter + cool summer). This is apparently what happened in 1660–1661; 1692–1694; in 1709 to some extent; and lastly in 1740;

b) *or, a slightly more complex combination, consisting of a very wet and possibly mild winter, flooding the sowing season, and a wet and cold spring and summer.* In this case, only the spring and summer are typical of the little ice age pattern (a). As for the wet and possibly mild winter, it is more associated with another, somewhat different climatic pattern (b); in any case it has nothing icy about it. It was the association of (a) and (b) within this second combination that created (in 1630) and prolonged (in 1662) some of the great famines of the seventeenth century (and possibly the famines of the 1310 decade). This second type of association however, proves to be comparatively rare, as we can see from the infrequency, all things considered, of very great crises during the Classical Age.

In methodology, Lebrun's work is therefore doubly fruitful, serving both pure historical climatology and the history of catastrophes such as famines. But these Anjou-based studies and also the convergent studies in which De Martin has gathered together the meteorological data contained in the letters of Mme. de Sévigné, will not take on their full significance[19] unless and until their results are eventually deposited in an "archive bank" or a "data bank". In the vaults of such a bank, the series of information collected by this or that scholar could be combined with other series gathered by different authors, thus constituting in the long run, a serial corpus of data relating to the climate. Such data would refer to a particular century, region, nation or continental area.

*

5. To turn now to the glaciological method it is sometimes suggested that it may have served its turn. Certainly, many workable documents on the Alpine and Scandinavian glaciers have already been identified, published, tabulated, and serialized. Perhaps the time of diminishing returns has arrived. And yet, even in this area, splendid archival scoops are still possible; John Grove,[20] whose field of study is Scandinavia, has recently, thanks to the fiscal registers,

brought to light fresh and precise knowledge of the destruc-
tion and impoverishment of the local farms caused by the
looming glaciers in Norway, in the Jodestal range, between
1695 and 1750, and also, possibly, as long ago as 1340. In
the Alps, any further discovery of new texts, by the standard
methods of archive historians, would require a medievalist
to delve into the municipal and ecclesiastical papers of
Chamonix, so rich and, as yet, so little-known, as far as the
fourteenth and fifteenth centuries, at least, are concerned.
Again, in German-Switzerland, the absence of centralization
—in other respects beneficial—has meant that many deposits
of archives remain intact and available, but scattered in the
villages, cantons and bishoprics close to the great glacier
systems (Grindelwald, Aletsch, Rhonegletscher, Allalin,
etc.); genuine discoveries are therefore still possible in
Switzerland even for the well-studied period of the "little ice
age" (1570–1850). Of course, the historian who undertakes
this type of research would have to be not only a forager
among old archives in the best Benedictine tradition, but
also, to some extent, a geomorphologist capable of field-work
on the spot. In any case, such a requirement should not daunt
French historians, who have been academically trained from
their apprentice days to meet the harsh demands of
geography.

But the new breakthroughs of knowledge, in this particular
territory of the history of the ice-fields, may come from two
other methods based on techniques utterly different from
those I have referred to or hinted at. Moreover, both methods
will tear us away from our usual research haunts and transport
us to that lost paradise of the history of the climate, situated
somewhere in the approaches to the ice-fields of Greenland.
The first of these two methods is specifically cartographical;
it is also—to say the least—uncertain and debatable. We
know that quite recently, thanks to the praiseworthy researches of the librarians of Yale University,[21] a new document,
as controversial as it is unusual, has emerged to supplement
the dossier of Scandinavian history—the sensational Vinland
Map, compiled perhaps in the middle of the fifteenth
century,[22] and thought to be possibly a representation in
condensed form of the discoveries made by Scandinavian

sailors in the course of their voyages during the tenth to the twelfth century. Contained in this map is a fairly accurate picture of the whole of the coastline of Greenland. As such (assuming of course that it is an authentic document) it might well be confirmation of Ivar Baardson's well-known chronology which subdivides into two periods:[23] in the first—from the late tenth to the end of the twelfth century—the southern half of the east coast of Greenland, to the latitude of the Gunnbjorn's Skerries[24] was relatively free of ice-floes, enabling navigators bound from Iceland to approach Greenland in a straight line from east to west; more generally, the Nordic settlers and sailors of this epoch—the "mid-Middle Ages"—are believed to have acquired an adequate knowledge —experimental and even quasi-cartographical—of the whole Greenland coastline, which is thought by some people to have found a distant echo in the Vinland Map.[25] Then, in the following phase (thirteenth to fourteenth century),[26] perhaps even as early as the twelfth century, the ice-floes drifted southward and blocked the former approach-routes to Greenland via the Gunbjorn's Skerries; they forced the Icelandic and Norwegian navigators making for Greenland to sail in a much more southerly line; consequently, circumnavigation of Greenland, if, that is, it had ever existed, ceased.

The attraction of such a periodization is that it agrees with the recent discoveries of American and Danish researchers[27], in their studies of the medieval fluctuations in Greenland's climate as measured by the "ice-cores". But—is the Vinland Map genuine? G.R. Crone[28] contests it categorically: his scepticism should make us cautious and at the very least should prompt us to await new evidence. The very fact that the Vinland Map includes a drawing of the whole Greenland coastline constitutes an additional motive for Crone's mistrust! And on this point, he argues in an exactly contrary sense to Skelton, who was one of the "discoverers" of the map. "Another difficulty [of the Vinland Map]", writes G.R. Crone, "is the apparent accuracy of the outline of Greenland, [which was] not circumnavigated until the nineteenth century. It is generally accepted that firstly, this great island could not have been circumnavigated at an early period despite a somewhat milder climate; secondly, that there seems to have been no motive for the Norsemen to have undertaken such a voyage; and thirdly, that the Norsemen did not use or make charts. It is possible that the map was reconstructed in or before 1448 from oral tradition and a study of the sagas, though even this hypothesis would not explain the Greenland outline. . . . For the present, it remains an enigma."[29]

For the moment then, let us leave this enigma and, still on the subject of Greenland, turn to the certainties with which the practitioners of fossil-ice methodology have recently presented us. Their findings will furnish our second, most up-to-date approach in this field. What happened was that during the year 1966 an American research unit, the C.R.R.E.L. (Cold Region Research and Engineering Laboratory) succeeded in extracting an ice-core cut vertically through the entire thickness of the ice-field in a place called Camp Century (Greenland). The sample thus obtained measured 12 cms. in diameter . . . and 1,309 metres in length. The approximate age of the different sections from top to bottom of this thin column of ice was worked out by the C.R.R.E.L. scientists by means of a complex formula which takes into account the speed of accumulation of ice (35 cms. per annum) and the speed of its progressive compression under the weight of the upper layers. More than a thousand centuries of ice piled layer upon layer, right up to the present day, thus became available for systematic research. Dansgaard and others have undertaken the study of this immense ice-core sample.[30]

Evidence of this type is of obvious and essential interest for the history of the climate; in the oxygen isotope O 18, present in varying quantities in glacier ice, we have, in fact, a first-class indicator for the "intra-glacial" exploration of the thermal conditions of past eras, since the concentration of O 18 in deposits of rain or snow (later to be "deep frozen" in the polar ice-caps in the form of fossil-ice) is principally determined by the temperature at which the deposits in question were condensed: "Decreasing temperature leads to decreasing content of O 18 in rain or snow; and vice versa."

The Camp Century ice-sample indicates, firstly, at the very top of the slender column (in the most recently formed layers) high concentrations of O 18. They correspond to the well-marked climatic optimum of the years 1920–1930. Then, when we dig deeper into the ice bed at Camp Century, below the recent high temperature years (1900–1950), we reach, and find characteristically poor in O 18, the levels of the "little ice age"; broadly speaking this age extends from the thirteenth to the nineteenth century, during which time there were three main cold waves, the first occurring between 1160 and 1300. It was followed, not without interruptions, by a moderate remission, not too icy (1310–1480). Then the lowest depths of cold, of which there had been intimations as early as the sixteenth century, duly arrived in the seventeenth century, and again from 1820 to 1850. In contrast, the eighteenth century (1730–1800) appears as a well-defined if temporary period of rising temperatures.

Of course, this periodization is neither definitive nor fixed once and for all. Other ice-cores from other ice-fields will be studied: they will correct or define this chronology more precisely. The important point is that through all the centuries-long fluctuations, corresponding to "cycles" of very approximately one hundred and twenty years, the great cold periods marked in the Alps by the forward movements of the glaciers in the thirteenth, seventeenth and nineteenth centuries, are found once more, precisely located in time, in Greenland; and this despite the considerable differences resulting from the geographical distance between the European continent and the sub-continent of Greenland.

And then, penetrating still deeper into the layers of ice, the Camp Century diagram eventually arrives at the warm indices of the "little optimum" of the Early Middle Ages! Abruptly, in the five centuries preceding A.D. 1125 (from, say, A.D. 610 to 1125) the graph rises and levels out; throughout this period the O 18 concentration remains constantly greater than it will ever be during the icy centuries which mark the "little ice age" (thirteenth to nineteenth centuries). This Early Middle Ages richness in O 18 clearly emphasizes the continuity of a phase of rising temperatures which persisted with sustained intensity for a period of some five hundred years (seventh to eleventh centuries). The Norsemen benefited,[31] there can be no doubt about it, from

the opportunities offered them at this time by certain of the
Arctic coasts which were freer of ice than usual. They vied
with one another in making landfalls on the marginal lands
of the kingdoms of Thule. The colonization of Iceland in the
ninth century, of Greenland in the tenth century—the former
possibly, the latter certainly—benefited from this climatic
bonus. In the "favourable" period which extends from 610
to 1185 A.D., two thermal maxima stand out quite distinctly
on the Camp Century graph, one during the last thirty years
of the tenth century, the other during the first quarter of the
twelfth century. We meet with nothing equivalent until
very much later, until the peaks of warmth in Greenland
which occurred at the very end of the eighteenth century
(1780–1800); and above all in the recent optimum (1920–
1930). It will be apparent that the two Early Middle Ages high
peaks of the "little optimum" in Greenland coincide in an
interesting manner with two critical episodes in the Arctic
sub-continent. From 978 to 986, first Snaebjorn Galti, then
Erik the Red, profited from the relatively ice-free seas to strike
due west from Iceland to reach Greenland on the latitude of
the Gunnbjorn's Skerries. From there Erik went towards
the south of the great island where he created, at the same
time as the *Eastern settlement*, his great Brattahlid farm.[32]
Two and a half centuries later, at the height of the climatic
and demographic fortune of this ultra-north settlement, a
Greenland bishopric was founded at Gardar[33] in 1126.

The great Camp Century ice-core thus confirms the
patient researches of the Danish archaeologists who had, as
early as 1925, first suspected and subsequently demonstrated
the existence of a medieval "little optimum" in Greenland.

Furthermore, if we reach further back still into the past,
the immense C.R.R.E.L. ice-core clarifies and confirms many
other important episodes: thus the maximum of the Alpine
glaciers, shown by the Fernau peat-bog to have occurred at
an indeterminate date somewhere between 400 and
750 A.D., now has its probable equivalent in Greenland,
with the cold episode registered by the Camp Century ice-
core between 340 and 620 A.D. As with the "little ice age"
of 1580 to 1850, the probability is that this was an intercontinental phenomenon affecting at least Europe and America.

Indeed, John Mercer in his important article, *Glacier varia-tions in Patagonia* (1965),[34] notes that, according to carbon 14 dating, the glaciers of the American continent (Alaska and and Patagonia) were showing signs of forward movement as early as 250 A.D. and reached their maximum about 450 A.D. If we go further back still[35] to the beginning of the first millennium A.D. (50 B.C.–200 A.D.), we see that the Camp Century graph strongly emphasizes the extent of the sub-Atlantic fall in temperature which lasted throughout the last millennium B.C. (the coldest period occurring between 500 and 100 B.C.). Here again, Mercer's analysis generalizes this conclusion; the entire complex of glaciers, not only in Green-land but also in the Alps, in Iceland, in Sweden, in New Zealand and in Patagonia—the latter magnificently dated—took a great leap forward between 500 B.C. and 300 B.C. to greet the coldest point of the sub-Atlantic temperature drop.[36]

Last but not least, the Camp Century ice-core definitively confirms the existence of the climatic optimum in prehistoric times. In Greenland, this reached its maximum temperatures between 5200 B.C. and 2200 B.C., and more precisely between 4000 B.C. and 2300 B.C.. So the fourth millennium before the Christian era (4000–3000 B.C.) in Europe as in Greenland, did indeed bring the "thousand years of sunshine" that the pollen graphs of the northern countries had long been indicating.

The prodigious "memory" of the polar ice-cap is thus able to preserve, thanks to O 18, a "record of the fluctuations of the climate" from the great ice ages[37] to the very recent tempera-ture rise.

*

Oxygen O 18 has helped us in other ways too: it has offered climatic history research an additional promising method. In 1967, Labeyrie and his colleagues[38] analysed the variations affecting the O 18 content of Calcium carbonate ($CaCO_3$) which is present in the different concentric rings of a white stalagmite of very pure calcite discovered in Aven d'Orgnac (Ardèche). The stalagmite is nearly seven thousand years old. The variations in O 18 content (*v. supra*) indicate changes in the ambient temperature of the cave. The results were as follows:

Tenth century A.D.	12.1 degrees C
circa 1150 A.D.	11.5 degrees C
circa 1450	11.0 degrees C
circa 1750–1800	12.3 degrees C
circa 1940	11.7 degrees C

With the customary reservations as to the very limited and preliminary nature of these results, Aven d'Orgnac would appear therefore to testify to optima in the year 1000, and in the eighteenth and twentieth centuries; and to a Late Medieval drop in temperature around 1450. Unfortunately Labeyrie gives no figures for the seventeenth century which saw the culmination of the "little ice age". But his pioneering work in this direction has opened up possibilities for further research which may well be taken up by historians.

*

To conclude this brief account of the recent and varied methods employed in the history of the climate with a general proposition, let me say that, in view of these very varied techniques, some of which can be regarded as traditional historical methods interpreted along new lines, and others of which, initially at least, are foreign to the orthodox procedures of history, one guiding principle stands out: as far as the Christian era is concerned, the only road towards a convincing history of the climate is by way of interdisciplinary and comparative research. From the study of the ice-fields to the study of the wine-harvests, from Oxygen O 18 to tree-rings, from the medieval chronicles to accurate thermometric readings, diachronic meteorology testifies in many different voices to the profound unity (despite diversity in method) of the knowledge it imparts.

BIBLIOGRAPHY

For a more complete bibliography and further information the reader is advised to consult my book *Times of feast, Times of famine: A history of climate since the year 1,000*, New York, Doubleday, 1971, and London,

Allen and Unwin, 1973. This book is the English edition of my work *Histoire du Climat depuis l'an mil*, Paris, Flammarion, 1967, much added to, corrected and brought up to date.

ANGOT, A., "Études sur les Vendanges en France", in *Annales du bureau central Météorologique de France*, 1883.
— "Premier catalogue des observations métérologiques faites en France depuis l'origine jusqu'en 1850", in *Annales du bureau central météorologique de France*, 1895, I.
CRONE, G. R., *The Discovery of America*, London, 1969.
— "How authentic is the Vinland Map?", in *Encounter*, Feb. 1966, pp. 75–78.
DANSGAARD, W., JOHNSEN, S. J., MOLLER, J., and LANGWAY, C., "One thousand centuries of climatic record from Camp Century on the Greenland ice sheet", in *Science*, 17 Oct. 1969, vol. 166, p. 377–381.
DANSGAARD, W. and JOHNSEN, S., "A time scale for the ice core from Camp Century", in *Journ. of glaciol.*, 1969, pp. 215–223.
FRITTS, H. C., "The relation of growth rings in American beech and white oak to variation in climate", in *Tree-ring Bull.*, 1961–1962, vol. 25, 1–2, pp. 2–10.
— "Dendrochronology", in *The Quaternary of the United States. A review volume for the VII Congress of the International association for Quaternary research*, Princeton, 1965, pp. 871–879
— "Tree-ring evidence for climatic changes in western North America", in *Monthly Weather Review*, 1965, vol. 93, no. 7, pp. 421–443.
— "Tree-ring analysis: for water resource research", *I.H.D. Bulletin, U.S. National Committee for International Hydrological Decade*, Jan. 1969.
— "Growth rings of trees and climate", in *Science*, 25 Nov. 1966, 254, pp. 973–979.
— "Bristlecone pine in the White Mountains of California", in *Papers of the lab. of tree-ring Research*, 1969, no. 4, (Tucson, Ariz).
— "Growth rings of trees: a physiological basis for their correlation with climate", in *Ground level climatology* (Symposium, Dec. 1965; Berkeley). *Amer. Assoc. for the advancement of Science*, Washington, D.C., 1967.
FRITTS, H.C., SMITH, D.G. and HOLMES, R.L., "Tree-ring evidence for climatic changes in western north America from 1500 A.D. to 1940 A.D.", in *1964 Annual Report to the United States Weather Bureau*, Washington (Project, dendroclimatic history of the United States), 31 Dec. 1964.
FRITTS, H.C., SMITH, D.G., CARDIS, J. and BUDELSKY, C., "Tree-rings characteristics along a vegetation gradient in Northern Arizona", in *Ecology*, 1965, vol. 46, n° 4.
FRITTS, H., SMITH, D. and STOKES, M., "The biological model for paleoclimatic interpretation of tree-ring series", in *Amer. Antiquity*, Oct. 1965, vol. 31, n° 2–2.
FRITTS, H.C., SMITH, D., BUDELSKY, C. and CARDIS, J., "Variability of tree-rings ... ", in *Tree-ring Bulletin*, Nov. 1965.

GRAENLANDICA SAGA in *The Vinland Sagas, The Norse discovery of America*, translation and introduction by M. Magnusson and H. Palsson, Penguin Books, Baltimore, 1965.

HOLLSTEIN, E., "Jahrringchronologische Datierung von Eichenhölzern ohne Wald-Kante (Westdeutsche Eichenchronologie)", in *Bonner Jahrbücher*, 1965, 165, pp. 1–27.

HUBER, B., "Seeberg ... Dendrochonologie", in *Acta Bernensia*, 1967.

HUBER, B., and JAZEWITSCH, W., "Tree-ring studies", in *Tree-ring Bulletin*, Apr. 1956, p. 29.

HUBER, B. and SIEBENLIST, V., "Das Watterbacher Haus in Odenwald, ein wichtiges Bruckenstück unserer tausendjahringen Eichenchronologie", in *Mitteilungen der floristischsoziologischen Arbeitsgemeinschaft*, N.F., 1963, Heft 10.

HUBER, B., SIEBENLIST, V. and NIESS, W., "Jahrringchronologie hessicher Eichen", in *Budinger Geschichtblatter*, 1964, Band V.

HUBER, B. and GIERTZ-SIEBENLIST, V., "Tausendjährige Eichenchronologie", in *Sitzungsberichten der Osterr-Akademie der Wiss.*, *Mathem. naturw. Kl.*, Vienna, 1969, Abt. 1, 178 Band, 1–4 Heft.

LABEYRIE, J., DUPLESSY, J.-C., DELIBRIAS, G. and LETOLLE, R., "Températures des climats anciens, mesure d'O 18 et C 14 dans les concrétions des cavernes", in *Radioactive dating and methods of low-level counting*, Monaco, Symposium 1967 (*International Atomic Energy Agency*, Vienna, 1967).

LABRIJN, A., "Het klimaat van Nederland gerudende de laatste twee en cen halve leuw", (with English summary), Koninklijk Nederlandsch Met. Inst., no. 102, *Meded. Verhandeligen*, Gravenhage, 49, 1945.

LAHR, E., *Un siècle d'observations météorologiques en Luxembourg*, Published by the Meteorology service, Ministry of Agriculture, Luxembourg, 1950.

LAMB, H.H., *The Changing Climate*, London, 1966.

LE ROY LADURIE, E., "Pour une histoire de l'environnement: la part du Climat", in *Annales*, 1970. (See also books mentioned above.)

MANLEY, G., "Temperature trends in Lancashire", in *Quart. Journ. of the Roy Met. Soc.*, 1946.

— "The range of variation of the British climate", in *Geog. Journ.*, March 1951, pp. 43–68.

— "Variation in the mean temperature of Britain since glacial times", in *Geologische Rundschau*, 1952, pp. 125–127.

— "The mean temperature of central England (1698–1952)", in *Q.J.R.M.S.*, 1953, pp. 242–262, et p. 558.

— "Temperature trends in England", in *Archiv. für Met. Geophys. und Bioklimatol.*, 1959.

— Manley's most important articles for our purposes are those of 1946 and 1959.

MARTIN, P. DE, "Dendrochronologie et maison rurale", in *Annales*, 1970.

MERCER, J., "Glacier variations in Patagonia", in *Geog. Rev.*, 1965, p. 390–413.

MULLER, K., "Weinjahre und Klimschwankungen der letzten 1000 jahre", in *Weinbau, Wissenschaftliche Beiheft*, 1947 Mainz, I, 83, 123.

—*Geschichte des Badischen Weinbaus (mit einer Weinchronik und einer Darstellung der Klimaschwankungen in letzen Jahrtausend)*, Lahr in Baden, 1953.

POLGE, H. and KELLER, R., "La Xylochronologie perfectionnement logique de la dendrochronologie", in *Annales des sciences forest.*, 1969, 26 (2), pp. 225–256.

RUDLOFF, H. von, "Die Schwankungen der Grossirkulation innerhalb der letzten Jahrhunderte", *Annalen der Meteorologie*, 1967.

— *Die Schwankungen und Pendelungen des Klimas in Europa seit dem Beginn der regelmässigen Instrumenten-Beobachtungen*, Braunschweig, Vieweg, 1967.

SCHOVE, D., "Contribution to Post-Glacial climatic change", in *Quart. Journ. of the Roy. Met. soc.*, 1949, pp. 175–179 and p. 181.

— *Climatic fluctuations in Europe in the late historical period*, M. Sc. Thesis, London University, 1953, (unpublished).

— "Medieval Chronology in the USSR", in *Medieval Archecology*, 1964, vol. 8, pp. 216–217.

— "The biennial oscillation", in *Weather*, Oct. 1969, pp. 390–396.

— "Fire and drought 1600–1700", in *Weather*, Sept. 1966; (correlation between narrow tree-rings and dry years).

SKELTON, R. A., MARSTON, T.E. and PAINTER, G.D., *The Vinland Map and the Tartar Relation*, with a foreword by A.O. Vietor, New Haven, Yale Univers. Press, 1965.

TITOW, J., "Evidence of weather in the account of the bishopric of Winchester, 1209–1350", in *Economic History Review*, 1960.

— "Le climat à travers les rôles de comptabilité de l'évêché de Winchester (1350–1450)", in *Annales*, 1970.

NOTES TO THE TEXT

1 THE HISTORIAN AND THE COMPUTER

1. This article first appeared in *Le Nouvel Observateur*, 8 May 1968.

2 THE QUANTITATIVE REVOLUTION AND FRENCH HISTORIANS

1. This article first appeared in *Le Monde*, 25 January 1969.
2. On this question, cf. articles by F. Crouzet, D. Richet and M. Lévy-Leboyer in *Annales* in 1966 and 1968.

3 QUANTITATIVE HISTORY: THE SIXTH SECTION

1. Lecture given at the American Historical Association Convention at Toronto, December 1967.
2. This lecture was prepared while the author was Visiting Professor at Princeton.
3. Fernand Braudel, *La Méditerranée et le monde méditerranéen à l'époque de Philippe II*, first French edition Paris 1949; second edition revised and enlarged, Paris 1966; English translation of second edition: *The Mediterranean and the Mediterranean World in the Age of Philip II* (trans. Siân Reynolds), London 1972.
4. Pierre and Henriette Chaunu, *Séville et l'Atlantique de 1504 à 1650*, Paris 1955–57. Pierre Vilar: *La Catalogne dans l'Espagne moderne*, Paris, 1962. Henri Lapeyre, *Géographie de l'Espagne morisque*, Paris 1959. J. Nadal and E. Giralt-Raventos, *La Population catalane de 1553 à 1717*, Paris, 1960.
5. Earl J. Hamilton, *American Treasure and the Price Revolution in Spain, 1501–1650*, Cambridge, Mass., 1936.
6. Bartolomé Bennassar, *Valladolid au Siècle d'Or. Une ville de Castille et sa campagne au XVIe siècle*, Paris, 1967. C. Carrère, *Barcelone, centre économique à l'époque des difficultés, 1380–1462*, Paris, 1967.
7. F. Braudel, *op. cit.*
8. Lucien Febvre, *Le Problème de l'incroyance au XVIe siècle : la religion de Rabelais*, Paris, 1947.
9. Marc Bloch, *Les Caractères originaux de l'histoire rurale française*, Paris, 1931, 1956.
10. Ernest Labrousse, *Esquisse du mouvement des prix et des revenus en France au XVIIIe siècle*, Paris, 1933.
11. Ernest Labrousse, *La Crise de l'économie française à la fin de l'Ancien Régime et au début de la Revolution*, Paris, 1943.

12. Pierre Goubert, *Beauvais et le Beauvaisis au XVIIe siècle*, Paris, 1960.
13. See below, p. 223 ff.
14. Full title: Micheline Baulant and J. Meuvret, *Prix des céréales extraits de la mercuriale de Paris*, Paris, 1960–1962.
15. P. and H. Chaunu, *Séville et l'Atlantique, op. cit.*
16. Pierre Chaunu, *Les Philippines et le Pacifique des îles iberiques (XVIe–XVIIe–XVIIIe siècle)*, Paris, 1960.
17. P. Jeannin, "Les comptes du Sund comme source pour la construction d'indices généraux de l'activité économique en Europe" in *Revue historique*, 1964.
18. F. Braudel and R. Romano, *Navires et marchands à l'entrée du port de Livourne (1547–1611)*, Paris, 1951.
19. Jean Delumeau, *L'Alun de Rome (XVe–XVIe siècle)*, Paris, 1963.
20. Louis Dermigny, *La Chine et l'Occident. Le commerce à Canton au XVIIIe siècle (1719–1833)*, Paris, 1964.
21. Frank C. Spooner, *L'Economie mondiale et les frappes monétaires en France*, Paris, 1956. Later published by Harvard U.P. as *The International economy and Monetary Movements in France 1493–1725*, 1972.
22. NB this lecture dates from 1967.
23. B. Boutelet, "La criminalité dans le baillage de Pont-de-l'Arche" in *Annales de Normandie*, 1962.
24. René Baehrel, *Une Croissance: la Basse-Provence rurale (fin XVIe siècle–1789)*, Paris, 1961.
25. Baehrel's ideas on the regularity of the "30 year cycle" within the century, on the other hand, are less convincing.
26. Emmanuel Le Roy Ladurie, *Les Paysans du Languedoc*, Paris, 1966, (English trans. by John Day, *The Peasants of Languedoc*, Urbana, 1974).
27. Lionel Rothkrug, *Opposition to Louis XIV*, Princeton, 1965, p. 268.
28. Pierre Vilar, *La Catalogne, op. cit.* (published by S.E.V.P.E.N.) 1962.
29. E. Baratier, *La Démographie provençale du XIIIe au XVIe siècle. Avec chiffres de comparaison pour le XVIIIe siècle*, Paris, 1961.
30. P. Deyon, *Etude sur la société urbaine au XVIIe siècle: Amiens, capitale provinciale*, Paris, 1967.
31. Ernest Labrousse, *op. cit.* Cf. also D. Landes, "The statistical study of French crises" in *Journal of Economic History*, vol. X, 1950, pp. 195–211.
32. Fernand Braudel, *Civilisation matérielle et capitalisme*, vol. I, Paris (English translation: *Capitalism and material life*, by Miriam Kochan, New York 1974).
33. Centre de recherches historiques: *Villages desertés et histoire economique, XIe–XVIIIe siècle*, Paris, S.E.V.P.E.N., 1965.
34. François Furet and Adeline Daumard, *Structures et relations sociales à Paris au milieu du XVIIIe siècle*, Paris, 1961.
35. Adeline Daumard, *La Bourgeoisie parisienne de 1815 à 1848*, Paris, 1963. J. Meyer, *La Noblesse bretonne au XVIIIe siècle*, Paris, 1966. B. Bennassar, *op. cit.*
36. J. Le Goff, *Les Intellectuels au Moyen Age*, Paris, 1957. *La Civilisation*

de l'Occident médiéval, Paris, 1967. R. Mandrou, *De la culture populaire aux XVIIe et XVIIIe siècles, la Bibliothèque bleue de Troyes*, Paris, 1964. A. Besançon, *Le Tsarevitch immolé*, Paris, 1967.

37. G. Bollème, J. Ehrard, F. Furet, D. Roche, *Livre et société dans la France du XVIIIe siècle*, Paris, 1965.

38. L. Perouas, *La Diocèse de La Rochelle de 1648 à 1724. Sociologie et pastorale*, Paris, 1964.

39. In this connection, see below, pp. 193ff. and the collective publication, *Les Fluctuations du produit de la dîme*, edited by J. Goy and E. Le Roy Ladurie Paris, 1972.

40. Cf. the work under the direction of Pierre Chaunu, *Maison et bâtiment dans l'histoire économique*, Paris, 1970; see also P. Couperie and E. Le Roy Ladurie, "Les loyers à Paris", *Annales*, July, 1970; and below, pp. 61ff.

41. M. Couturier, "Vers une nouvelle méthode mécanographique. La préparation des données" in *Annales*, 1966.

42. W.S. Robinson, "Ecological correlations and the behaviour of individuals", in *American Sociological Review*, 1950, pp. 351–357.

43. For some of the results of this survey, see below, pp. 33ff.

44. One joint project carried out by the Sixth Section and the Inter-University Consortium of Ann Arbor and the CNRS has been the transfer on to machine-readable tapes of the volumes of the *Statistique générale de la France, 1800–1950*.

4 THE CONSCRIPTS OF 1868

1. This article first appeared in *Annales de démographie historique*, 1971; it was written in collaboration with N. Bernageau.

2. For all details of the archival, documentary and methodological basis of this article, the reader is referred to the following article: E. Le Roy Ladurie, N. Bernageau and Y. Pasquet: "Le conscrit et l'ordinateur. Perspectives de recherches sur les archives militaires du XIXe siècle français", which appeared in *Studi Storici*, vol X, no. 2, April–June, 1969. Strictly speaking the present article should be read in connection with this earlier publication. (Translator's note: the earlier article is in French and has not been translated into English. It contains details of the system of classification used, particularly concerning the occupations of the conscripts as listed on the registers; in order to help readers of the present article a note has been added to Table II on this point.)

3. Notably theft and fraud, violence and vagrancy.

4. *Le remplacement*: the system by which those who could afford it paid another man to carry out their military service; it remained in force as long as military service was subject to the drawing of lots.

5. For a more detailed explanation of the contents of this table, see the full version of this article in *Annales de démographie historique*, 1972.

6. When one comes to the "medium" and "higher" occupational groups, delinquency is (predictably) much lower. If we add together all

categories of conscripts in which a large number of individuals could be said to belong to medium and higher groups (the following categories: clergy, landowners, rentiers, students, liberal professions, administrators, artists, teachers, state employees, other white collar workers) and also those from the category *food and trade* (which contains an unidentifiable mixture of young men from humble backgrounds and others who rightly belong to the petit-bourgeoisie— shopkeepers etc.—or to the middle classes), we have a total of 1,367 young men, of whom 24 have a record of delinquency; that is 1.76 per cent, whereas the average delinquency rate for the entire sample is 2.40 per cent.

7. To be precise, the "popular" or lower income groups consist of the following occupational categories: "farmers", forestry workers, resin-tappers, charcoal-burners, vine-growers, gardeners, agricultural labourers, general labourers, servants, household offices, unskilled workers, street and field trades (e.g. molecatchers), sea-faring trades, traditional transport trades (e.g. carters), building trades, artisan and traditional industry, large-scale industry and textile workers. See also note to Table II.

8. i.e. the non-replaced. This term does not include those who were themselves substitutes.

9. Again, excluding substitutes.

10. i.e. a combination of the categories: building trades; artisan and craft production; large-scale and textile industry.

11. Cf. Table III below.

12. See also Table I above.

13. Men who could neither read nor write: they were coded "O" in the recruiting registers which are our source.

14. That is able both to read and to write, coded "2" in the recruiting registers. We have not used the figures for those coded "1", i.e. able to read but not to write, since we wanted in this particular instance to be able to contrast two clearly separated groups of young men: the illiterate and the educated.

15. The problem presents itself rather differently perhaps in contemporary society.

16. 17 delinquents out of a total of 702 individuals.

17. 4 delinquents out of the 832 individuals in this group.

18. See Table II: in these six categories, that is: total of non-replaced delinquents: $12 + 27 + 14 + 0 + 4 + 4 = 61$; total of non-replaced delinquents and non-delinquents: $172 + 412 + 348 + 6 + 64 + 28 = 1,030$; total of replaced delinquents: zero; total of replaced delinquents and non-delinquents: 117.

19. We asked the computer to sort out the young men who were resident in a different *département* from that of their parents. This type of geographical mobility is more radical and drastic than a mere change of address from, say, one village to another within the same *département*.

20. See Table VI.

21. Columns E and F of Table VI.
22. Columns E and F, top line.
23. Cf. Table VII.
24. See Table VI.
25. Table VII, bottom line.
26. P. 43.
27. This category includes both "farmers" *(cultivateurs)* and those who worked in the forests.
28. In this section of our study, where we were interested in the conscript's birthplace being different from the "present address" of his parents, the computer was asked to register not only mobility between *départements* but *any change of address*, from one *commune* (municipality) to another, whether within the same *département* or not. Our results in this case were based on the random movement of the conscripts and their families, and not only as in the preceding example on more distant removals, from one *departement* to another. The conclusions that may be drawn concerning the relation between the various data (replacement-delinquency-education etc.) and the mobility of the conscripts are not, however substantially different, whichever of the two types of mobility one chooses to take.
29. That is, agricultural labourers, general labourers, servants, household staff, unskilled workers (Table IX).
30. We have identified with this group the categories: building trade, artisan and craft production, large scale industry and textile workers (Table IX).
31. That is 99 replaced out of a total (non replaced plus replaced) of 743.
32. That is 329 replaced out of a total (non-replaced plus replaced) of 1,625.
33. That is 131 illiterate out of 713 conscripts whose educational level is recorded.
34. That is 212 illiterate out of 1,766 conscripts whose educational level was recorded.
35. That is: state employees, other white-collar workers, liberal professions, administration, artists, students and higher occupational groups; we have not included conscripts described as "teachers" or "members of the clergy", because they could get special exemptions.
36. 118 replaced out of a total of 202 replaced plus non-replaced.
37. 244 replaced, out of a total of 395 replaced plus non-replaced.
38. *Studi Storici*, 1969, *art. cit.*, p. 291.
39. Cf. Table XVI.

5 CHANGES IN PARISIAN RENTS

1. This article first appeared in *Annales*, July–August 1970 (in collaboration with P. Couperie).
2. For the years 1783–1791, our graph for rents received by institutions is based on a decreasing number of houses, within which there is a striking contrast between the "modern", large multi-occupied build-

ings and the hovels surviving from the sixteenth century and even the Middle Ages. The Minutier samplings of 1784 and 1788 are therefore the only reliable sources here (cf. the tables at the end of this article).

6 RURAL CIVILIZATION

1. Article "Rural Civilization" in *Encyclopaedia Universalis*.
2. On rural demography, see Part Three of this book.

7 THE "EVENT" AND THE "LONG TERM" IN SOCIAL HISTORY

1. This article first appeared in *Communications*, no 18, 1972.
2. Ed. Flammarion, 1971.

8 IN NORMANDY'S WOODS AND FIELDS

1. Introduction to the new edition of *Un Sire de Gouberville*, by Abbé Tollemer, Paris and The Hague, Mouton, 1972 (First published in the *Journal de Valognes* 1870–1872).
2. *Traité du Pommé*, by the doctor Paulmier, quoted by President La Barre, *Nouveau formulaire des élus*, 1628, VII, 3.
3. Research in quantitative history carried out at Caen under the direction of Pierre Chaunu.
4. There is one exception to this pattern: the workers threshing the grain in the barn received 13 per cent of the threshed corn on Gouberville's estate, as against the 5 per cent received by those who trod out the corn in the Languedoc. But the amount of human labour required in treading out, using horses, was much less than that required to thresh with flails, as was the custom in Normandy—hence the difference probably.
5. In this connection see Marc Bloch's outstanding chapter in *The Cambridge Economic History of Europe*, vol. I, *Agricultural life*, chapter VI (Cambridge 1966, new edition).
6. It does appear, but *after* the outbreak of the civil wars and in an essentially religious context.
7. G. Duby.
8. In the *Annales de Normandie*, 1962.
9. Mme. Nicole Bernageau, who is working on a full-length study of Gouberville, tells me that the heaviest items of expenditure in the household were *clothes and material*; then came *wages*; next *lawsuits*, *travel* and *meat*; and the rest comes very far behind.
     Financial receipts (e.g. 99 *livres twelve sous* per year from the sale of stock, wool and some grain) fell far below the level of expenditure.
10. Abbé A. Tollemer: *Un Sire de Gouberville, gentilhomme campagnard au Cotentin*, Paris—The Hague, Mouton, 1972. The reissue of this book by Mouton will make it available to a wider audience.
     The Journal of the Lord of Gouberville for the years 1553–1562 was published in a single very large volume by the *Société des Anti-*

quaires de Normandie (Rouen and Paris, 1892), with an introduction by Eugène de Robillard de Beaurepaire, who used the Tollemer copy of the original manuscript. A second volume, for the years 1549–1552 was published by the same *Société des Antiquaires* and with the assistance of the Count A. de Blangy, in 1895.

9 THE CHIEF DEFECTS OF GREGORY KING

1. This article first appeared in *Annales*, September–October, 1968.
2. J.-C. Toutain, "Le produit de l'agriculture française de 1700 à 1958. 1° Estimation du produit au XVIIIe siècle" in J. Marczewski, "Histoire quantitative de l'économie française", *Cahiers de l'Institut de Science économique appliquée* (I.S.E.A.), no. 115, July 1961, pp. 1–216.
3. In spite of some initial empirical references to Normandy (Vauban, *La dîme royale*, 1933 edition, p. 39 ff) and to the Morvan (*ibid.*, p. 127ff) the square league is undoubtedly, in its very principle, a theoretical model in the least ambiguous sense of the term. The only thing its inventor could be reproached with is his assumption, for not entirely invalid reasons, that the model could be applied without modification to the whole of France (*ibid.*, p. 165 ff). The operation was carried out as follows: from his extensive experience as a rural economist, Vauban imagined how much arable and pasture land, vineyards, forests etc. might be contained within a square league, as representing a fictitious plot of land, itself to be regarded as typical of the average French parish in the time of Louis XIV. In the course of the calculations, the model would be slightly adapted by its inventor, who added a few utopian embellishments and gave it some finishing touches *ad usum delphini* (*ibid.* p. 169). Lastly, Vauban calculated the total agricultural income from this square league (35,000 *livres tournois, ibid.*, p. 176). Then all he had to do was multiply this income by the 30,000 square leagues generally assumed at this time to be the total area of France (cf. Mousnier, *La Dîme de Vauban*, Paris, 1968, C.D.U., p. 80 ff). He then had a figure representing the total revenue of French agriculture (*ibid.*, p. 176).
   It is in no way my intention here to deny Vauban's efforts to acquire information on this subject (see Saint-Simon, *Mémoires*, 1899 edition, vol. XIV, pp. 324–325, a reference kindly supplied by P. Couperie). I simply wish to point out that such efforts did not eliminate certain gaps in his knowledge (cf. for example his misunderstanding of biennial crop rotation) (Vauban, 1933 edition, p. 176). And I would strongly emphasize that the square league, even in its finished form, is much more akin to a logical construct, albeit a very brilliantly-conceived one, than it is to any empirical reconstitution. To establish any such empirical validity would have required the careful preparation of an adequate series of regional models, which was not the case here.
4. Toutain, *op. cit.*, pp. 75–76.
5. Cf. also in the *Cahiers des Annales*, a fascinating study by M. Morineau

on the non-occurrence of the agricultural revolution, "Les faux-semblants d'un démarrage économique".

6. Vauban, *Dîme royale*, Paris, Alcan, 1933 edition, p. 169.

7. The application of the system known as the *dîme royale* would have meant establishing an immense network of tax constituencies (Vauban, 1933 edition, p. 47). When Vauban proposed this procedure, he was fascinated by a number of ancient, remote or utopian models (cf. the examples he mentions, drawn from the Bible, the Grand Mogul and the "King of China", *ibid.*, p. 12 of the 1933 edition). Cf. also J. Ganiage, *Les Origines du protectorat français en Tunisie*, Paris, 1959, pp. 99–100; F. Braudel, *Civilisation matérielle et Capitalisme*, vol. I, Paris, 1967, pp. 422–423, (English trans., by M. Kochan). On the Chinese sources for Vauban's ideas on this theme, see R. Mousnier, *La Dîme de Vauban*, Paris, 1968, p. 18–20, quotation from Père Lecomte, *Nouveaux mémoires sur l'état présent de la Chine*, Paris 1696.

8. During the Second Empire (1858), average French yields were only about 17 hectolitres to the hectare, according to the *Statistique de la France*.

9. Cf. the earlier quotation, p. 176.

10. On land clearances during the French Revolution, cf. in particular François Crouzet's article on the development of the French economy during the Revolution, based on the observations of Sir Francis d'Ivernois, in *Annales historiques de la Révolution française*, 1962, pp. 336 ff (second section).

11. Toutain, p. 33.

12. Gueuvin de Rademont, *Nouveau traité sur la dîme royale*, 1715, esp. pp. 146–148.

13. Moreau de Jonnès, *Etat économique de la France ... jusqu'en 1715*, Paris 1867, claims, following Vauban that the timber product was 1/20 that of cereals.

14. Michel Devèze, *La Vie de la forêt française*, Paris, 1961, vol. I, p. 267.

15. I have found Paul Studenski's analysis in *The income of nations*, New York, 1958, pp. 26–40, most helpful on this question.

16. Gregory King, *Natural and Political Observations ...*, 1696. I have used the 1936 Baltimore edition (*Two Tracts by Gregory King*), 1936, which reproduces the original; see p. 56.

17. M.O. Piquet-Marchal, "Gregory King, précurseur de la comptabilité nationale", in *Revue économique*, 1965, pp. 212–245.

18. *Ibid.*, p. 241 and 245.

19. Dupâquier, in *Revue historique*, 1968, p. 47, 48 and 49.

20. King, from his calculations referred to below, reckoned that there were 14 million inhabitants in 1688, and 13½ million in 1695 because of losses through war and hardship.

21. *Two Tracts by Gregory King*, The Johns Hopkins University Press, Baltimore, 1936.

22. Cf. King, 1936 edition, p. 49; for the geographical basis for his calculation, cf. p. 35.

23. King, *ibid.*, p. 49, and for more exact figures Vauban, 1933 edition, p. 159 and Dupâquier, 1968, p. 54 and note 3.
24. King, *ibid.*, p. 50.
25. Toutain, *op. cit.*, p. 193.
26. *Ibid.*, p. 187.
27. Toutain, p. 176.
28. *Ibid.*, p. 189.
29. *Ibid.*, p. 176.
30. *Ibid.*, p. 176.
31. Still according to M. Toutain.
32. Quoted by D.V. Glass, "Two papers on Gregory King", in *Population in History*, London, 1965, p. 164.
33. *Art. cit.* n. 19.
34. According to D.V. Glass, *art. cit.*
35. Cf. Toutain, *op. cit.*, table 53.
36. Toutain, *op. cit.*, p. 191.
37. Cf. above, p. 176.
38. F. Crouzet, "Croissances comparées de l'Angleterre et de la France au XVIIIe siècle, *Annales*, March-April, 1966.
39. J. Marczewski, "Histoire quantitative . . . " *Cahiers de l'I.S.E.A.*, no. 115, July 1961, p. XLI.

10 TITHES AND NET AGRICULTURAL OUTPUT (FIFTEENTH TO EIGHTEENTH CENTURY)

1. This article first appeared in *Annales*, May-June 1969. I should like to thank M. Joseph Goy, without whose collaboration this study of tithes could not have been accomplished. The full results appeared in a jointly written book *Les Fluctuations du produit de la dîme*, Paris, Mouton, 1972.
2. To deflate: in other words, given a certain income of which one knows the money value at various successive times, to calculate the equivalent of these values in some form of real goods. Let us suppose for the sake of argument that the income from a certain tithe in the year 1599 is 100 *livres tournois* and that the normal price of a hectolitre of wheat in an average year between say 1594 and 1605 is 10 *livres tournois*. The deflated value of the tithe in question is the equivalent of 10 hectolitres of wheat. The same calculation can be repeated for previous or following years.
3. That is whether the tithe is 1/10, 1/11, 1/13 etc. Changes in the rate cannot be ruled out.
4. For details of Monsieur Toutain's research, which is not described here, see the article above, p. 173, "The chief defects of Gregory King".

11 MÉLUSINE DOWN ON THE FARM

1. This article first appeared in *Annales*, 1971, pp. 603–622.

2. *Ibid.*, pp. 587–602.

3. This section of the article is concerned exclusively with the indisputable traces (known *indirectly* from the evidence of witnesses) left by Mélusine in the *unwritten* culture of the "modern" era. But the serpent-woman also occupies an important place (which would merit its own separate study) in the subject matter of books associated with the *Bibliothèque bleue de Troyes*: in this connection, see the bibliography of Léo Desaivre, in *Le Mythe de la Mère Lusine*, Saint-Maixent, 1883, pp. 249–252. Cf. also, among "written" accounts, the rather poor *Mélusine* by Nodot, 1698.

4. I have used the edition given of it by Pierre Jourda, *Conteurs français du XVIe siècle*, Bibl. de la Pléiade, Paris, Gallimard, 1965; particularly p. xxiii, and pp. 620–621.

5. On the story known as "Anette's skin" (*Cuir d'Anette* or "*Peau d'Ane*", literally "ass's skin", a story similar to *Coat o'Rushes*) see the Breton version which is also entitled *Peau d'Anette*, in Sébillot, *Littérature orale de Haute-Bretagne*, pp. 73–78, quoted by P. Delarue and M.-L. Teneze, *Le Conte populaire français*, Paris, Maisonneuve et Larose, vol. II, p. 264.

6. A. Aarne, translated and augmented by S. Thompson, *The Types of the Folktale*, Helsinki, 1961, pp. 21–22. In the early years of the seventeenth century *Mélusine* and *le Roman de Renart* were among the nursery stories told to little children (Ph. Ariès, *L'Enfant et la vie familiale sous l'Ancien Régime*, Paris, 1960, p. 59).

7. Aarne and Thompson, *ibid.*

8. N. du Fail, *Contes et discours d'Eutrapel* (in chap. 33, entitled "De la Moquerie"), p. 483 of the Natoire edition, Antwerp, 1587.

9. "The relics of Saint Rigomer were preserved at Maillezais and were highly revered in Poitou" (Rabelais, *Oeuvres complètes*, Bibl. de la Pléiade, N.R.F., Paris, 1951, p. 666, note 1, ed. J. Boulenger). It is worth noting that it was precisely in the Abbey of Maillezais that Geoffrey-of-the-Great-Tooth, the "son" of Mélusine was "buried".

10. Rabelais, *Quart livre*, chap. 38. Quoted here from the Urquhart and Motteux translation of Rabelais, vol. III, 1904 ed., p. 110. The final reference to Brittany (see, in connection with the dances referred to, Guilcher, *La Tradition populaire de danse en Basse-Bretagne*, Paris, 1963), is interesting in that the texts of Du Fail and of Etienne de Lusignan indicate an extension of Mélusine's influence in the XVth-XVIth centuries into Brittany (Etienne de Cypre de Lusignan, *Les Généalogies de 67 très nobles et très illustres maisons ... Paris, 1586, p. 49).

11. *Pantagruel*, chap. 30.

12. Interesting though it may appear at first glance, Mélusine's connection with the kitchen (*cuisine*) derives perhaps quite simply from an over-persuasive rhyme. See also, in this context, Corneille, *Le Menteur*, Act 1, scene vi: "*Urgande et Mélusine/N'ont jamais sur le champ mieux fournie leur cuisine*".

It is the case though, that lavish and miraculously served meals were a feature of Melusine's wedding feasts (*Mélusine* by Jean d'Arras, ed. by Ch. Brunet, Paris, 1854, p. 62); and in Poitou, at least, Mélusine is edible, having given her name and her shape to a local cake (Nodot, *Mélusine*, 1698, p. 13 in the Favre edition; cf. also M. de la Liborlière, in "Gâteaux d'une forme particulière", *Bull. de la Soc. des Antiq. de l'Ouest*, 1840, and L. Favre, *Glossaire de Poitou*, ed. 1867, p. 225). On the question of the name of this cake and its likely connection with the fairy's reputation as a corn-harvest fertility symbol, v. *infra*, note 15.

13. *Oeuvres complètes de Brantôme*, ed. 1869 by L. Lalanne, vol. V, *Grands capitaines français*, p. 19.

14. On the subject of gifts of precious metals and precious stones with which Mélusine was always very generous, cf. *Mélusine*, by Jean d'Arras in the 1854 edition already quoted, pp. 41, 124 and 357.

15. This name, misspelt by Perrault, is comparable with the similar *Coiraults* and *Koirots* (local names for "Merlusin" cakes, according to La Liborlière in *Bull. de la Soc. des Antiq. de l'Ouest*, 1840).

16. M. Mazet, "*Mémoire sur la Mellusine du Poitou*", *Athénée de Poitiers*, 8th. public session, *11 fruct de l'an XII*, Poitiers, Catineau, 1804, pp. 42–54.

17. His text is "reproduced" by B. Fillon and O. de Rochebrune, *Poitou et Vendée*, Fontenay-le-Comte, 1861, pp. 27–28. Unfortunately, B. Fillon is not to be trusted as a historian, and the text he claims to be by Biaille-Germont is suspect. We may wonder whether the tradition it incorporates, attributing to Melusine the acclimatization of the haricot bean is of genuinely popular origin. This is possible but not certain.

18. On the subject of Melusine's links with the Chabot family, see Mazet, *op. cit.* 1804, p. 49.

19. "Big-Tooth" i.e., Geoffrey-of-the-Great-Tooth.

20. According to Fillon, *op. cit.*, p. 27, in actual fact, Saint Louis fought against Geoffrey de Lusignan, besieging him in Vouvent in 1242.

21. Fillon's account is full of such patois expressions.

22. Nowadays, a farm known as *la Funerie*, in the *commune* of Jazeneuil. The change of *m* into *n* is quite common in the Poitevin patois: *sener* (*semer*), *gerner* (*germer*). Cf. L. Desaivre, *op. cit.*, p. 154.

23. Properly speaking, we should add to this collection the numerous instances of oral evidence circulating in the Poitevin country-side in the nineteenth century, gathered and grouped, directly or through intermediaries, by Léo Desaivre, *op. cit.*: appearing belatedly, and published in much condensed form, this evidence chiefly emphasizes the fairy's prowess as builder.

24. Jérémie Babinet, *Mélusine*, Poitiers, 1850, p. 50.

25. On the subject of the presence of serpents in the folklore and pre-Christian cults of Savoy and Dauphiné, see Louis Christillin, *Mémoires historiques sur la vallée d'Aoste*, vol. I, Aosta, 1884 p. 149.

26. N. Chorier, *Histoire généalogique de la maison de Sassenage*, Grenoble, 1669, pp. 10–20.

27. Denis Salvaing de Boissieu, *Septem miracula Delphinatus*, Grenoble, 1656, pp. 99–106 *(Melusina, sive Tinae Sassenagiae)*. On the subject of forecasting the harvest from the level of the water on the eve of Epiphany, or from the density of the foggy vapours above a stream, in a cave or some craggy spot, cf. the periodical *Mélusine*, 1, 1884 (in connection with the village of Neuville-Chant-d'Oisel); see also the report of Father Boisot in the *Journal des Savants*, 1686, on Froidière-de-Chaux (Jura).

28. Jean d'Arras, *op. cit.*, ed. 1854, p. 74 and pp. 116–118 (deduced from the age of the eldest children, p. 118; and from the birth intervals of the subsequent children, pp. 116–117. Added to these eight children, there were later born two more, Remonnet and Thierry the youngest.

29. P. Goubert, in F. Braudel and E. Labrousse, *Histoire économique et sociale de la France*, Paris, 1970, p. 32.

30. *L'Europe classique*, P. Chaunu.

31. Léo Desaivre, *op. cit.*

32. However, Couldrette, in *Mellusine, poème ... composé à la fin du Moyen Age*, published by F. Michel in the Niort edition, Robin et Favre, 1854, p. 182, makes the point—which Jean d'Arras does not—that before flying away for ever, Melusine, speaks about her "horrible" son who must be killed so that Poitou may survive, in the following words:

> "Entens Raimon: ton fils orrible
> fay mourrir ...
> s'il vit jamais ne faudra guerre,
> En tout le pays poitevin;
> *et n'y croistra ne pain ne vin*
> *... Tant que rien croistre ne pourroit*"

(Hear me Raimon: kill your horrible son ... if he lives, war will never be absent from all Poitou; *and neither bread nor wine will grow there, and indeed nothing will grow there*). This highly important text brings out two points: a) Melusine was actually concerned, as early as the fifteenth century and no doubt very much earlier still, with the problems of agricultural fertility; she was particularly interested, just as she was to be later on at Sassenage, with the vine and the grain harvest. b) If we are to trust the evidence of these few lines, Couldrette was not content simply to present a mere compilation of Jean d'Arras' work; he was also thoroughly conversant with earlier and very pertinent versions of the myth, certain important details of which, Jean d'Arras, for once misguided, had omitted.

33. Cf. *supra*, texts of passages taken from Cl. Perrault, N. Chorier and later from Biaille-Germont.

34. See *supra*, p. 211. On the subject of the spread of the cultivation of the haricot bean, the *mojette* or *mongette*, see E. Le Roy Ladurie, *Les Paysans de Languedoc*, Paris, 1966, vol. I. pp. 71–72.

35. *Infra*, conclusion of this article.

36. 1854 edition, p. 65.

37. In this connection, see a text written in the reign of Louis XIII,

reproduced in Langlet-Dufresnoy, *Recueil de dissertations anciennes et nouvelles sur les apparitions, les visions et les songes,* Avignon, 1752, vol. I, part 2, p. 127.

38. M. de Certeau, *Les Possédées de Loudun,* Paris, 1970.
39. See *supra,* note 16.
40. Jérémie Babinet, *Mélusine,* Poitiers, 1850, pp. 55–59 (faulty translation). And chiefly, *Anzeiger für Kunde des deutschen Mittelalters,* pub. by Auffess and Mone, 1834, 3rd. year, pp. 87–91 (original text taken directly "from the lips of popular story-tellers" by a Baden scholar at the start of the nineteenth century).
41. The story of Sebald is part of the Peter von Stauffenberg cycle, the earliest versions of which date from the beginning of the fourteenth century (Lütz Röhrich, *Erzählungen des späten Mittelalters und ihr Weiterleben in Literatur und Volksdichtung,* vol. I, Francke, Berne, 1962, p. 243–244).
42. Ch. Prieuret, "Histoire de la grosse communauté des Jault (1580–1847)", *Bull. de la Soc. nivernaise des lettres, sciences et arts,* vol. 28, 1929 (pub. 1930), pp. 333–386.

12 FROM WATERLOO TO COLYTON

1. A version of this article appeared in *The Times Literary Supplement,* 8th Sept. 1966.
2. On these areas of more liberal moral attitudes, see Ganiage, *op. cit.;* Daniel and Henry, *Sainghin, art. cit.;* and Girard "Sotteville" in *Population,* 1959.
3. "*La mercuriale*" was the market register on which the price of grain was regularly recorded.

13 FROM BRANTOME TO PAUL VI

1. This article first appeared in *Franco Observateur,* 1st April 1965.
2. *La Prévention des naissances dans la famille; ses origines dans les temps modernes,* Paris, P.U.F.
3. The best-informed experts on seventeenth-century contraception, in particular M. Philippe Ariès and Fr. Venard have not yet been able to determine what these mysterious "restringents" were.

14 DEMOGRAPHY AND THE "SINFUL SECRETS"

1. This paper was given in 1964 to the *Société des Études robespierristes.* It was later published in 1965 in *Annales historiques de la Révolution française.*
2. The notes refer to the bibliography of the article on pp. 253–254.
3. P. Vilar, 1962, II, p. 64–65.
4. R. Baehrel, 1961, p. 277 and note 1 on the same page.
5. Reinhard and Armengaud, 1961.
6. According to the most recent census.

7. Departmental Archives of the Hérault C 15, extract from the letter sent by the *Intendant* to Necker.
8. Reinhard and Armengaud, 1961, p. 193.
9. According to the annual population and birth tables drawn up by the *Intendant* of Hainaut, published in 1964 by Esmonin.
10. Henry, in Bergues, *La Prévention des naissances*, 1960, p. 375.
11. Bourgeois-Pichat, 1951 and 1952.
12. R. Mandrou, 1958, II, p. 73.
13. Féline, ed. 1880, p. 7–9.
14. On these figures given by Young and Ballainvilliers, cf. Duthil, 1911.
15. The diocese of Lodève being counted twice, first in the original sample of the twelve dioceses, and then with the five dioceses of present-day Hérault.
16. Departmental Archives of the Hérault C 10.
17. Godechot and Moncassin, 1964; and, for Blagnac, Y. Ben Samoun.
18. Fleury and Valmary, 1957. Vilback, 1825.
19. Ben Samoun.
20. E. Labrousse, 1953, p. 346; Goubert, 1960.
21. Diagrams in Le Roy Ladurie, *Les Paysans du Languedoc*. Earlier still (about 1720) according to a thesis by M.G. Frèche.
22. Godechot and Moncassin 1964.
23. Armengaud, 1960, p. 53.
24. Malthus recognized three ways in which population increase could be held in check: catastrophic poverty, the death factor; "virtue" (abstinence); and "vice" (including contraception).
25. Henry, in Bergues, 1960, p. 375.
26. Ganiage, 1964.
27. J. Biraben at the European demographic Conference in Strasburg (Council of Europe, 1966).
28. Cf. for example Hilaire, 1964, p. 109. Bergues, 1960, p. 230. Zola. Freud, ed. 1956, p. 50, 61–65, 70–71, 78–83, 88, 103, 149, etc.
29. *Ibid.*
30. In this connection, cf. the decisive eighteenth and nineteenth century texts quoted by Hélène Bergues, esp. Bouvier's (the Bishop of Le Mans) ("husbands are abandoning religious practice, murmuring against their confessors, because they command them, on pain of mortal sin to renounce contraception"); and the response sent to Bouvier in 1842 by the Grand Penitentiary of the Vatican, a response widely circulated in the seminaries by the writings of Bouvier in very many editions: in cases of *coitus interruptus*, said the Penitentiary, the man is responsible and sinning (and if he persists in this sin he must abstain from religious practice); the woman on the contrary, is to be considered as passive, and therefore remains innocent (and she can continue to attend mass and receive the sacraments) (Bergues, 1960, p. 229–230).

N.B.—Since writing this article I have learnt of a recent study by J.-C. Perrot confirming the existence of very great regional contrasts in the national figures of birth and death rates during the latter years of the *ancien régime* (J.-C. Perrot, in *Contributions à l'histoire démographique de la Révolution française*, Paris, 1965).

15 AMENORRHOEA IN TIME OF FAMINE

1. This article first appeared in *Annales*, Nov.–Dec. 1969.
2. J. Meuvret, "Les crises de subsistance et la démographie de la France d'Ancien Régime", in *Population*, 1946, pp. 643–650. See also D.S. Thomas, *Social and Economic Aspects of Swedish Population Movements, 1750–1933*, New York, 1941.
3. P. Goubert, "Une richesse historique: les registres paroissaux", in *Annales*, 1954, p. 92.
4. J. Ruwet, "Crises démographiques: problèmes économiques ou crises morales, le pays de Liège sous l'Ancien Régime" in *Population*, 1954, pp. 451–476.
5. Étienne Gautier and Louis Henry, "La population de Crulai, paroisse normande", in *Travaux et documents de l'I.N.E.D.*, Paris, 1958. But the "sinful secrets" of contraception spread to the towns, big and small, in the eighteenth century especially after 1750: cf. particularly studies by A. Chamoux and C. Dauphin on Châtillon-sur-Seine (*Annales*, 1969, pp. 662–684); by M. Lachiver, on Meulan (E.P.H.E., 1969); by El Kordi, on Bayeux; by students of P. Goubert, on Argenteuil; and, of course, for a period a little earlier, Louis Henry's thesis "Anciennes familles genevoises. Étude démographique", in *Travaux et documents de l'I.N.E.D.*, Paris, 1956.
6. P. Goubert, *Beauvais et le Beauvaisis*, Paris, 1960, pp. 49–50.
7. Moheau, *Recherches et considérations sur la population de la France*, 1778, quoted by P. Goubert, *ibid.*, p. 50.
8. *Ibid.*, p. 50.
9. For a medical statement on the question, the reader is advised to consult A. Netter, *Comment soigner les aménorrhées*, Paris, 1955, p. 61, and also, by the same author, in collaboration with P. Lumbroso, *Aménorrhées, dysménorrhées*, Paris, Baillière, le Précis du Praticien, 1962, p. 58 and *passim*: in this chapter malnutrition amenorrhoea is classified among the various *secondary* forms of amenorrhoea. Cf. also a recent study, "Les aménorrhées non ménopausiques", *Les Assises de médecine*, vol. XXIII, 26th year, number 2, May 1968, particularly p. 102.
10. J. V. Jaworski, "Mangelhäfte Ernährung als Ursache von Sexualstörungen bei Frauen", *Wiener Klinische Wochenschrift*, August 1916, number 24, p. 1068 *et seq.* It is worth noting that in times of peace (1898), in the poorer, backward areas of Polish Galicia, they were still recording the harmful effects of bad harvests and high corn prices on the numbers of births; and this at a time when this particular correlation, characteristic of the *ancien régime* grain crises, had long disappeared in the developed countries of Europe. "In Galicia, after the very bad harvest of 1897, the number of marriages fell by 3,506, but births fell by 45,438", according to Buzek, "Der Einfluss der

Ernten, resp. der Getreidepreise auf die Bevölkerungsbewegung in Galicien, 1878–1898", *Der statistische Monatschrift*, 1901, quoted by Julius Wolf, *Der Geburtenruckgang*, Jena, G. Fischer, 1912, pp. 124–125.

11. On these phenomena, clinical data and the associated biological syndrome, and also on the quoted exceptions, cf. "Les aménorrhées non-ménopausiques", *op. cit.*, pp. 101–102.

12. A. Giesecke, "Zur Kriegsamenorrhoe", *Zentralblatt fur Gynäkologie*, 1917, 2, pp. 865–873.
K. Czerwenka, "Über Kriegsamenorrhöe", *Zentralblatt. f. Gyn.*, 1917, 2, pp. 1,162–1,165.

13. *Ibid.* See also F. Spaeth, "Zür Frage der Kriegsamenorrhöe", *Zentralbl. f. Gyn.*, vol. 2, number 27, pp. 664–668.
C. Kurtz, "Alimentäre Amenorrhöe", *Monatschrift für Geburtshilfe und Gynäkologie*, 1920, pp. 367–378.

14. Kurtz, *art. cit.*, 1920, pp. 371–372.

15. Czerwenka, 1917, *art. cit.* Czerwenka is very insistent on the lack of carbohydrates: this was also of course a feature of the seventeenth century famines in France.

16. Hilferding, "Zur Statistik der Amenorrhöe", *Wiener Klinische Wochenschrift*, 1917, number 27, reviewed in *Zentralblatt f. Gyn.*, number 50, 1917, col. 2, p. 1,139.

17. Spaeth, *art. cit.*, 1917.

18. G. Teebken,: "Amenorrhöe in der Kriegs-und Nachkriegszeit, ein Rückblick um 10 jahre nach dem Kriege", *Zbl. f. Gynäk.*, vol. 52, 1928, vol. III, pp. 2,966–2,978.

19. M. Boucher, *L'Aménorrhée de guerre dans les régions envahies*, Thesis of the Faculty of Medicine of Lille, Lille, Imp. Centrale du Nord, especially p. 24.

20. *Ibid.*, p. 51.

21. *Ibid.*, p. 28.

22. The median weight of these twelve women fell from 65 kg. to 49.5 kg. (*ibid.*, p. 29).

23. T. Heynemann, "Die Nachkriegs-amenorrhöe", *Klinische Wochenschrift*, 26 March 1948, pp. 129–132.

24. H. Selye, *Stress, The physiology and pathology of exposure to stress . . .* , Montreal, 1950, pp. 366–367.

25. In addition to the articles already quoted, see: Schilling, "Kriegsamenorrhöe", *Zentralblatt für innere Medizin*, 1917, number 31, (quoted also in *Zentralblatt für Gynäk.*, 1918, 2, p. 712).
Graefe, "Über Kriegsamenorrhöe", *München Med. Wochenschrift*, 1917, number 32, (quoted in *Zentralblatt für Gynäkologie*, number 50, 1917, 2, p. 1,140). In 1916 an important debate took place between, on the one hand, A. Hamm of Strasbourg ("Geburtshilflich-Gynäkologische Kriegsfragen", *Zentralblatt für Gynäk.*, 1918, 1, p. 82) who was of the opinion that psychological shock played the greater part in the onset of war amenorrhoea, and on the other hand, those who held that malnutrition was chiefly to blame (the latter opinion expressed

notably by Graefe and Spaeth, *art. cit.*; by Dietrich and Pok, *Zblt. f. Gynäk.*, 1917, numbers 6 and 20: also by Schweitzer, *Munch. med. Wochenschrift*, 1917, number 17).

26. L. Von Lingen, "Kriegsamenorrhöe in Petersburg", *Zentralblatt für Gynäkologie*, vol. 45, Sept. 1921, pp. 1,247–1,248.

27. W.H. Stefko, in *Virchows Arch.*, 252, year 1924, p. 385, quoted by T. Heynemann, *art. cit.*, 1948, pp. 130 and 132.

28. The case of the occupied territories excepted, of course (Boucher, *op. cit*).

29. *Art. cit.*

30. "Amenorrhoea in Wartime . . . ", 1918, *The Lancet*, p. 712.

31. In the case of France, the bibliography on the subject this time is immense: cf. particularly *Questions gynécologiques d'actualité* (vol. III, 1943, symposium); also, G. Laroche and E. Bompard, "Les aménorrhées de guerre", *Paris médical*, 30th August 1943, pp. 217–219; the same authors plus J. Trémolières, "Les aménorrhées de guerre", *Revue française de gynécologie et d'obstétrique*, March 1943, p. 65 *et seq.*; G. Cotte, in *Lyon médical* vol. 169, 28th March 1943, p. 263 (insisting on psychological factors as paramount); M. Sendrail and J. Lasserre in *Revue de Pathologie comparée et d'hygiène générale*, vol. 48, Jan-Feb 1948, pp. 63–75 (important bibliography). Items of information which follow are taken, except when indicated, from one or other of these articles.

32. E. Olivier-Pascual, in *Clinica y laboratorio*, Nov. 1941, quoted by Sendrail and Lasserre, *art. cit.*

33. Laroche and Bompard, *art. cit.*

34. F.L. Quémeré, *Les Aménorrhées de guerre*, thesis, Paris, 1942.

35. But it is true that this figure represented 5.11 per cent of a sample entirely composed of hospital patients.

36. Theses of S. Vidal, 1945 (Toulouse) and Castan-Pollin (Montpellier), quoted by Sendrail and Lasserre, *art. cit.*

37. On this point, the essential and most notable articles are by C.A. Smith, Effects of maternal undernutrition upon the new-born infant in Holland (1944–45)", *The Journal of pediatrics*, vol. 30, March 1947; and "The effect of wartime starvation in Holland upon pregnancy", *Amer. J. obst. and gynec.*, April 1947, pp. 599–608.

38. J.A. Stroink, "Kriegsamenorrhöe", *Gynaecologia*, vol. 123, 1947, pp. 160–165.

39. Selye, *op. cit.*, 1950, pp. 366–367.

40. A Binet, "Les aménorrhées chez les déportées", *Gynécologie et obstétrique*, vol. 44, numbers 1-2-3, "1944" (1945), p. 417. See also L.S. Copelman, "L'aménorrhée des déportées", *Revue de path. comp. et d'hyg. gén.*, 48th year, 1948, pp. 102–107 (386–391), who concludes his detailed study with these remarks: "The proportion of amenorrhoea cases is directly related to the intensity of the famine . . . (in the camps). Ovarian activity recommenced immediately after the food shortage ended."

41. K. Horvath, C. Selle, R. Weisz, "Beiträge zur Pathologie . . . der

Kriegsbedingten Amenorrhöe", *Gynaecologia*, vol. 125, 1948, pp. 368–374. The conclusions of these authors on the renewal of ovarian activity when famine conditions ceased, are less positive than those, previously quoted, of L. Copelman.

42. A. Netter, *op. cit.*, 1962, p. 59 ff., and 1955, p. 61.
43. Cf. also, in this connection, the symposium already quoted, in *Assises de médecine*, 1968, pp. 102–103.
44. F. Whitacre and B. Barrera, "War amenorrhoea, a clinical and laboratory study", *Jour. of the Amer. med. assoc.*, vol. 124. number 7, 12th Feb. 1944, pp. 399–403.
45. A. Sydenham, "Amenorrhoea at Stanley Camp, Hong-Kong, during internment", *British medical journal*, Aug. 1946, (vol. 2), p. 159.
46. J.S. Sweeney and collaborators, "An observation on menstrual misbehaviours", *The Journal of clinical endocrinology*, vol. 7, 1947, p. 659 *et seq.*
47. Cf. *Ibid.*, p. 660.
48. The reader will not need reminding of Alfred Netter's conclusions on this matter: "Amenorrhoea is a symptom, like fever or loss of weight ... it is never an illness, it is only a symptom, a disturbing manifestation of a lesion or a functional trouble attacking the complex mechanism which causes the menstrual cycle ... very often amenorrhoea is just a *cry of suffering* the physical suffering caused by infectious or cachectic diseases, or the psychological suffering caused by disturbed emotions; investigation must consider the malady in its total somatic, social and psychological context ... amenorrhoea is not solely dependent on a lesion of the uterus, of the ovaries or of the hypophysis, it can result from a number of causes, attacking other organs, other functions ... amenorrhoea may be "the symptom of organic suffering", or else "the symptom of psychological suffering, a sudden shock, situation of conflict, or nervous exhaustion" (A. Netter, *op. cit.*, 1955, pp. 5, 61 and *passim*).
49. T. Heynemann, *art. cit.*, 1948.
50. C. Lévi-Strauss, *La Pensée sauvage*, p. 326.
51. R.L. Strecker and T.T. Emlen, "Regulatory mechanisms in housemouse populations: the effect of limited food supply", *Ecology*, 1953, p. 375 ff. See also B. Ball, "Caloric restriction and fertility", *Amer. journal of physiology*, 1947, vol. 150, p. 511 ff.
52. A. Netter, *op. cit.*, 1962, p. 59.
53. Abstinence, of course, figures as one, among other factors, and also perhaps some forms of attempt at birth control; the problem that remains to be solved is to know what weight to attach to these various factors in the total phenomenon of the fall in the rate of conception in times of acute food shortage.
54. Cf. *supra*, at the start of this article.
55. H. Boerhave, *Institutions de médecine*, with a commentary by M. de La Mettrie, Paris, (trans.) Vol. I (ed. 1743), p. 231 and vol. VI (ed. 1747), p. 108 ff. There are also other publications which deal with late puberty, especially marked in the poorer regions. Cf. for example

(in data supplied to me by J.-P. Peter) references to Bressuire and Brittany: "Girls in these areas are often of pale complexion and seldom menstruate before the age of eighteen, nineteen or twenty" (*Archives départementales*, Deux-Sevres, C 14, sub-district of Bressuire: "Topographie de la ville et de la subdélégation de Bressuire" by Dr. Berthelot, July 1786); and again, "Among the girl population, those who do *not* work on the land menstruate between eleven and fourteen years of age, those who *do* work do not menstruate until they are fourteen to eighteen" (Académie de Médecine, *Archives S.R.M.*, Carton 179, Dr. Baudry, "Topographie de Vieillevigne, Bretagne", Oct. 1787).

56. *Animal dispersion in relation to social behaviour*, London, 1962, esp. Chap. 21.
57. A. Netter, *op. cit.*
58. My thanks to Jean-Pierre Peter, Antoinette Chamoux and Dr. Michel Bitker for the bibliographical or medical information they have kindly supplied to me.

16 CHAUNU, LEBRUN, VOVELLE: THE NEW HISTORY OF DEATH

1. An address given at the annual meeting of Catholic intellectuals, Paris, 1972.
2. The article appeared in *Les Informations*, 1972.
3. Michel Vovelle's thesis on the history of wills of Provence studied serially was published in 1973: *Piété baroque et déchristianization en Provence au XVIIIe siecle; attitudes devant la mort d'après les clauses des testaments* Paris, Plon, 1973.

17 WRITING THE HISTORY OF THE CLIMATE

1. Cf. on this subject L. Lliboutry, *Traité de Glaciologie*, 1965, vol. 2.
2. *Phenology*: a branch of plant biology concerned with the "appearance" of vegetative phenomena.

18 THE HISTORY OF RAIN AND FINE WEATHER

1. This article was first published in a collection of essays under the title *L'Histoire nouvelle et ses méthodes*, edited by Jacques Le Goff and Pierre Nora (Gallimard, Paris) 1973.
2. See Manley and Labrijn (except where expressly indicated, the footnotes refer to the detailed bibliography to be found at the end of this article).
3. Angot, 1883. Le Roy Ladurie (L.R.L.), 1967 and 1971.
4. Titow, 1960 and 1970.
   Schove, 1949.
5. L.R.L., *op. cit.*
6. L.R.L., 1970; and especially H. Lamb, 1966.

7. G. Manley, article in *Quart. Journal of the Roy. Met. Soc.*, 1946 and 1953, pp. 242–252 and p. 358, and in *Archiv für Met Geophys. und Bioklimatol.*, 1959.

8. H. von Rudloff, *Die Schwankungen und Pendelungen des Klimas in Europa seit dem Beginn der regelmassigen Instrumenten Beobachtungen*, Brunswick (Vieweg, edit), 1967. See also the long resumé of this book I published in *Annales*, Sept. 1970.

9. J. Dettwiller, *Évolution séculaire du climat de Paris ...* , *Mémorial de la Mét. nat.*, Number 52, Paris, 1970.

10. See the inquiry into these archives by the author and others in the collection of essays *Climat, médecins, épidémies*, Mouton, 1972.

11. Fritts (see bibliography pp. 316–317).

12. On the problems of absolutely precise dating of ancient timbers by *cross-dating* with living trees, see my *Histoire du Climat*, 1966, chap. 11; cf. also the bibliography, the articles quoted by Hüber and Hollstein.

13. L.R.L., *ibid.* (1967 and 1971), chap. vi.

14. Polge, *infra*.

15. De Martin.

16. See details of these corrections in the article by M. Baulant and E. Le. Roy Ladurie, which appeared in the *Mélanges* in honour of Fernand Braudel, Privat, Toulouse, 1973.

17. See in this connection the research studies of F. Lebrun, *Les Hommes et la mort en Anjou*, Paris—The Hague, Mouton, 1971 *(in fine)*.

18. Cf. the table on pp. 371–375 in the English edition of my *Histoire du Climat*, New York, 1971.

19. Lebrun, De Martin, in the magazine *La Météorologie*.

20. Article in *Arctic and Alpine Research*, 1972.

21. Skelton, Marston, Painter and Vietor, 1965, p. 3.

22. Skelton, *ibid.* 1965, p. 156 and p. 230.

23. See Skelton, 1965 pp. 169–170 (map) and p. 186; Baardson's text is in L.R.L., 1971, pp. 153–258.

24. Skelton, 1965, p. 170, and *Graenlandica Saga*, ed. 1965, p. 16.

25. Such at least is Skelton's opinion, 1965.

26. From the thirteenth century onwards, if we are to accept Ivan Baardson's text. From 1140 A.D. onwards if we rely on the climatic datings of the Camp Century ice-core *(infra*, p. 314 ff.) and L.R.L., 1971, pp. 257–264.

27. Dansgaard, 1969; cf. *infra*, p. 314 et seq.

28. G.R. Crone, 1966, pp. 75–78. M. George Kish, whom I questioned on the subject, considers the map is authentic. But he reserves judgement on the extreme western margins of this map (Vinland and Greenland) ... ; on this point, also, it would seem to be best to "wait and see".

29. Crone, 1969, p. 23.

30. Dansgaard; and L.R.L., 1971, pp. 257–264.

31. Dansgaard, 1969, *ibid.*, p. 378.

32. *Graenlandica Saga*, pp. 17–18 and p. 50.

33. *Ibid.*, p. 21 and p. 52.
34. Mercer, 1965.
35. Dansgaard, etc., 1969, fig. 4.
36. Dansgaard, *ibid.*; Mercer, pp. 410–412.
37. The Camp Century ice core, the bottom layers of which are more than 100,000 years old, also provides corroboration of the great quaternary ice ages.
38. Labeyrie, Duplessis, Delibrias, and Letolle.

GLOSSARY

Weights, measures, money

livre tournois	: unit of account in France under *ancien régime*, minted at Tours and originally worth a pound of silver, but devalued so much that it was worth under 5 grams by 1801 when the decimal franc was introduced.
sou(s)	: There were 20 *sous* in one *livre* or franc.
deniers	: There were 12 *deniers* in one *sou*.
quintal	: approximately a hundredweight under the *ancien régime* (a metric quintal = 100 kg).
setier	: grain measure, somewhere between 150 and 300 litres.
hectare	: land measurement = 10,000 m² or 2.47 acres.
arpent	: land measurement = approximately 1 acre.

*

ancien régime	: used of the historical period and system of government in France before 1789.
assignats	: promissory notes (paper money in effect) issued by the Revolutionary government 1790–1796.
bailli	: magistrate, or functionary administering justice either on behalf of the Crown or of a noble.
ban	: the summons to arms of the nobility by the sovereign.
bocage	: the landscape typically found in north-west France, where the fields are divided by many hedges and woods.
cahiers de doléance	: registers of grievances presented by the Estates-General in 1789.
canton	: administrative subdivision within a constituency, essentially for electoral purposes.
cens	: quit-rent, i.e. dues paid by landowner to feudal overlord.
champart	: right to share of crop exercised by feudal landlords.
châtelain	: the lord of a manor or *château*.
Chouan	: Royalist rebel against French Revolution. The Chouannerie was an uprising in western France one of whose leaders was "Jacques Chouan" (= "owl") by nickname.
commune	: the smallest territorial and administrative division in France; approximately "parish" or municipality.

343

conjoncture	: used particularly in economic history to describe the dynamic combination of circumstances determining the economic situation at any one time. Not as long as a trend, not as short as an event.
conseil de révision	: the board which pronounces conscripts fit to serve or not.
corvée	: unpaid and compulsory labour owed to a feudal overlord.
croquant	: peasant rebel during the reigns of Henri IV and Louis XIII.
cru	: vintage
département	: administrative division of France, introduced in 1790 and administered by the prefect.
dictier	: poem or song, usually learnt by heart.
dîme royale	: *dîme* or *dixième* (= 1/10) is the usual word for tithe(s) the levy on crops payable to the Church. In 1698, Vauban proposed the *dîme royale* or royal tenth as a tax to be levied indiscriminately across the country and to all classes. His proposal, published in 1707 was not accepted by Louis XIV (and Vauban is said to have died of a broken heart).
Eaux et Forêts	: department of French administration responsible for waterways and forests.
Ecole des Chartes	: Specialist institute for training of archivists.
Ecole pratique des Hautes Etudes	: Institute of advanced studies and research in Paris, divided into different sections for different disciplines. The 6th section (economic and social sciences) has become well-known for history, and many of the historians associated with it also write in the journal *Annales.*
événémentielle (histoire)	: literally the history of events, often used of the traditional narrative history or biography as opposed to quantitative and interdisciplinary research in history. Sometimes, but not always, derogatory.
gabelle	: salt tax under *ancien régime.*
grand siècle	: the seventeenth century, especially the reign of Louis XIV.
Intendant, Intendance	: the royal administration under the *ancien régime*; the *Intendant* had very wide-reaching powers over one of the old provinces.
Jacques, jacquerie	: Jacques was the traditional name for a peasant, and became particularly associated with the peasant risings in the fourteenth century, *jacqueries*; later used generally of peasant revolts.
laboureur	: literally one who ploughs, and can mean ploughman

or farmer who works his own land. Often found meaning "well-off peasant" as opposed to day-labourer.

livre de raison : journal kept by head of family, who put down in it as well as accounts, events such as births and marriages, etc., and his own reflections.

Midi : the south of France.

Minutier : store for legal documents. The *Minutier central* refers to the section of the archives to which all notarial documents are transferred after 125 years.

Montagnard : originally used of the most radical members of the National Assembly during the French Revolution, and by extension used of radical politicians during later regimes.

notable : a person of note, influence and standing, usually used of local rather than national figures.

réserve : the home farm, or part of an estate farmed directly by the landowner.

remplacement : when military service was subject to the drawing of lots in the nineteenth century, those who could afford it paid a substitute to do their service for them if they had drawn a bad number. The institution was the *remplacement*, the substitute the *remplaçant*.

rois fainéants : = "do-nothing kings" used to describe the succession of Merovingian kings between 639 and 751, none of whom lived longer than the age of 25; the throne was frequently vacant and the real ruler was the *maire du palais* "the palace mayor".

seigneurie : the area over which the feudal overlord *(seigneur)* had rights, e.g. to ask for *cens* or *corvée* even if he did not own or work all the land himself.

subdélégué,
subdélégation : local administrative division of a province under the *ancien régime*; the *subdélégué* was the local official.

sans-culottes : the most ardent supporters of the French Revolution, especially in 1792–1793, so called because they wore trousers and not the noble breeches *(culottes)*.

taille : tax under the *ancien régime* paid mainly by commoners.